WAR WITHOUT VICTORY

By the same author

The War in the Mediterranean, 1803–1810
The War for America, 1775–1783
Statesmen at War: the Strategy of Overthrow, 1798–1799
The Coward of Minden: the Affair of Lord George Sackville

WAR
WITHOUT VICTORY
THE DOWNFALL OF PITT
1799–1802

Piers Mackesy

CLARENDON PRESS · OXFORD
1984

Oxford University Press, Walton Street, Oxford OX2 6DP

London New York Toronto
Delhi Bombay Calcutta Madras Karachi
Kuala Lumpur Singapore Hong Kong Tokyo
Nairobi Dar es Salaam Cape Town
Melbourne Auckland

and associated companies in
Beirut Berlin Ibadan Mexico City Nicosia

Oxford is a trade mark of Oxford University Press

Published in the United States by
Oxford University Press, New York

British Library Cataloguing in Publication Data
Mackesy, Piers
War without victory: the downfall of Pitt
1799–1802.
1. Great Britain — Politics and government —
1789–1820
I. Title
941.07'3   DA535
ISBN 0-19-822495-8

Typeset by Hope Services, Abingdon
Printed in Great Britain at the
University Press, Oxford

To My Colleagues

The Master and Fellows of Pembroke College, Oxford

Preface

War without Victory is the last of four volumes devoted to the warfare of the reign of George III. Its predecessors described the history of the Mediterranean theatre, the global war for America, and Britain's European strategy during the period when her forces had been expelled from the continent.[1] All three books were concerned with statesmen and commanders in adversity; and adversity again broods over the final volume.

The unifying theme of all the books has been men under stress, exercising their judgement on difficult options. There was Lord Collingwood's long Mediterranean vigil, when he bore responsibilities that ranged far beyond the task of managing his scattered fleets. In America the Howe brothers and Sir Henry Clinton were challenged by military and political problems beyond the scope of any historical experience they could consult. Sir Ralph Abercromby and the Duke of York contended in Holland with difficulties not of their making. Above the commanders, the statesmen tried to control the struggle: North, Germain and Sandwich; Pitt, Dundas and Grenville; Castlereagh and Canning.

The original plan for the present book was that it should follow the pattern of its predecessor, *The Strategy of Overthrow*, in which the political shaping of strategy led naturally into the military campaign. There was unity in that arrangement, for the Dutch campaign of 1799 was close enough to London for the build-up of the army in Holland to take place under the ministers' supervision. They could make daily comments on the progress of operations, and hope to exercise political control of military events. Not so, however, in the present volume. The operations on the coast of Spain and in Egypt were too far off to be influenced from London, while the foreground came increasingly to

[1] *The War in the Mediterranean, 1803-1810* (1957); *The War for America, 1775-1783* (1964); *Statesmen at War: The Strategy of Overthrow, 1798-1799* (1974).

be dominated by the crumbling of the ministry under the stress of war.

The military operations therefore remain in the background, and Pitt and his colleagues hold the centre of the stage. If such a story can have a hero, it is not Pitt but Henry Dundas, a statesman whose limitations have been stressed more often than his stature. It was he who first identified the Coalition's failing fortunes, and made it his task to adjust policy and strategy to the coming collapse of the alliance. Yet paradoxically his success may have hastened the end of the ministry; for the discord generated in the Cabinet by his reappraisal increased the stress on the Prime Minister to the point where his health and mental resilience could no longer cope. Having lost the confidence of the King during the military misfortunes of 1800, Pitt faced a royal confrontation over the Catholic question at a moment when his command of the Cabinet was weakened by high conflict over war and peace. His strange behaviour during the last months of his ministry reflects the pressures on a statesman faltering under accumulated blows. The themes of the book are the intractable problems of war organization; the restricted options in British strategy; conflict over the purpose of the struggle; and the stresses endured by statesmen at war.

A guiding principle in the four volumes has been to renounce the hasty and didactic judgements which characterize so much historical writing on war: to prefer explanation to denunciation. Only when the restricted options and resistant medium of war have been defined is one entitled to judge the actors. This has led me to avoid the all-seeing historian's Olympian overview of past events, which confuses historical truth because it provides knowledge not available to the participants. Sometimes it has been necessary to unfold the enemy's plans in advance, in order perhaps to explain a great strategic surprise, as at Yorktown and Marengo, when the initiative and the control of events were slipping from the grasp of the British; or to measure the stakes for which the parties were playing, such as the value Bonaparte placed on Egypt in 1801 or on Corfu in 1808. There is a price to be paid for seeing only one side of the hill, and I am aware for instance that by seeing the French Chouans through the eyes of British officers one diminishes their heroism and self-sacrifice. The designs of Tsar Paul and the fears and suspicions of the Austrian court also yield place to the British viewpoint. Nevertheless I have held to the belief that to see both sides of the hill consistently is to distort the persepective of those who planned the strategy and directed the operations. They took their decisions in the fog of war, and it would be wrong to disperse the drifting smoke.

I have to thank the Earl of Crawford and Balcarres, Viscount Sidmouth and Sir Ralph Verney for permission to consult their family papers; and Colonel A. C. Barnes for lending me a piece of his family correspondence.

I must also express my gratitude for their help to Sir Robin Mackworth-Young; to Mr John Ehrman; to Professor Ole Feldbæk of the University of Copenhagen; to Miss Glenise Matheson of the John Rylands Library; to Mrs Arlene P. Shy of the William L. Clements Library; and to the staff of the National Register of Archives (Scotland), especially to Miss D. Young.

Finally, I would like to thank the Rockefeller Foundation, and Mr Roberto Celli, for a happy month spent at the Villa Serbelloni where I started to write this book.

Pembroke College, Oxford
January 1983

Contents

The Cabinet, 1799–1801

First Lord of the Treasury and Chancellor of the Exchequer	William Pitt
Lord Privy Seal	Earl of Westmorland
Lord President of the Council	Earl of Chatham
Lord Chancellor	Lord Loughborough
Home Secretary	Duke of Portland
Foreign Secretary	Lord Grenville
Secretary of State for War	Henry Dundas
First Lord of the Admiralty	Earl Spencer
President of the Board of Trade	Earl of Liverpool
Secretary at War	William Windham
Minister without Portfolio	Earl Camden

The Master-General of the Ordnance (Marquis Cornwallis) had formerly been a member of the Cabinet, but vacated his seat on going to Ireland as Lord-Lieutenant in 1798.

The Commander-in-Chief had ceased to be a member in 1795 when the Duke of York succeeded Lord Amherst.

Maps

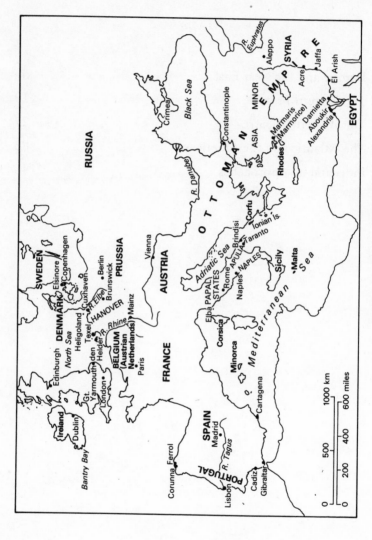

Map 1. Europe and the Near East

PART ONE:
THE PHANTOM OF VICTORY

CHAPTER I

To Overthrow or Outlast?

1. *Disaster Appraised*

On the morning of 14 October 1799 Colonel Brownrigg stepped from his post-chaise in Downing Street, at the end of his
five-day journey from the headquarters of the Anglo-Russian
army in Holland. He brought a personal report from its commander the Duke of York, and at two o'clock that afternoon
a hastily convened Cabinet met to consider the army's situation. The news from the front was grave. It was seven weeks
since the spearhead of the expedition had stormed the beaches
south of the Helder, and a month since the Duke of York's
first attempt to break out of his beachhead had been shattered
by General Brune at Bergen. Since then the weather had
broken, and incessant rain delayed the Duke's regrouping for
his next attack while enemy reinforcements were marching
up from the south to strengthen Brune's defences. A successful attack at Egmond on 2 October dislodged Brune from the
Bergen position and produced a transitory gleam of hope; but
four days later the allied advance was checked under a tor-
rential downpour in a confused encounter battle at Castricum.
For the Anglo-Russian army this was the end. With the
autumn rains breaking up the roads and filling his hospitals
with sick, and the enemy's strength increasing daily, the
Duke withdrew across twenty miles of hard-won sand-hills
and polder to his start-line on the Zijpe dike. Now Colonel
Brownrigg brought York's bleak assessment of the future.

As Pitt took his place at the Cabinet table he faced two
heart-sick men, the creators of the ill-starred expedition.
They were his closest colleagues. Henry Dundas, the Secretary
of State for War, was the forthright elderly Scot who had
organized the operation and assembled the troops with their
shipping and naval escorts, their supplies and ordnance. But
the real begetter of the campaign was the Prime Minister's
solemn cousin, the Foreign Secretary Lord Grenville, and for
him the frustration was deepest. This year 1799 should have

marked the climax of his policy and brought decisive victory
to the Coalition. To destroy the Jacobin wickedness in Paris,
his diplomacy had forged a chain of Austrian and Russian
armies along the eastern frontiers of France, and had caused
the Tsar to ship another Russian corps from the Baltic to reinforce a British invasion of Holland. Grenville had expected
that by this autumn Marshal Suvorov's Russians would be
surging across the Swiss frontier towards Lyon, supported on
their flanks by Austrian armies advancing through the Belfort
gap and over the Maritime Alps. In the north the Duke of
York's British and Russians should have been driving south
across the Waal and into Belgium, perhaps dragging the wary
Prussians into the war in their wake. All would then have
been set for a final converging advance on Paris in the spring
of 1800, to overthrow the Jacobin republic and restore the
Bourbon monarchy.

It was not to be: Grenville's insubstantial pageant of victory
had faded. In Holland the western front had sunk into stagnation. In the east the news was perhaps worse. The major Swiss
offensive had dissolved in the acid of conflicting political
aims, and Grenville knew that he had been snared in an
Austrian trap. Indifferent to the counter-revolutionary
crusade which Grenville and Tsar Paul were waging against
the French republic, the Austrians saw their national interests
in terms of expansion in south Germany and Italy. The
Chancellor Thugut was not planning to march on Paris, but
looked forward to consolidating the Habsburg lands in Italy
by further acquisitions, and to reoccupying the lost province
of Belgium in order to exchange it for Bavaria. These gains
would be underwritten by a peace of compromise and barter.
The hated Prussians would acquire nothing; France would
remain a strife-torn republic; and the Russian armies would
retire frustrated to the steppes.

Thugut's policy had now ripened, and Grenville seethed
with anger at its disastrous harvest. He had played into
Thugut's hands by shifting Suvorov's Russian army north
from the Po valley into Switzerland, leaving a clear field in
Italy for Austrian politics. And the prospect of Suvorov's
arrival in Switzerland provided a further opportunity for the
Austrians. Grenville had intended Suvorov to reinforce the

Russians and Austrians already in Switzerland for a decisive offensive; but instead the Austrians had used his approach as an excuse to release their own army from Switzerland. Its commander Archduke Charles did not even wait for Suvorov, but marched northwards into Germany to besiege Mainz and prepare to enter the Netherlands, leaving Korsakov's Russian army isolated at Zurich. He had scarcely departed when Masséna attacked the Russians and drove them out of Switzerland; while Suvorov, still toiling over the passes from Italy, was likely to be trapped in the Alpine valleys by the victorious French.

When these disasters had stopped the main offensive in the east, what hope was left for the Duke of York's 34,000 sickly troops in Holland? Cooped up in a narrow neck of dune and polder south of the Helder, with the enemy free to send reinforcements from the Rhine now that they had nothing to fear from the Russians, the Duke of York could only expect misfortune: at best a wasting winter with uncertain supplies, at worst another Yorktown surrender. The French might also renew their attempts against rebellious Ireland; and when Colonel Brownrigg arrived in Downing Street Pitt was already convinced that the Dutch campaign should be abandoned. The Cabinet reached its decision within the hour, and at three o'clock its advice was on its way to the King at Windsor: the army in Holland must be withdrawn.[1]

This resolution meant that within days the Cabinet would be faced with a greater decision. Should Grenville's quest for decisive victory be maintained, to reduce France to her ancient limits and restore the monarchy? Or should Britain abandon her continental strategy, and withdraw into limited maritime warfare?

The decision to withdraw the army from Holland was greeted with a general sense of relief, which became overwhelming a few days later on the news that the Duke of York had secured his embarkation by an agreement with General Brune. Under

---

[1] The above events are described in my earlier volume on the Second Coalition, *Statesmen at War: the Strategy of Overthrow, 1789-1799*, hereafter cited as *Strategy of Overthrow*.

French attack it would have been impossible to embark the rearguard and artillery, and if wind and weather had delayed the shipping the whole army could have been lost. Now it was safe, at the cost of a capitulation by which the British would return 8,000 French prisoners from England. The price seemed cheap, and even the Dutch fleet which had been captured at the beginning of the campaign remained in British hands. 'We have our army again for better times and seasons' rejoiced George Canning, an Under-Secretary in the Foreign Office.[2]

What better seasons? The Cabinet met again four days later to consider future plans, but it could well have discussed whether the war should be continued at all. Apart from the military failures, there were economic clouds to sap the country's will. Already the reverberations of a slump in north Germany had been felt; and now the harvest failure was pushing up the price of bread, for the August gales which had scattered the expedition on its voyage to Holland and turned the Dutch roads into swamps had spoiled the corn. Grain merchants and farmers were withholding their stocks from the market to wait for higher prices; and to nurse the grain supplies the government banned the distilling of spirits to the detriment of the revenue. 'The bad harvest threatens a scarcity of grain this winter', Canning warned Lord Mornington in India, 'which may put spirits into both Jacobins and Opposition.' The price of wheat crept up, from fifty shillings a quarter to sixty-seven. In the dearth of 1796 it had gone to seventy-eight; but at that time there had been more barley and oats to make up the shortage, while this autumn all grains were scarce. If the price went much higher there would be hunger and riots; and gold would be drained abroad to pay for corn imports. When this happened, Parliament's enthusiasm for the war would wilt.[3]

In spite of these fears the bellicose and ambitious young Canning asserted that the resolute and confident spirit of the past year would continue. 'The country is more right than it has been at any time within my remembrance,' he assured

[2] Canning MSS, 29 Oct. 1799 to the Revd W. Leigh.
[3] Dropmore, V. 225; Canning MSS, 20 Oct., to Mornington; Add. MSS 38311, ff. 19, 27.

Lord Mornington. 'The only doubt entertained . . . seems to be between the two systems of endeavouring to overthrow, or determining to outlast the present state of things in France.'

To 'overthrow' or 'outlast': if this was the doubt, the word 'only' was misleading, and in spite of his bombast Canning knew it. For the choice was fundamental. To overthrow the revolutionary government meant continuing continental warfare, with huge armies and staggering loans and subsidies; a march on Paris; and a new government imposed on a defeated nation. To outlast the enemy meant withdrawing into maritime warfare and waiting on events. It meant surrendering supremacy in Europe to the French, and hoping that they would not use it to create a naval challenge. Britain would have to hope that the French Revolution would destroy itself from within, or that France would succumb to war-weariness and economic pressures before the British did. It meant forgoing the grand decisiveness of Grenville's continental strategy, and waiting for something to turn up; and the likeliest outcome was a peace of compromise. The question the government faced, wrote Canning, was whether to mount another effort on the huge scale of the last campaign; 'reserving the power of returning at the end of the campaign . . . to that system of limited expense, and sober defensive, by which if we cannot succeed in overthrowing the present power of France, we must keep ourselves secure against it, while it lasts, and survive till it is exhausted.'[4]

2. *Lord Grenville's Challenger*

To Canning's question his Foreign Office master Lord Grenville would have given an unhesitating answer. The country should mount another colossal effort, with no reservation about carrying on if the coming campaign should fail to achieve a decision; for only thus could the evil government of France be overthrown and tranquility restored. But a powerful challenger to Grenville's view was soon to emerge in the Cabinet. Henry Dundas, the Secretary of State for War, was about to

---

[4] Canning MSS, 20 Oct. to Mornington.

declare himself the advocate of a reduced political aim and a return to limited warfare. Dundas's views and character were discussed in my earlier volume. But since he was to dominate the final phase of the war, it is proper to look again at this remarkable man.

Together with Pitt and Grenville, he had been recognized for many years as one of the three 'efficient' members of the Cabinet. He had joined the inexperienced Pitt in the winter of 1783 to challenge the Fox–North coalition, an act of calculated courage which was characteristic of the man. The violence of opposition and the unpopularity of the North ministry in the latter years of the American War had never deterred him from supporting Lord North when other colleagues shrank back; and in the precarious early days of the Pitt ministry he was the hero of debate and the sure rock of the minority government. To Pitt, who was his junior by some seventeen years, he remained loyal, generous and affectionate. When both were out of office, he gave and collected money to pay Pitt's debts, with 'heartfelt pleasure . . . that at so immaterial an expense we had at once set at ease a friend whom we all love and venerate'. And when Pitt died Dundas told an old friend, 'I have no resources in store by which I can meet such a calamity.' Yet he knew Pitt's weaknesses, and was able to compensate for them. If Pitt was not, as an enemy described him, a 'mere moral effeminate', his close colleagues considered him to be easily influenced. 'You know by experience', Lord Spencer wrote to Dundas in 1801 after the fall of the ministry, 'how open Pitt is to be influenced by friends whose minds are not of sufficient strength and calibre to lead a mind like his.' Dundas called it 'facility of disposition', and coupled this weakness with another one: a tendency to adopt a new plan with headlong enthusiasm, without sufficient reflection and without the staying power to see it through when difficulties later arose. Dundas referred to this propensity as 'an over-eagerness to aim at the object immediately in contemplation. He is either in a garrett [*sic*] or a cellar.' It was a trait which Dundas said he had often had occasion to check. Strong-minded and decisive, sanguine yet canny, he was the ideal political friend for Pitt, complementing his strengths and compensating his weaknesses. In Dundas's house at Wimbledon a room was permanently reserved for the Prime Minister, and they often drove down there together after a debate or a Cabinet meeting to discuss the day's problems over supper and a bottle. Dundas's decisiveness, his friend Lady Anne Barnard believed, was 'necessary to fix Pitt's resolutions, which weaker judgments might have overturned, for he had no inflexibility of thinking'. Pitt had been, she said, 'a young man who looked up to him, for whom he had all the fondness of a father'. In Dundas's own words he was 'a cement of political strength'.[5]

So forceful a character made enemies, and they depicted Dundas as an unscrupulous, intriguing jobber. The political manager of Scotland had to be tough and ambitious, and he has been called a philistine. The King disliked his familiar manners and broad Scots dialect, and complained that his handwriting was 'the worst and most ungentlemanlike he had ever met with'. Pitt and Grenville, reared in the classical mould of Cambridge and Oxford, laughed at his grammar; and even fellow Scots marvelled at his diction. Lord Minto described his oratory as 'strange, barbarous but forcible', and Lady Anne Lindsay complained after dining with him and his daughters, 'my ears grated with the Scots dialect in all its purity'. North Britons were regarded with suspicion in English politics, and a Scot could scarcely win, for if he kept his native accents he was treated as a barbarian, yet if he modified his voice like Mansfield and Loughborough, he was condemned as sly. But on balance Dundas turned his Caledonian ways to his advantage. Like many compatriots in later times he used his Scots accent to project an image of frank directness. His commanding presence and strong, clear voice could force the attention of a clamorous House or an impatient Cabinet. In private society that intellectual soldier Sir Henry Bunbury found him 'a particularly agreeable man . . . notwithstanding his advanced age, his strong Scotch accent and Scotch peculiarities. There was a sort of jovial, fearless *abandon* about him that entirely removed from one's mind at the time all thought of the deep,

---

[5] Harlow, II. 249; Wraxall, I. 426; Matheson, 316, 318-19; A. D. Harvey, *English Literature and the Great War with France*, 70 (quoting Philip Francis); Rylands Library, Memoirs of Lady Anne Barnard, IV. 16; Add. MSS 40102, f. 102; Ehrman, 132, 322, 441, 457.

astute and wily character which was assigned to him in political life.'[6]

Dundas has been dismissed as a Scots adventurer; but he came of a family which had been distinguished in the law and politics for generations, and had been an able advocate till he abandoned the bar for politics. He was not uneducated, and had attended Edinburgh University; nor did he despise education. It was thanks to his pressure that his ward the future Earl of Aberdeen, destined one day to be Prime Minister, was allowed to enter St. John's College at Cambridge in opposition to his grandfather's prejudices: 'I take it for granted', Dundas told the young man, 'you do not mean to acquiesce in the principle that your rank supersedes the necessity of education.' But his own life and conversation were all politics, from which he only escaped during his autumn visits to his cottage on the banks of the Earn in the Perthshire highlands, 'my paradise in the north'. There his days were spent in shooting on the hills, and his evenings in non-political talking with his friends. He would walk by himself in the heavy highland rain, 'admiring the beauties I have already created in this sequestered paradise . . . a great deal of the beauties of Dunira depend on the rapidity of the torrents and the little cataracts rolling from the tops of the mountains, the rain . . . is the parent of much beauty . . . my rocks are ever rugged; my mountains are ever lofty . . .'. It was a far cry from Lord Grenville's arboretum in the Chilterns.[7]

Between Dundas and Grenville there was no long-standing history of disagreement, and they had worked together with

[6] Burges, 88; Matheson, 338; Rylands Library, Memoirs of Lady Anne Barnard, IV. 157; Bunbury *Memoir*, 23. There is an entertaining article by Richard Pares on the Scots in English politics in *History* 1954. Specimens of Dundas's speech have been phonetically recorded by his fellow Scots. Lord Glenbervie reports that he was alleged to have ended a speech with the words, 'I shall say no more but content myself with bagleaving to bring in a Bŭll.' More authentically, perhaps, Lady Anne Barnard recorded one of his disquisitions on Pitt: 'I often envy that rogue, while I am lying tossing and tumbling in my bed, and canna sleep a wunk for thinking of expedeshons and storms and bauttles by sea and laund, there does he lay doon his head in his bed, and sleep as soond as a taup.' (Glenbervie, I. 216; Rylands Library, Memoirs of Lady Anne Barnard, IV. 160.)

[7] Matheson, 297; Rylands Library, Balcarres Papers 27/2/57, 5 Nov. 1788, and 27/2/60, 21 Oct. 1791, Dundas to Lady Anne Lindsay.

Pitt for many years as an inner Cabinet. If Dundas was supreme in Indian affairs, Pitt and Grenville usually signed with him the secret directives of the Board of Control for the governors in India; and before the war the three had been in unison in extending the British empire of trade. Nevertheless Dundas was the initiator in colonial matters. He had been educated in Indian affairs by Charles Jenkinson, now an ageing Cabinet colleague and Earl of Liverpool, and he had been the effective head of the India Board since its inception in 1784. His efforts to push British exports into the markets of south-east Asia and China were paralleled by Jenkinson's support of the free port system in the Caribbean to insinuate British goods into South America. Dundas's aim was not to conquer territory but markets; and Asia was far from being his exclusive interest or even his clear first priority. We shall see that in 1800 he turned his attention first to the markets of Spanish America, and only later under pressure for peace negotiations did he give priority to Egypt and the security of India. In 1797, before the Second Coalition was formed, he had been pushing for the newly conquered island of Trinidad to be used as a base to open the Spanish markets on the Orinoco; and, weighing the probable revolt of Spain's American colonies, he was more favourable than was the cautious legitimist Grenville to a forward policy of encouraging their independence and penetrating their markets.[8]

Since the beginning of the war in 1793 Dundas had questioned the wisdom of pouring British resources into continental warfare. 'There exists [*sic*] in this country', he had warned within weeks of the outbreak of war, 'many strong prejudices against continental wars; and, with many, a strong

[8] Harlow, II. 113-14, 227, 244-6, 651-3. A different view of Dundas's priorities has been advanced in Edward Ingram's *Commitment to Empire: Prophecies of the Great Game in Asia, 1797-1800* (1981). The book provides an interesting perspective on the War of the Second Coalition, and is indispensable for affairs east of Suez. Its interpretation of British policy, however, is marred by lack of proportion. Ingram's theme is that previous historians of the Coalition have fought 'the wrong war in the wrong place'. Pitt's government ought to have been pursuing the 'heartland' theory of national power put forward a hundred years later by Halford Mackinder instead of defending the balance of power in Europe. He sees Britain as already a declining power; its naval supremacy a useless fraud; its greatness founded on the British Raj in India; its real defensive front the land boundaries of British India, with forward positions reaching towards the Middle East.

prepossession against the strength of the country being directed in any other channel than that of naval operations.' These prejudices he shared in some degree. They were supported by his reading of recent history, for in the war of 1739-48 Marshal Saxe had dominated the continent, yet the naval victories of 1747 had forced the French to surrender their European conquests. Dundas's doubts were strengthened by the crumbling of the first Coalition in 1795 and the expulsion of the British army from the continent. Thereafter he was cautious about plans to reopen a British front on the continent by invading France. 'My principle', he wrote, 'has been . . . to employ British force for the purpose of gaining and retaining a communication with the coast, but that the operations *in the interior* must be carried out by the French themselves.' His dislike of mixing British regulars with the French royalists brought him into conflict with William Windham, the Secretary at War and the Cabinet's link with the royalists. For Dundas all such efforts were secondary to imperial defence. 'It is my conviction unalterably fixed', he told the Duke of York at that time, 'that either with a view to peace or war . . . a compleat success in the West Indies is essential . . . No success in other quarters will palliate a neglect there. . . . By success in the West Indies alone you can be enabled to dictate the terms of peace.' His conviction led him to the colossal military effort of 1796 in the West Indies.[9]

Though Dundas acquiesced in the forming of the Second Coalition in 1798, he continued to question the continental commitment. When the naval victory at Camperdown in 1797 restored the national confidence on which Grenville began to rebuild the coalition, Dundas's reaction was to urge that England should adhere to the 'narrowest line' of limited warfare; and he encouraged Pitt's doubt whether the British public would support the renewed uncertainties and expense of continental war. As President of the India Board he was the first member of the Cabinet to catch the alarm for Egypt and India when Bonaparte sailed from Toulon in 1798. He was rightly sceptical in the following year about Grenville's promise of a Dutch insurrection to support the invasion of

⁹ Duffy, 21, 193-4; Add. Mss 40102, ff. 5, 9, 39.

Holland. And when the combined fleets of France and Spain were locked into Brest in August 1799 he saw an opportunity to destroy them for the sake of which he was prepared to withdraw the British army from its offensive in the Low Countries. To attack Brest and capture the enemy fleets would 'give the death blow for half a century to the power of France'. 'I am sure', he wrote to his friend the First Lord of the Admiralty, 'that country will always be the natural enemy of this, and if it is in our power we ought to use our best exertions to annihilate their naval power. . . . We are a small spot in the ocean without territorial consequences, and our own power and dignity as well as the safety of Europe, rests on our being the paramount commercial and naval power of the world.' In that observation he summarized his philosophy of war.[10]

As a minister Dundas has been variously judged. Historians of the government of India have acknowledged his sound work at the India Board, which he regarded as his greatest achievement: 'vigorous and competent' was the verdict of Dame Lucy Sutherland. But his tenure of the War Department was mercilessly caricatured by Sir John Fortescue, the intemperate historian of the British army. 'How many and how shameful had been Dundas's failures', he exclaimed: all the minister's enterprises had been inspired by 'ignorance, folly, and presumption . . . He knew no more of war than a monthly nurse, but had not the wisdom to be conscious of his ignorance.'[11]

Fortescue was not one to allow for the problems of conducting so difficult a war with such limited options, or for the pressures from Dundas's colleagues in the Cabinet. Dundas was admired by a distinguished soldier of the day, Lord Moira, for the energy and detail he brought to the deployment of military forces. Another military man, however, damned him as an ignorant civilian. 'What alas are we to expect when lawyers are allowed to think themselves Generals, and plan our military operations?' the Duke of Northumberland declaimed.

[10] *Strategy of Overthrow*, 3, 37, 161, 176; Spencer, III. 110–11, 162.
[11] Sutherland, *East India Company*, 352; Harlow, II. 113–14 and *passim*; Fortescue, *History of the British Army*, IV. 801, 865, and *The British Army 1783–1802*, 37.

The cobbler should stick to his last: 'I am certain no one would trust Mr. Dundas to make a pair of shoes for them, and why they should imagine that less knowledge and experience are necessary to form the plan of a campaign and conduct a war than to make a pair of shoes, I cannot conceive.'[12]

In a century which has seen the British army reorganized by Lord Haldane one can scarcely write off Dundas merely for being a lawyer; and even in the eighteenth century the Secretaries of State who directed the wars were usually civilians. If the Elder Pitt and Lord George Germain were soldiers, they scarcely constituted precedents against civilians; the one a very political cornet of horse, the other tarnished by the sentence of a court martial. What was novel in Dundas's situation was his office. Until the end of the American War the Secretaries of State had divided the world and its wars into the northern and southern departments and the colonies; and it was the reorganization of 1782 which, by creating the Foreign and Home Departments, first demarcated the Secretaryships by executive functions instead of by geographical areas. Dundas's War Department was a still later creation, an artifice of the coalition of 1794 to make room for the Duke of Portland at the Home Office by moving Dundas. The new War Department absorbed most of the former military responsibilities of the Home Office.

It was Dundas's new office, suggesting that he had special qualifications for directing a war, which provoked Northumberland's sneer at his legal training. Dundas himself accepted the change ungraciously. He complained that a War Department was superfluous, for the real War Minister must be Pitt himself, as controller of the purse; and with no troops to spare for overseas expeditions, military administration and home defence could be managed by the Home Office and the Commander-in-Chief. Dundas asserted that he would prefer to concentrate on his old love, the government of India, and continued to complain. In 1798 he twice protested angrily to Pitt about his situation: once about the overlapping powers of the Home Office, which still controlled the militia and volunteers; and again with a rambling and intemperate diatribe

[12] Hastings, III. 266; Simcoe Papers, 12 Jan. and 23 Oct. 1799, Northumberland to Simcoe. Northumberland had served in the American War as Earl Percy.

against Cabinet interference in the details of his office. 'Our Cabinet is a pretty large society of men', he wrote, 'and it is pretty obvious that on this subject as little as any other it is likely we should not always agree, is the majority to decide on the position of every regiment in the service and on the propriety of every position which the general of the district is to occupy?' This outburst shows why Pitt and Grenville derided Dundas's grammar; it also reveals Dundas's impatience with his colleagues and discontent with his office.[13]

In 1799, however, an expeditionary force was created, and it was Dundas who organized the expedition to Holland. He could no longer complain that he lacked a role; but the real weakness of the new organization of the Secretaryships became apparent. Instead of one Secretary of State being responsible for the military operations in his geographical area in their entirety — diplomacy, planning and execution — these functions were divided between two specialized departments. At the Foreign Office Lord Grenville devised the strategy which launched the British and Russians into Holland, and made the arrangements with the Tsar. But the parallel preparation of the British expedition did not proceed in step with the plans of Grenville, whose timetable was too rapid for the War Department which had to improvise the forces. Neither Grenville nor Dundas had overall responsibility; they lacked the practice and temperament for co-operation; and there was no superior authority to co-ordinate them. Unless the Prime Minister would accept the ultimate power of co-ordination, the new structure of the Secretaryships could not work smoothly.

The blame for the defeat in Holland fell heavily on Dundas, though he had performed marvels of improvization and the plan had not been his but Grenville's.[14] He smarted at the defeat, for which he blamed the atrocious and unpredictable weather; and though his optimism scarcely flagged, his temper was affected. The cheerful disposition of this handsome, courageous Scot was being undermined by weariness and poor health, the natural effect on a man in his late fifties of seven

[13] Add. MSS 40102, 3 Nov. 1799, Dundas to Pitt; PRO 30/8/157, 10 Feb. 1798, same to same; Rylands Library, Engl. 907, 31 May 1798, same to same.
[14] *Strategy of Overthrow*, 315.

years at the centre of a great war. He had already been begging for relief: 'You may naturally believe that after thirty-five years of active and laborious business, any relief from any part of my present labours must be highly gratifying to me and my family.'[15]

After the Dutch expedition Dundas's relations with Grenville, never cordial beneath the surface, became more acrimonious. In background and character Pitt's two closest colleagues could scarcely have been more different. Grenville was the younger man by seventeen years in age, but not in temperament. The aloof classical scholar and rigid man of principle, ponderous in build and gait, contrasted with the genial Scots pragmatist, the lover of good jokes and women's company and drink. When they collided over the terms of the Duke of York's capitulation, Grenville's sharp pen was bound to irritate. Since no Cabinet was called to discuss the terms Grenville sent his views in writing. They were of characteristic rigidity and lack of realism: Grenville insisted that the Duke was not entitled to give up prisoners in England who had not been taken by his own army, and wanted to repudiate the capitulation. This course could have led to the army's unconditional surrender, and Dundas, who had been in office at the time of Yorktown, well knew the peril of an army with its back to the sea. He replied that he took personal responsibility for accepting the terms; and if the Cabinet had met and rejected them, he would have refused to sign the order and would have resigned. 'I am afraid you and I unfortunately see this whole subject in so different a point of view that there is little chance of our agreeing upon almost any part of it . . . every channel of information I can apply to, public and private, leads me to a conclusion directly the reverse of what your information has induced you to believe.'[16]

Dundas's collision with the Foreign Secretary was followed immediately by a quarrel with George III. The point in dispute concerned military administration, the special interest of the King. Pitt's friend Lord Granville Leveson had raised the Staffordshire Volunteers, and the question was whether to disperse the battalion as additional companies in established

[15] PRO 30/8/157, 10 Feb. 1798, Dundas to Pitt.
[16] Dropmore, V. 501–4.

regiments, or preserve its separate identity. The King complained that Dundas's instructions to the Adjutant-General were not what he had said they would be, and when Pitt intervened he told him: 'I am thoroughly convinced of the propriety of my conduct, and . . . of the great impropriety of that of Mr. Dundas from the beginning of the business.' The King prevailed. 'Well,' he boasted publicly on the terrace at Windsor, 'I have got the better, for I have gained a victory over Dundas.' Some people thought that the King never forgave the quarrel; and Dundas's response was to ask Pitt again to relieve him of the Secretaryship of State.[17]

For some time Dundas had probably resented Grenville's influence with Pitt, on which other people had commented with surprise and disfavour. He had complained of being insufficiently listened to and supported in his 'arduous and responsible situation';[18] and now there were 'some recent circumstances which have made my situation even more disagreeable'. Whether this referred to his dispute with Grenville or with the King one cannot be sure; but he was clearly tired and unwell, and had been warned by his distinguished physician Sir Walter Farquhar to change his lifestyle. 'Let the very few years of talents and powers of business that remain to me', Dundas now implored Pitt, 'be devoted to the service of India which is in truth my proper element, and let the remainder of my time be appropriated to domestic happiness and the enjoyment of a few select friends.'

Pitt's rejoinder was unpitying: Dundas must not go. In the wake of the Dutch failure and with another great offensive to be prepared for the spring, the public interest required him to remain in office; so did Dundas's own reputation and peace of mind. 'There is *no* mode of your quitting your situation under the present circumstances which would not in my opinion be injurious to your own credit, and produce irreparable public mischief . . . let me therefore entreat you . . . to reconcile yourself to a duty which, however difficult and painful, you are at this moment not at liberty to relinquish.'

In the light of the latest reverses on the continent, Dundas

---

[17] Matheson, 275-6; Gower, *Private Corr.*, I. 270-2; Glenbervie, I. 181.
[18] Rylands Library, Engl. 907, 31 May 1798, Dundas to Pitt.

could only agree. Shackled to his galley-bench, he continued to 'ply the tough oar.'[19]

3. *The Continental Commitment*

The Cabinet discussion of future war plans on 18 October was long and inconclusive. They talked round the situation in Holland and the future of the war, and considered three possible ways of using a force against France. But military planning was premature till it was clear who Britain's allies were to be and what pressure they could mount in the east. When Austria's 'perfidy' in Switzerland had been unmasked, the three men who dominated British strategy had agreed on at least one thing: that Russia must in future be treated as Britain's only true ally. But about the quality of that ally they differed. The Russian army's performance in Holland had been deplorable; accounts of Korsakov's force in Switzerland were little better; and there were even disquieting rumours about Suvorov, the hero of the Italian campaign.

Grenville's faith, however, was restored after the Zurich disaster by an extraordinary report on Suvorov, confirming his stature and refuting the stories which were circulating about his senile eccentricity. In a two-hour interview with Colonel Clinton on the eve of his plunge into the Alpine passes, Suvorov had given a lucid, unfaltering account without notes of his Italian operations, his troubles with the Austrians, and his fears about the coming march into Switzerland. This interview, wrote Grenville, destroyed the Austrian nonsense of denigrating the Russian commander, 'the only General that has yet shown any knowledge of the nature of the enemy he had to cope with'.[20]

Grenville had written this in early October, when Suvorov's fate in the Alpine valleys was still unknown. By the end of the month he was safe, after a series of desperate mountain marches and combats. Instead of taking the safer route from

---

[19] Furber 123; PRO 30/8/157, 27 Feb. and 4 Nov. 1799, Dundas to Pitt; *GL* III, p. 294n, 304n.

[20] Wickham, II. 206–12 (Wickham's no. 28 of 12 Sept., received 27 Sept. 1799: FO 74/24); Stowe Papers, 1 Oct., Lord Grenville to Thomas Grenville.

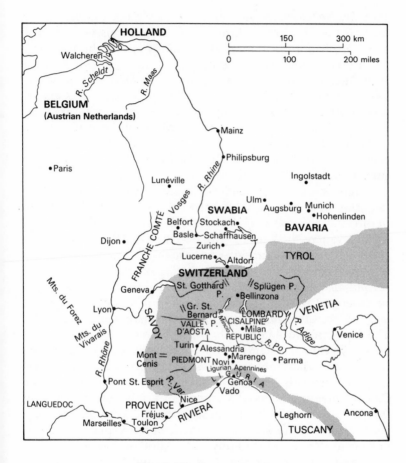

Map 2. The Eastern Front.

Italy by an eastward detour over the Splügen pass, he had crossed the St. Gotthard, intending to fight his way through the French cordon to Korsakov's aid. Forcing the pass with his infantry and a few mountain guns, he emerged from the high Alps at Altdorf near the head of the Lake of Lucerne to find that Korsakov had been routed and Masséna was marching to attack him with a superior force. He turned eastward over the Klausen pass into the Linth Thal, fighting off his pursuers as he headed for Glarus; found his way blocked by Soult; and crossed the Col de Panix in snow at 7,000 feet to gain the valley of the Rhine.

Surely such troops under this great leader could be the mainstay of next year's offensive? So Grenville believed; and before the collapse in Holland and Switzerland he had already offered to pay the Tsar for 100,000 men in 1800 and support them with 30,000 subsidized Germans.[21] This proposal was left unaltered by the Cabinet meeting on 18 October. But a second ally was still needed, for the Russian force alone would be swamped by the French; nor could it be deployed in the west without the collusion of one of the major German powers. The Prussians would certainly continue to sit on the fence and prosper in their 'enchanted circle' of neutrality; and Pitt feared that the Austrians too would make peace with France now that they had virtually secured what they wanted in Italy. At the Cabinet meeting he aired a scheme of bribing them to stay in the war, probably by promising them Piedmont. But till Austria's collaboration was secured, military planning could not begin. Her excellent army of 230,000 men was indispensable; and without her the Russians would have no overland route to western Europe. That would mean the end of continental warfare, and Britain would be compelled to revert to her maritime defensive, using such Russian troops as could be sent to England by sea to threaten and harass the enemy coasts. With these uncertainties, nothing firm could emerge from the Cabinet meeting. No decision was recorded, and nothing seems to have been agreed except that the next campaign should be carried on with all possible resources and energy.[22]

[21] Stowe Papers, 1 Oct., Grenville to Whitworth.
[22] Dropmore, V. 404, 414–16, 432–3; Windham *Diary*, 415, 416; FO 65/44, 18 Oct., Grenville to Whitworth.

But how? The meeting had not been well conducted, as
Grenville complained to Dundas: 'On the general question we
were led into more discussion that I think useful in our large
Cabinet.' Dundas agreed; an opinion which would have infuriated his colleague William Windham, the Secretary at War.
Windham had protested, during the planning of the Dutch
expedition, about the looseness of procedure which allowed
the Cabinet to drift imperceptibly from one decision into
another. He was now an angry man; angry about the failure
in Holland which he had predicted, and angry about the
scanty aid being given to his friends the French royalists
because all resources had been committed to Holland. The
Dutch expedition, he complained sarcastically a few days
after Grenville and Dundas exchanged their dismissive opinion
of the Cabinet, 'was not one of the measures of which Cabinet
could be supposed to take any cognizance'. He could see the
same process at work again. The Cabinet was being eddied
through desultory discussions into enormous new commitments to the Russians. To them England was to pay out
millions while aid to the French royalists was measured in
hundreds. Windham wished Britain would spend her money
in France, instead of squandering it on the Russians whose
lamentable performance at Zurich was now exposed. How
fatal to build a great offensive on such troops! He wondered
whether to push his dissent to the point of resigning, but
hoped his colleagues had learned from their failure in Holland.
'Defeat and miscarriage renders men a little more tractable in
their opinions.'[23]

With much of this Dundas would have agreed. He regarded
the Austrians as incorrigible, and did not believe that they
could be bribed into loyalty by promising them Piedmont.
Better to leave the nursing of the Austrian alliance to the
Tsar, promising that the British would fall in with his arrangements, for if there was any hope of renewing the offensive it
rested on the Russian army. Yet even with the Russians
Dundas doubted whether much could be done. Their pillaging
and indiscipline in Switzerland were notorious, and Korsakov's

[23] Dropmore, V. 487, 494; Nat. Library of Scotland, Minto Papers, 25 Oct.,
Windham to Minto. For Windham's earlier complaint about Cabinet procedure see
Strategy of Overthrow, 177–80.

retreat from Zurich had resembled Essen's flight from Bergen in Holland. His troops looted the villages as they fled, sold half-worked plate in the streets of Schaffhausen, and tore up the palisades in the fortified Rhine bridgehead for fuel. So oppressive was their haphazard foraging that the diplomat William Wickham predicted a general insurrection if they returned to Switzerland. Dundas regarded the Russian army as unfit for the field, and believed that it would take a year to reform and retrain it. He doubted, therefore, whether the next campaign could be decisive.[24]

But Grenville was not to be deflected. He seldom listened to arguments against his settled opinions; and from Bavaria his old and trusted friend Wickham was urging that with an increase of pay and a regular commissariat the brave and enduring Russian troops could become the best in the world. Grenville remained convinced that his war aims could be attained by a vast strategic combination of the great powers. 'What may we not hope if the French are pressed by Suvorov on one side, by the Archduke on the other, and on this side, harassed by the operations which we can undertake with a superior fleet, and a disposable force of 60,000 men?'

He admitted that the Russian army needed administrative reform and an Austrian staff; but those he thought could be arranged. His doubts were still focused on the Austrians rather than the Russians. 'I fear we shall have endless difficulties when we come to treat for magazines and supplies with the most shabby set of people in Europe. It will require no small degree of firmness at the outset to convince them that we are not at their mercy, which we really are in this respect, though we must not let them think so.' He carried the Cabinet with him. On 26 October it was agreed to offer Russia a subsidy for 80,000-90,000 men to invade France through Switzerland; to treat jointly in Vienna for Austrian co-operation; and to offer Piedmont to the Austrians.[25] The strategy of the great offensive lived on.

To this Cabinet minute Windham gave a hesitating assent, still anxious because all the available funds were being

[24] Dropmore, V. 498-9; Wickham, II. 249, 257, 262.
[25] Wickham, II. 262; Dropmore, V. 456, 504-5 and VI. 1; *GL* 2072; Windham *Diary*, 416; Duffy, 376-7.

absorbed by the eastern allies at the expense of the French royalists. But Windham, wrote a female victim of his fine black eyes, was 'a man spending his life in regretting and being too late for everything'.[26] The doubts which he had lacked the nerve to press in the Cabinet grew stronger after the decision, and he began to push his view when the opportunity had passed. He canvassed Canning on the way home from a dinner, called on Pitt and walked with him to Lady Chatham's, and thought he had made some impression. The more he considered it, the clearer it seemed that this was not the moment for a grand assault on the French Republic. If Grenville's armies could be assembled, which he doubted, their real effectiveness would be less than their numbers, and the Russian army was not fit to be left unsupported in the presence of a French force of equal size. Yet for the delusive hope of an Austro-Russian offensive, Britain was sacrificing the legitimate ruler of Piedmont and the principles for which Windham believed the war should be fought. Better to revert to the defensive than throw away Britain's last stake on such an unpromising gamble. We should 'lie on our oars for the present', he said, and reserve Britain's strength for a better opportunity.[27]

The opinions of the vain and capricious Windham seldom carried much weight; and Dundas, who agreed with him, was engaged in his quarrel with the King and his attempt to resign. There was no effective opposition to Grenville's Coalition policy till a private letter arrived from Wickham in which he abruptly changed his advice about the Russian army. Ten days in the company of Suvorov and the Russian generals had convinced him that even if the Russian army were remodelled its commanders were incapable of using it. The Tsar's younger son, the Grand Duke Constantine, was 'one of the greatest brutes that ever disgraced the human shape'; and the great Suvorov, who had talked so lucidly to Colonel Clinton in Italy, seemed to have gone out of his mind. He dined at eight in the morning, served by dirty servants with food so disgusting that even the Croatian General Jellachich could not swallow a mouthful. In the evening Suvorov's head was often clearer,

[26] Rylands Library, Memoirs of Lady Anne Barnard, IV. 87, and V. 31.
[27] Windham *Diary*, 416; Windham *Papers*, II. 132-5.

and his long discourses seemed to confirm the impression Clinton had formed of a vigorous mind and sound judgement. But as soon as Wickham raised an awkward subject the marshal retreated behind a smoke-screen of senility, garbling Wickham's point in an unintelligible tone he often used in public, and evading or pretending not to understand his questions.

Frustrated and infuriated by the atmosphere of the Russian headquarters, Wickham denounced Suvorov as 'an ignorant designing mountebank', surrounded by scheming nephews and by hangers-on 'as cunning and treacherous as they are ignorant and brutal . . . they are shag all over'. But in calmer mood Wickham sensed that this 'cunning, artful' Muscovite was playing a game; the eternal secretive Russian stalling a negotiation. Wickham guessed that he was trying to conceal the collapse of his army's morale, its homesickness and its dread of being tested against the French. In rational discussions Suvorov admitted that his army was not fit for independent operations and needed a stiffening of Austrian troops and an Austrian staff. Wickham went further. 'I am now thoroughly persuaded', he warned Grenville, 'that the Russian troops cannot possibly be kept together in the shape of an army.'[28]

Wickham's revised portrait of the Russian army went to the Cabinet on 7 November, and it was clear that the Russians could not be treated as Britain's 'only true ally'. But Dundas arrived late and missed much of the discussion, and his views were not put to the meeting; and instead of concluding that an Austro-Russian alliance was impracticable, as he would have wished, the Cabinet merely resolved that Austria must be more fully integrated into the military planning. This meant bringing the Austrians into the discussions, consulting Thugut about the Russians' problems, and asking him to provide them with Austrian troops and supplies. Grenville was being sucked back into dependence on the Austrians. He had gambled on their co-operation in his war plans of 1799, though he knew that their political aims conflicted with his

[28] Dropmore, V. 485; Wickham, II. 261, 272–5, 277, 292, 324, 340, 409–10. A very different interpretation of Suvorov from that perceived by his British contemporaries is to be found in C. Duffy, *Russia's Military Way to the West*, 189–95.

own and the Tsar's, and he had lost his stake when the Arch-duke Charles deserted the Russians at Zurich. Yet from now on, as his confidence in the Russians faded, he was to be lured even deeper into dependence on Austria by his quest for decisive victory.

The Cabinet agreed that British financial support for the next campaign should depend on 25,000-30,000 Austrian troops being permanently attached to the Russians, with an Austrian staff to be selected by Suvorov, and magazines, transport and bridging train to be provided at Austria's expense. This meant that the next grand offensive, like the last one, would depend on Austrian co-operation; and Pitt's approval of the plan was guarded, though he had agreed to it with Grenville before the meeting. If Austria could be per-suaded to act in earnest and pursue her aims through a com-mon allied strategy, he still saw hope of 'saving Europe' in two more campaigns. 'The decision of Vienna is however wholly uncertain, and our best comfort is that if it fails us, we can return to our defensive system with unbroken spirits and resources, and trust to our own anchors to ride out the storm.'[29]

Dundas's objections to the plan were stronger. Had he been present at the beginning of the meeting, he told Grenville in a courteous letter, he would have been unable to see any advantage in cobbling the Coalition. He still believed that the Russians and Austrians should be left to their own arrange-ments, with a promise of a subsidy for the Russians if they agreed on a satisfactory plan. Dundas remained convinced that no effective operations could be expected of the Russian army in the coming year. Suvorov's force would have to be totally remodelled to fight in western Europe, a process so complicated and expensive that it would fail; and then the British public, disillusioned by repeated disappointments in the alliance, would cease to support the war. Perhaps the Russians could be used to garrison the Italian fortresses, and release enough Austrian troops to mount an offensive with a reinforcement of subsidized South Germans. But it was useless to depend on the Russians as the main force of the Coalition.

[29] *GL* 2079; FO 7/57, 8 Nov., Grenville to Minto; William Clements Library, 6 Nov., Pitt to Mornington.

If Austria would not co-operate, the government must use its resources 'to maintain at all costs the power and independence of Great Britain'.

With equal courtesy, Grenville disagreed. On balance he thought it best to do what one could with the Russians; and he did not see why a reorganized Russian force should not succeed. In spite of Pitt's doubts and Dundas's outright hostility, he proceeded to implement his plan by opening negotiations in Petersburg and Vienna, and arranged for Sir Home Popham, the naval officer who had arranged shipping for the Russian expedition to Holland, to return to Petersburg. As an expert in obtaining transports, Popham's presence would be the more necessary because Grenville was playing with other ideas for obtaining Russian reinforcements. If it proved difficult to obtain overland reinforcements for Suvorov, he thought of shipping the Russian troops from Holland to the Mediterranean to join him, and perhaps bringing other Russian troops from the Black Sea.[30]

4. 'The interior of France'

Parallel with these far-flung schemes for the eastern front, Lord Grenville had plans for the west. He promised the Tsar that Britian would support a Russian offensive in Switzerland by invading western France with 60,000 or 100,000 troops. These were loose figures, and the larger one must have included the Russians then in Holland; but Dundas did not quarrel about numbers, and assured Grenville that the offensive force at home could be raised to 80,000 without the Russians. But the problem was how to use them, and the experience in Holland was discouraging. Grenville, with his talent for analysis, distinguished two types of attack on France: a second front, or a major raid. An attack on the combined French and Spanish fleets in Brest was still being examined, and this Grenville defined as a 'limited object' which might be achieved by a correct calculation of time and force. Was it possible to do more, he asked Dundas. Could a

[30] Dropmore, VI. 12-14, 16; FO 7/57, 8 Nov., Grenville to Minto (two dispatches); FO 65/45, 10 and 12 Nov., Grenville to Whitworth.

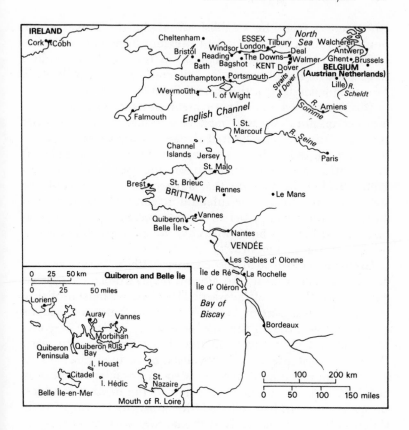

Map 3. The Western Theatre.

true second front be established? Might the Russians and South Germans exert sufficient pressure from Switzerland to make a British campaign feasible in the west? Or could a large enough British force be collected to maintain itself in France independent of the eastern front?

Dundas replied that a permanent western front would be 'perfect insanity' without massive pressure on France from the east. But even the limited stroke against Brest ought not to be attempted without a strong allied offensive in the east. If an offensive were mounted on the eastern front with 100,000 men, he thought that a magnificent blow could be struck against Brest: 'one splendid attempt, at one stroke, to annihilate the naval power of France and Spain.' The operation would have to be a swift *coup de main*; relying on surprise, and over in a month.[31]

Grenville embellished his enquiry with a lecture on the danger of being drawn into adventures in France by royalist enthusiasm. 'If we fail', he warned Dundas, 'we must probably lose the greatest part of the only army we have ever had, or ever shall have, during the war.' It scarcely became Grenville, who had staked so much on the Dutch Orangists, to warn Dundas against the French royalists, or to urge him 'not to let your mind proceed step by step to consider the plan as decided'. This was a fair description of the manner in which Grenville himself had allowed the army to be engulfed in Holland; but Dundas received the homily with good temper. He assured Grenville that he was as sceptical about the royalists as he had been about the Orangists, and that only pressure from Pitt and Grenville himself had induced him to prepare a few supplies for them.[32]

The minister who did believe in the royalists was Windham, but his faith was unseasonable; for the failure of the Dutch to rise should have been a warning against basing strategic plans on insurgents. So thought the King. 'I trust', he wrote, 'that we shall learn experience from this severe lesson and not place

---

[31] Stowe Papers, 1 Oct., Grenville to Whitworth; Dropmore, V. 487, 493; Dundas MSS, Duke University MSS, XVIII F, memorandum on disposable force (undated, but evidently about this time). For the origins of the Brest plan, see *Strategy of Overthrow.*

[32] Dropmore, V. 487, 493.

so much confidence in the assertions of those who thought
the Dutch would have . . . acted more suitable to the assistance that has been afforded them.' But as I argued in my
earlier volume, it was not so easy to omit insurgency from
the calculation. Lacking an organized bridgehead and allied
armies in western Europe, the small British army could not
hope to maintain a foothold without military aid from the
population. Lord Grenville continued to rest his hopes for
the west on counter-revolution. In the case of Holland his
hopes had been fed by his brother Thomas, who was in touch
with Orangist exiles in Berlin and promised a massive explosion as soon as a British force appeared. Now it was Windham
who promised a decisive insurrection in France. Put 20,000
troops ashore with a French prince, he urged, and the whole
of western France would explode 'and give more soldiers
than you would know what to do with'. It was almost exactly
the language that Tom Grenville had used about the Dutch.
And to strengthen the lure, Grenville's old friend William
Wickham, writing from southern Germany, promised a rising
in the eastern provinces of France. Two French generals,
Pichegru and Willot, had recently escaped from exile in
Surinam to lead the insurrection. Pichegru was now with the
'Swabian agency', the royalist group led by General de Précy
at Augsburg, and was to enter Franche Comté with a royalist
force in the rear of the Austrians. Willot, who was lying low
in England after recovering from the effects of his imprisonment, had commanded the Marseilles military district before
the Jacobin coup of 1797 and asked to be used in Provence.
He was sent off to the continent to meet Wickham, who was
establishing communications with Lyon in preparation for
the allied invasion.[33]

The time certainly seemed propitious. The latest Paris
revolution had left Sièyes in precarious power and openly
dedicated to rewriting the revolutionary constitution. The
French were war-weary, the financial deficit was still growing,
and the army's depleted numbers had scarcely risen since
conscription had been reimposed in the spring. British intelligence sources indicated a prevailing sense of instability in

[33] *GL* 4060; Dropmore, V. 219, 407–8; Mitchell, 237; Hall, *Pichegru*, 266 ff.

Paris. Everyone was saying that the present government could not last and a change was inevitable. 'Par qui et comment se fera-t-il?' The question was soon to be answered. On 9 October a frigate from Egypt had landed General Bonaparte at Fréjus.[34]

In the meantime ill-concerted royalist risings had been exploding like firecrackers. The royalists of Toulouse had risen on 4 August, but failed to enter the Jacobin-controlled town and seize the arsenal. The Bordeaux royalists then rose sporadically before they were really organized. In the west, the *Vendée militaire*, the rising was timed for mid-August like the others, but the local leaders did not even assemble till mid-September, a month after the south-west had been put down.

Hitherto it had been the British government's policy to discourage a royalist rising till the allied armies were in a position to support it. But in the late summer it had become apparent that the royalists could not be held back, and Windham began to press for supplies and weapons. It was agreed that arms should be purchased abroad immediately, to supplement the 10,000 stand of arms which was all that the Board of Ordnance would spare. A cruiser squadron was to be stationed in Quiberon Bay, and an Ordnance transport was to be prepared to load a cargo of arms for the insurgents.[35]

On 30 October came news that the whole of western France had burst into revolt. But by then the Cabinet had edged deeper into the financial commitments to the eastern powers at which Windham had protested so bitterly.

[34] Stowe Papers, 19 and 26 June, de la Palu to T. Grenville; 29 June, François d'Ivernois to same.

[35] Add. MSS 37844, ff. 202-3; Windham *Diary*, 414-15.

CHAPTER II

War or Peace?

1. *The Coming of Bonaparte*

By the middle of November 1799 the British ministers had
been groping their way for a month through the dust clouds
which swirled from the ruins of the year's collapsed offensives.
Still they continued to patch the tattered alliance, pragmati-
cally adjusting their plans, their aims, their principles with
every fresh scrap of news. With each adjustment their cohesion
as a Cabinet was shaken a little looser. Hitherto, however,
Lord Grenville's large views had prevailed. On 19 November
he composed an immense dispatch for Petersburg, in which
he covered the war aims of the concert and the building up of
Suvorov's force. It was to form a mass of 125,000 men composed as follows:[1]

Suvorov's existing force	30,000
Reinforcements from Russia	60,000
Bavarians to be treated for	10,000
Attached Austrians	25,000
	125,000

But on that very day came a fresh shock to his system. A
letter from the Tsar informed his ambassador in London,
Count Simon Vorontsov, that he had broken with the Austrians
and was withdrawing his army from the eastern front.

Paul's anger with Austria originated in Suvorov's summer
operations in Italy. Having overrun Piedmont, the marshal
found that Thugut was preventing the return of the King to
Turin while he arranged to annexe Piedmontese territory to
link Austria's Italian possessions with the port of Genoa. This
evidence of the Austrians' 'insatiable spirit of aggrandisement'
was followed by the Archduke Charles's desertion of the
Russians in Switzerland. Paul did not at first oppose the

[1] FO 65/45, 19 Nov. 1799, Grenville to Whitworth.

Austrian plan, for he understood the difficulty of supplying such large forces in Switzerland, and was allowed by the Austrians to believe that Korsakov's right flank would be protected by a South German force. In this delusion he remained till the end of September, when he learned with consternation that the Archduke had marched away without providing for the Russian flank. Paul's advisers had long suspected that the plans to move Suvorov out of Italy were designed to further Austria's political ambitions at the expense of the Russian armies; and on hearing of Korsakov's defeat at Zurich the explosive Tsar resolved to withdraw his armies from the Austrian front.[2]

This news might have signalled the moment for the British government to give up its plans for continental warfare. Since the collapse in Holland and Switzerland, ministers had been saying that if efforts to regenerate the continental war should fail, Britain must fall back on a maritime defensive and 'ride out the storm'. Had not the time now come for the country to rest on its oars and husband its strength? So at least the King believed: we must 'keep our exertions within such bounds that we may continue the war for many years and thus by time overcome the enemy'.[3] But just at this moment, when every indicator in the east signalled that it was time to withdraw from the continental war, the ministers had to assimilate an electrifying event in France: the coup of 18 brumaire.

A *coup d'état* in Paris was neither novel nor suprising. The Directory had used force three times to circumvent the ponderous constitution or put down its opponents; and it had organized numerous coups in the satellite republics with the help of its generals. There was no want of practice; and since the summer the Director Sièyes had been 'looking for a sword' to stabilize his regime against the Jacobin left. General Moreau was considered and rejected; Joubert was groomed for the part, but was killed while qualifying himself in the battle of Novi. Then providence placed in Sièyes's hands the most determined and brilliant adventurer of them all.

---

[2] FO 65/43, Whitworth's of 28 July, and FO 65/44, Whitworth's of 22 Aug., 5, 14 and 27 Sept.; Stowe Papers, 23 Aug., Whitworth to T. Grenville; Vorontsov, VIII. 240-1, 246, 259.   [3] *GL* 2082.

Bonaparte, home from Egypt to pluck the ripening pear, was placed in command of the Paris garrison. On 9 November his troops dispersed the Legislative Councils, and a provisional government of three Consuls was set up of which he assumed the leadership.

It was virtually certain that a peace offensive would follow, and the Consuls immediately mounted a propaganda campaign in France to promote the belief that they were seeking peace. But was the new government any more capable of negotiating a stable settlement than its revolutionary predecessors had been? A military despotism, which could not guarantee its own existence for twenty-four hours and faced a general insurrection in its western provinces, could promise little. The western insurgents had already at various times occupied Nantes, Le Mans and Saint-Brieuc; and thanks to Windham's efforts, arms were being sent to help them survive till British troops could come to their aid in the spring. Windham had battered at the doors of Whitehall and Downing Street. He had badgered Dundas and Huskisson at the War Department, Frere at the Foreign Office; had written to Pitt. 'For God's sake, let us at length exert ourselves to support these people . . . Delay is destruction. The crisis is such that we must count by hours.' At last Pitt exerted himself. Twenty thousand stand of arms were released from the Tower, and 7,000 from store at Portsmouth; and there was a prospect of more arms being purchased abroad or handed in by disbanding militiamen. All this was desperately late in the day, and since all the transports were needed to evacuate the army in Holland even the store-ship promised weeks earlier was not ready. Nevertheless when the news of Bonaparte's coup arrived, the British government was already committed to helping the insurgents. By the end of the year 22,000 stand of arms, 32 pieces of ordnance, and 18,000 sets of shoes and gaiters had been sent to the French coast or to depots at Falmouth, Jersey and St. Marcouf.[4]

Windham himself had been pessimistic about the royalists' capacity to survive through the winter, neglected as their needs had been before the rising. But Bonaparte's adventure

[4] Windham *Papers*, II. 136–8, 145–7; Dropmore, VI. 1, 3, 5; Windham *Diary*, 16–17; Add. MSS. 37872, ff. 243–4; Add. MSS. 37878, f. 216.

changed the outlook. If the Consulate were pressed hard between the western insurgents and external attacks, Bonaparte could not find the military force to fend off his Jacobin opponents. Pinched between the left and the right, he might be forced to play the role of General Monk and restore the monarchy. If the allies refused him peace he would be forced, in Grenville's words, to 'prepare for his voyage to Cayenne, or throw himself upon the Royalists'. It was therefore decided that in spite of the Russian rupture with Austria, one final effort should be made to resuscitate the Coalition.[5]

But a final effort it must be: 'one more campaign is its utmost limit', Grenville warned his trusted envoy Wickham. 'We are quietly making preparations for an immense effort next year against France itself in support of the Royalists . . . The situation of affairs at Paris appears to be in the highest degree favourable to the establishment and progress of the Royalist cause.' With this Pitt agreed. He saw 'every reason to be persuaded, that one more campaign, if our Confederacy *can any how* be kept together, will secure all we can wish'. But that *if* was everything. 'All these hopes', wrote Grenville, '. . . are dependent on the co-operation of Austria and Russia for another war.'[6]

Not that real co-operation was probable; for Wickham's latest reports made it clear that the Austrians had no intention of providing the support the Russian army needed to make it capable of independent operations. The British ministers, however, believe now that the Austrians had enough troops of their own to beat the run-down French army if their 'perverse and crooked' policy did not deflect them. If the Tsar could be induced to change his mind and allow his troops to fight alongside the Austrians, 30,000 Russians might still be used on the eastern front in an auxiliary role. But the main role for the Russians would be to join the British in surrounding France with concentric amphibious thrusts. Bonaparte was to be overwhelmed in the spring by

[5] Windham *Papers*, II. 143–4; Windham *Diary*, 417; *GL* 2082; Canning MSS, 23 Nov., Pitt to Canning, and 29 Nov., Hammond to Canning; Dropmore, VI. 53; Spencer, IV. 88.

[6] Dropmore, VI. 52–2; *GL* 2082; Canning MSS, 23 Nov., Pitt to Canning.

converging thrusts from the Alps, the Mediterranean and the English Channel.

The British role in these attacks was clear in outline. In the west 30,000 infantry would be landed in Brittany to attack Brest and sustain the royalists, and these would be doubled to 60,000 as reinforcements became available. In the Mediterranean about 5,000 British troops could be spared from the garrisons for offensive operations. On both the British fronts, in the west and in the Mediterranean, Russians would also be deployed; but how, and in what proportions? The question exercised the triumvirate, with Dundas questioning Grenville's ideas but changing his own mind or having fresh inspirations almost daily, and Pitt swithering between the two of them, composing a memorandum in the morning with Grenville, and falling into doubt again after dining with Dundas at Wimbledon. There were real problems: shortage of shipping, the unsuitability of Russian and British troops to act together, and the uncertainty whether the Tsar would spare more troops. Eventually it was agreed to propose to Paul that the Russians from Holland, perhaps 15,000, should be shipped to the Mediterranean as soon as possible, to form an Anglo-Russian force under General Stuart at Minorca and harass the Spanish or French coasts. To replace them 15,000-20,000 more Russians should be shipped from the Baltic to England, and used for a spring attack on Walcheren reinforced by the 5,000 Dutch troops. Paul was also asked to send 6,000-8,000 troops from the Black Sea to the Mediterranean, to garrison places captured by Stuart's force. A further possibility was added on the suggestion of Dundas, who as we shall later see, was deeply concerned about the transport tonnage on which these plans would depend. If the Tsar persisted in withdrawing Suvorov's army from the Austrian front he might be persuaded to place it at Britain's disposal, and march it down to the Mediterranean to form the offensive force under Stuart. No troops need then be shipped from the Black Sea; the Russian troops in England need not be shipped to the Mediterranean; and only 10,000-12,000 reinforcements would be needed from the Baltic for the Walcheren attack.[7]

[7] These confusing discussions and conclusions may be traced in Dropmore, VI. 35-6; 39, 48, 52-4, 80-1; Canning MSS, 23 Nov., Pitt to Canning; Windham

These plans were based on the British government's assessment of the Bonaparte coup; and to confirm that its view was correct an agent was sent to Paris. This was Philip Masseria, whom General Stuart had brought home with him from Minorca and recommended as a suitable agent to discover the real views of Bonaparte and his family: perhaps he was a fellow-Corsican. He was asked to find out what the new government was likely to bring, and whether it was durable; whether Bonaparte would prefer restoring the monarchy to being overthrown by the Jacobins; whether he thought peace or war best suited his interests; whether he would make an overture for peace, and on what terms. On the answers to these questions hung the success of the maritime offensives with which France was about to be encircled.[8]

2. *War Aims and the Ministers*

Through the twists and turns of Austrian and Russian policy the British ministers had contrived to sustain a thread of strategic planning. Even now their plans had to allow for several contingencies: the return of Suvorov's army to the eastern front, the total breakdown of Austro-Russian co-operation, or even a separate Austrian peace. To cope with a situation so fluid the full Cabinet was a clumsy machine, and Pitt had constructed his plans with his 'efficient ministers' Dundas and Grenville and with little reference to the rest of the Cabinet. No wonder its other members sometimes felt excluded and confused. 'We have so changed backwards and

Diary, 418; PRO 30/8/140, n.d., memo on application of forces; FO 65/45, 22, 23, 28 and 30 Nov., Grenville to Whitworth; Add. MSS 38759, 28 Nov., memo by Dundas for Huskisson.

[8] The instruction for Masseria is printed in Stuart Wortley, 322–3, where it is suggested that the questions are address to General Stuart himself. If this had been so, it would have indicated that Stuart's opinions carried extraordinary weight with the ministers (towards whom he was not politically very sympathetic), and would have strengthened the story of his alleged Mediterranean plan which is described on pp. 60–1 below. The original drafts in PRO 30/58/2 are endorsed as being 'sent to General Stuart for a person going to Paris Dec 1st 1799' (the rougher draft is dated 30 Nov.). Masseria is identified in PRO 30/58/3. He returned from France via Hamburg in April 1800, and complained that he had received no gratitude or acknowledgement from Pitt.

forwards,' Windham complained on 3 December, 'have so shrunk and expanded our views of Russian assistance, and subsidised force, that Cabinet, which has but a slight and imperfect view of these things, hardly allows the opportunity of knowing where one is.'[9]

Yet speculative though the plans might be, they were based on the solid hope that the Consulate's instability could lead to the return of the French monarchy. On that point the uneasy Windham was in agreement with Pitt, Grenville and the King. Dundas however had reservations. He was uneasy that nothing had been done to remove the French from Egypt; and he discovered that Grenville was willing to return most of England's colonial conquests to France and Holland if the Bourbons and the House of Orange were restored. This Dundas regarded as too high a price to pay for the goodwill of the exiled rulers' subjects; and he would rather abandon Louis XVIII and the Stadtholder than buy their restoration with the captured colonies. To him the security of the East and West India trades was more important than the monarchs of rival powers. In asserting this he challenged Grenville's view of the purpose of the war. He believed that solid British interests must not be sacrificed to ideology, for the Jacobin contagion was dead. In effect he was asserting that he supported the coming military effort in Europe only to secure material British interests. It was not necessary to march into Paris, overthrow the republic, and then buy popularity for the Bourbon monarchy at the cost of British colonial security and trade by handing back Britain's conquests. If his colleagues disagreed with him, he said, they would be unwise to retain him in the government.[10]

Grenville's reply showed that he had not moved an inch from his declaration in the previous summer that the republican government of France was 'the real root and origin of all its wickedness'. Jacobinism was far from dead. 'The Jacobin principle', he replied to Dundas, 'has remained unshaken, the

[9] Nat. Library of Scotland, Minto Papers, 3 Dec. 1799, Windham to Minto.
[10] Dropmore, VI. 37-9. Dundas was commenting on Grenville's dispatch of 19 November to Petersburg, which said that Britain was unlikely to consent to the restoration of the Cape, Ceylon and the conquests in India, but was silent on the West Indies (FO 65/45).

centre of all the hopes and wishes of the adherents of that principle in every other part of Europe; and so it will be, as I believe, for a hundred such revolutions, *till the principle itself be attacked and subdued in its citadel at Paris.*'[11]

With this exchange the divergence between Dundas and Grenville came further into the open. For Grenville, the aim of the war remained the overthrow of French republicanism. Dundas replied that the struggle was not being waged for ideas, but for power and wealth; implying that it was a war of limited and quantifiable aims, which could one day be resolved by a peace of compromise with the existing government of France.

Dundas was still willing to fight on, to safeguard England's maritime power and security, but regardless of who might rule in Paris. In the coming months, however, as his doubts of the country's capacity to win a decisive victory increased, he came to fear that the people's will to continue the struggle would break if their army suffered a disaster on the continent. Perhaps it is a reflection of Dundas's doubts that immediately after this clash of views with Grenville he made a fresh attempt to escape from the War Department. He was preparing for his usual winter visit to Scotland, and before his departure he appealed to the King against Pitt's refusal to relieve him. The King was adamant. He would not discuss the matter unless Dundas had Pitt's permission to resign, 'which I do not at present expect'. Dundas therefore departed for Edinburgh on 13 December still bearing the burden of the coming offensives. He left instructions with his under-secretary Huskisson to continue the military planning; but the handling of the expected French overture he was leaving to Pitt and Grenville.[12]

Pitt, indeed, shared some of Dundas's doubts. At the birth of the Coalition in 1798 he had questioned whether the country was willing to shoulder the burden of a renewed

[11] Dropmore, V. 147; VI. 46-7. Author's italics. Grenville's Petersburg dispatch of 19 November declared that a Bourbon restoration would be the best termination of the war and should be pursued by the allies. It added, however, that Britain could not look on this as the *sine qua non* of peace: Britain might seek future security in a diminution of French power rather than in the restoration of its internal tranquillity (FO 65/45).

[12] Add MSS 40100, ff. 421-3.

continental war; and he now feared that, if moderate peace terms were offered by a stable French government of the centre, the British public would refuse to prolong the war. His young acolyte Canning remained confident that the country would bear the burden and if necessary fight on alone; but Pitt thought this was too sanguine. He believed that Canning underestimated the financial cost of a limited maritime war; and he rejected as the reverse of the truth Canning's fear that peace would cause a trade recession.[13] In Pitt's doubts lie the seed of his ministry's break-up a year later; of his connivance in the compromise peace signed by his successors; and of the end of his alliance with Grenville. But these developments still lay far in the future; and when Bonaparte's expected overture arrived, Pitt would be on the side of those who rejected it.

The intermediate position which Pitt so often adopted between the views of Dundas and Grenville presents a puzzle. Was he projecting into the conduct of the war the patient politics of compromise which had served him well in peace? Was he exercising a balance of power between them, and reserving his position as chairman till the moment when issues clarified and his own will could prevail? Did he use the differences between Dundas and Grenville in order to divide and rule? Sometimes one senses that he is merely falling in with the views of the last person to whom he has spoken; and the minister to whom he was closest was his cousin Grenville. Three years later Dundas lamented Pitt's pliability, 'which has often, too often, led him to give up his better judgment to the perserving importunity of Lord Grenville'.[14]

Grenville shared none of the doubts of Pitt and Dundas. He was sure that the country could stand alone on the defensive for several years if necessary; and by this confidence he was liberated from weighing the need for peace. His choice when faced with an overture had already been made, and his declaration that Jacobinism must be subdued in Paris showed which way he would move. Yet how deep was his commitment to what the *Annual Register* called 'a war of opinion'?[15] There

[13] Canning MSS, 23 Nov. and 10 Dec., Pitt to Canning; J. H. Rose, *Pitt and Napoleon*, 319-20.   [14] Add. MSS 40102, f. 102; also Ehrman, 322.
[15] *Annal Register* 1798, Preface iii.

are apparent contradictions in his attitude: conflicts of ideology and pragmatism, reason and prejudice, wisdom and inflexibility. What was totally lacking was humility. His great aim was to restore stability among the powers of Europe; and he had always insisted that a stable peace could not be negotiated with an unstable government in Paris, whether they were the Thermidorians who had overthrown Robespierre to save their necks, or the Directors precariously balancing on a tightrope between Jacobins and royalists. Grenville had been reluctant to talk peace at Paris in 1796 when Pitt had favoured it, and his doubts seemed to have been justified; and to be justified again at Lille in 1797, when the coup of fructidor hardened the French terms and aborted the negotiations. It was from that time that he made peace contingent on restoring the monarchy, though he knew it was imprudent to say so in public. When the Russian subsidy of 1799 was debated in Parliament, he went along with Pitt in declaring that the ministry would negotiate with any stable French government; but his sincerity is questionable. He had to tread carefully to avoid giving a handle to the opposition; nor was it prudent to identify the British government with the absolutist Ultra wing of the French royalists.[16] In private, nevertheless, he declared that only a Bourbon restoration could lead to a durable peace. He said so repeatedly to his brother Tom on the eve of the great offensives of 1799: 'nothing will terminate this war but such a success in France as enables us to restore the monarchy.' His plans for invading France 'afford the only prospect of peace for Europe . . . our attack on the territory of France itself . . . affords the only means of trying the experiment of the Royal Standard'. And to Lord Mulgrave: 'peace with the Directory . . . can only be an armed truce; and . . . Europe can never be really restored to tranquility but by the restoration of monarchy in France'. Whatever it might be expedient to say in Parliament, his conviction had been strongly and repeatedly expressed that only a Bourbon restoration could produce stability.[17]

---

[16] *Strategy of Overthrow*, pp. 68–9, 86–7.
[17] Dropmore, V. 147–8, 159, 243.

3. *Peace Repelled*

Grenville was therefore implacably opposed to a compromise peace with the Consulate, and hoped that the Revolution would collapse under the stress of renewed external attacks and counter-revolution. There were also particular arguments against treating at this moment. One was that the French government could not afford to make peace, and was simply buying time by negotiating. This was argued by the Orangist General Stamford in a letter from Brunswick. Peace would bring home to France huge armies led by Jacobin generals like Masséna who were hostile to the Consulate. If the armies remained in being, they would have to be supplied from French resources, instead of living at free quarters in the occupied territories. If they were disbanded, the Consulate would lose the patronage and lucrative contracts with which a war government could buy support. And economic stagnation would follow. 'They need war, both as a Government and as individuals.'[18]

If this analysis was correct, why were the Consuls proposing peace? Two of the answers were obvious: to appease French opinion which was tired of the war, and to split the allies. Stamford suggested a third: to buy time for the army. An armistice would allow the French to withdraw troops from Switzerland where they could not be fed in the winter, and use them to put down the western rising. As for wrecking the Coalition by negotiation, the French had played this game of disruption as recently as 1798 at the Rastatt conference. They would use the coming overture 'to amuse Great Britain and induce her to give offence to her allies'.[19]

This argument, that the French were using negotiation as an arm of warfare, led to the further proposition that peace itself would be no more than an extension of war. There is no need to borrow the wisdom of hindsight and refer to Napoleon's later career, when intervals of peace were to be used for further encroachments; for the pattern was already recognized in 1799. General Bonaparte's character was known; and he had already employed the techniques of

[18] Weil, 293–303.   [19] Grenville in *Parl. Hist.* XXXIV. 1217.

Rastatt in the negotiations of 1797 with Austria which closed his precarious Italian victories. 'Negotiations', General Stamford observed, 'had always been part of French tactics, when those of their armies had been insufficient, or when their exhaustion had imposed a momentary need of repose.'[20] Canning made a parallel point to Pitt. If Bonaparte could whitewash his reputation in France by making peace, he would soon be stirring up new sedition in England, and the whole struggle would have to be fought again. With youthful recklessness Canning had rejoiced at the news of Bonaparte's coup. 'I am in raptures . . . The destroyer of the National Representation of the French Republic is a public benefactor to Europe. I care not whether he restores a King or becomes a despot, so that he be bloody and tyrannical enough . . . But as to peace — peace with a government six weeks old! No — no — no!'[21]

The first peace feeler arrived on Christmas day, and when the official overture arrived on 31 December Pitt and Grenville had already agreed to reject it. Pitt believed that if Bonaparte established his rule firmly and then offered good terms, public opinion would force the ministers to treat. But Bonaparte was not secure as long as the western insurrection survived; and news of an armistice between General Hédouville and the insurgent leaders, in terms much to the royalists' advantage, swelled Pitt's optimism about their future. Captain Keats was also home from the Bay of Biscay with reports which Grenville regarded as 'highly satisfactory' about the insurgents' strength and good order. Pitt made the characteristic reservation that the door should not be closed for ever on negotiation with the Consuls: 'we ought on no account to commit ourselves to any declaration that the restoration of royalty is the sine qua non condition of peace.' Nevertheless 'we ought peremptorily to reject all negotiations at present'. It is sometimes forgotten that when Bonaparte's overture arrived from Dover, Pitt was immersed in planning an invasion of Brittany to support the royalists.[22]

[20] Stowe Papers, 25 Nov. 1799, to T. Grenville.
[21] J. H. Rose, *Pitt and Napoleon*, 319-20; Gower, *Private Corr.* I. 273.
[22] Bowman, 101; Add. MSS 37846, 17 Dec., Grenville to Windham; SRO, GD 51/1/529/4, 18 Dec., Huskisson to Dundas; Canning MSS, 3 Dec., Pitt to Canning. For further intelligence of the Consulate's weakness, see Dropmore, VI. 71-2.

The overture took the form of a direct letter to the King from Bonaparte, claiming to have been 'called by the wishes of the French nation to occupy the first magistracy of the republic' and signing himself simply 'de votre Majesté, Buonaparte'. How, he asked, could the two most enlightened nations of Europe sacrifice to ideas of vain greatness the benefits of commerce, prosperity and family happiness? Why did they not feel that peace was the highest need as well as the greatest glory? 'These sentiments cannot be foreign to the heart of your Majesty, who reigns over a free nation with the sole view of rendering it happy.'[23]

This 'sentimental letter' as Canning called it seemed to breathe a large and generous spirit of enlightenment. Or was it something else: the empty rhetoric with which Siéyès had beguiled the King of Prussia, and countless revolutionary diplomats had manipulated their enemies? Canning saw in the letter the desperation of a tottering regime. 'I like the tone of everything I hear today, better than I ever did before. And I am persuaded that the whole game is in our hands now, and that it wants little more than *patience* to play it *well, to the end*.' For Pitt and Grenville, to play the game well meant rejecting the overture on the grounds, as Pitt explained to the absent Dundas, that 'the actual state of France does not as yet hold out any solid security to be derived from negotiation'. The reply, however, had to be carefully phrased to appeal to French and English opinion, to which Bonaparte's letter had been patently addressed. The British government must express its willingness to treat whenever solid security seemed to be attainable. It should also convey to the French people that the quickest road to peace was to restore the monarchy, though not in words which would later preclude the British government from treating with the Consulate if it consolidated its rule. Grenville was confident that British opinion would approve the rejection of the overture, 'provided proper care can be taken to give a right tone in the first instance'.[24]

A small cabinet met on the morning of 2 January 1800 to consider Bonaparte's letter, and the five members who could be collected agreed to the general terms of the reply. On the

[23] Translation in *Parl. Hist.* XXXIV. 1197–8.
[24] Add. MSS 37844, ff. 267–8; Stanhope, III. 206–7; *GL* 2095.

6th it was handed by the Collector of Customs at Dover to the French courier, who had been kept on board his ship since his arrival; and to avoid any suspicions among the allies, Grenville immediately forwarded copies to Petersburg and Vienna.[25]

The British answer took the form of a note, enclosed in a covering letter from Lord Grenville to the French Foreign Minister Talleyrand which rebuked the First Consul for addressing himself directly to the King. The note, much longer than Bonaparte's, denied that Britain was fighting for a vain and false glory: she was fighting for secure and permanent peace in Europe. She had been forced into the war by an unprovoked attack; and before she could make peace it was necessary for the parvenu Consulate to show that the causes of the war had been removed.

Grenville's note went on to denounce the record of revolutionary France. Its indiscriminate urge to destroy established governments had sacrificed Belgium, Holland and Switzerland; had ravaged Germany and plundered Italy; had involved the remotest quarters of the globe in the calamities of war. While such a system prevailed, no defence could avail but open and steady hostility. 'The most solemn treaties have only prepared the way for fresh aggression.' Peaceful words were therefore not enough: they had repeatedly been mouthed by the French destroyers of Europe. Britain would rejoice when the gigantic ambitions of France were relinquished. 'But the conviction of such a change, . . . can result only from experience, and the evidence of facts.'

The best security for such a change would be to restore the monarchy; but Britain did not insist that this was the only road to a solid peace: 'His Majesty makes no claim to prescribe to France what should be the form of her government.' Whenever Britain thought security could be attained, she would seek peace in concert with her allies. 'Unhappily no such security hitherto exists: No sufficient evidence of the principles by which the new government will be directed; no reasonable ground by which to judge its stability.[26]

[25] Windham *Diary*, 421; *GL* 2097; Add. MSS 57444, f. 13; FO 7/58, 6 Jan. 1800 to Minto; FO 65/46, 7 Jan. to Whitworth.
[26] *Parl. Hist.* XXXIV. 1198–1200.

Grenville's note was a fine piece of rhetoric, and Pitt was pleased with it. 'We . . . have drawn up our answer as a sort of manifesto both for France and England, bringing forward the topics which seem most likely to promote the cause of royalty.' But by historians the answer has been almost universally condemned. 'It ranks', wrote Pitt's biographer Holland Rose, 'among the greatest mistakes of the time.' In the light of later events this may be true; but in the situation when the overture was rejected, the error is less clear. Nevertheless one must distinguish between the substance of the note and its phrasing. To appeal in the same note to both French and English opinion was an impossible task.[27]

The imperious and declamatory language of the note is unmistakably the voice of Grenville: so is the foolish emphasis on protocol. Whether the language was well calculated to rally the country members of Parliament was a matter of political judgement. But more important were the consequences of the policy to which they were being rallied. The British government had rejected an opportunity to negotiate with a new French government. By doing so they left Bonaparte to triumph at Marengo and Hohenlinden, and after much expenditure they were forced to negotiate peace a year later in less advantageous circumstances. The sequel was predicted. Britain was saying, in Fox's words, 'If I succeed, well; but if I fail, then I will treat with you.' 'When well beaten', Lord Holland foretold, 'they would pretend to have had experience of Bonaparte's government, and then see other and speedier means of peace than the restoration of the Bourbons.'[28]

Yet one must distinguish between the manner and the policy. Historians have underrated the diplomatic and military arguments for rejecting the overture. There was the hopeful but precarious Coalition: would it surivive the shock of a negotiation? However carefully the British government avoided falling out of step with Austria, could they match the disruptive tactics of French diplomacy? Was it not likely that Austria would use the opportunity to push her own interests and make a separate peace? And would the legitimist

[27] Ziegler, 87–8; J. H. Rose, *Pitt and the Great War*, 384.
[28] *Parl. Hist.* XXIV. 1384, 1437.

Tsar Paul allow his troops to support allies who were negotiating with a usurper? Bonaparte's aim, said Pitt in the House,
was 'to engage this country in separate negotiation, in order
to loosen and dissolve the confederacy'.[29]

One might have argued that there could be no harm in an
armistice, which was Bonaparte's next proposal. But in every
way an armistice favoured the French. It would enable them
to recuperate their armies, now in desperate straits, and put
down the royalists at home. At sea they could either evacuate
or reinforce Egypt, and either course at this moment would be
damaging. To bring back from Egypt the élite of Bonaparte's
Army of Italy would reinforce the ailing armies in Europe
and offend the continental allies. A fortnight earlier the
Cabinet had learned that the Turks were negotiating with the
French commander in Egypt to grant his army a safe passage
home to France. This had to be prevented, and orders had
been sent on 15 December to the naval Commander-in-Chief
in the Mediterranean to intercept the French transports and
force them back. A naval armistice now would allow the
return of these troops to France; and the allies on whom
their return would have an immediate and devastating impact
were the royalists of the interior.[30]

The royalists: it was on these that the British ministers
based their hopes, their strategy, and their refusal to treat
with Bonaparte. To them they looked for the reconstruction
of stable government in Paris; for them they were planning
their 'immense effort' against the coasts of France. To
negotiate while the royalists were in arms would betray
them. It would give Bonaparte the time to crush them, and
encourage them to make terms with the usurper. Bonaparte
was not called to power by the French nation as he claimed,
but had been installed by the Paris garrison and was surrounded by ambitious generals and intriguing rivals. The
French armies were run down, the finances in chaos. Was
there sense in betraying the royalists and throwing away the
chance of restoring the monarchy, for the sake of a negotiation with this shaky and unprincipled government?

With hindsight one knows that the British calculation was

[29] Ibid., 1326.
[30] Windham *Diary*, 419; Spencer, IV. 89; Keith, II. 203-4.

wrong. The royalist insurgents had been disconcerted, not cemented, by the advent of Bonaparte; they were defeated within weeks of the British decision not to negotiate; and Bonaparte then consolidated his power and provided the stable authority for which the British government was waiting. Pitt and his colleagues had indeed miscalculated the royalists' strength. But about Bonaparte they were not altogether astray. To judge them fairly one must not look only at the year 1800 and the speculative military gamble at Marengo which consolidated Bonaparte's power. One must also look at the next fifteen years which led to Waterloo: at the rapid breakdown of the peace of 1801-2; the successive wars, peacetime encroachments and broken treaties; the reckless march to Moscow, and the bullying of Metternich in 1813 which finally sealed Napoleon's fate. Here was an unstable regime; not through weakness, but because of the ruler's personality. And this judgement is not pure hindsight. As Pitt observed at the time, Bonaparte was no stranger. 'The Corsican tyrant' was not a Cromwell or a Washington, as Fox and his friends were pretending. He was an adventurer and a gambler, contemptuous of human life and the human race, incapable of defining or limiting his goals, with a long record of violence and breach of faith abroad and at home. General Stamford's judgement that he lacked the prudence to make his successes durable was widely echoed. 'The new constitution', Pitt had written before Christmas, 'is a more undisguised contrivance for giving absolute power to Bonaparte than I expected, and, as such, must I think do good.' It was an accepted truism that military despotism was an unstable form of government; and who would dispute this in the twentieth century? 'One is inclined,' wrote a diarist on the day before the peace overture was received, 'to think Bonaparte more ambitious than wise. I think he will overreach himself and accelerate his ruin and the overthrow of the Constitution he has set up.' Before many years were to pass Talleyrand would be thinking the same. The proclamations using the royal 'we', and the letter addressed as an equal to the King of Great Britain, suggested that the Corsican adventurer's 'head was not quite strong enough for the eminence on which he was suddenly placed'.[31]

[31] Dropmore, VI. 84-5, 94; Add. MSS 57444, f. 11, journal of J. C. Herries; Sidmouth Papers, 9 Jan., Addington to Hiley Addington.

To ask whether Bonaparte's overture was 'sincere' is a mis-directed question. With callow youthfulness behind him, Bonaparte wrote letters only to manipulate. He liked to keep his options open; and his political option of peace or war is not dissimilar to his military option in 1798 of invading England or Egypt, or in 1805 of invading England or striking a pre-emptive blow against Austria. On the news in 1805 that his naval concentration in the Channel had been foiled, he instantly set in motion the strategy already worked out in detail in his head which led to the encirclement of Mack at Ulm. In the same way, on receiving the final British rejection of his peace overture in January 1800, he set in motion the alternative manœuvre. General Brune, newly arrived in Paris from his victorious campaign in Holland, was ordered to the Vendée in the wake of his demi-brigades to put down the insurgents with the utmost speed. At the same time Bonaparte gave orders to form the Army of Reserve at Dijon, for the manœuvre which was to win the campaign of Marengo. If the British government had agreed to treat, he would certainly have treated, for he would have gained by doing so. But to believe that he would have negotiated a durable peace is to assume that his future political habits were created by the British rejection. They were already fully formed.

4. *The Cracks in the Foundations*

For such reasons Bonaparte's overture was rejected. The British ministry would continue to fuel a continental war, and strive for victory and the overthrow of the enemy's government. Certainly there would have been risks to British foreign policy if they had opened a negotiation with the Consulate; but the great risk of refusing it was the effect on opinion at home if victory were long deferred. For war usually leads to domestic crisis, and the pattern of Britain's past wars was about to recur. After some years of indecisive warfare the country gentlemen would rebel against the high taxation of incomes hit by a bad harvest or a glut of corn, and would cease to support the war. In 1800 the struggle against revolu-tionary France was approaching its eighth year. The end was

not in sight; and a harvest failure had hit the country gentlemen's pockets and would soon undermine public order.

Much of the phrasing and argument of the British government's note was aimed at British public opinion. The ministers
were trying, in the jeremiad phrases of their Holland House
opponents, to rally 'those country members whose warlike
spirits may have been subdued at the sight of the universal
suffering throughout the country — a suffering aggravated,
if not caused, by the horrors of war'. Another hard winter
had set in early. The first snow fell on the Grenville palace at
Stowe by 19 December, and before the New Year ministers
were skating again. To sharpen the cold, the price of grain
and coal was rising steeply, and both rises could be blamed
on the war; the coal shortage on the use of colliers as horse
transports for the Dutch expedition, and the grain shortage
on the quantity of corn diverted abroad to feed the expedition. The real cause of the grain shortage, of course, lay
deeper. It was the wet harvest weather which Lord Auckland
asserted had almost halved the wheat yield. The price continued to rise, towards a record annual average of 113 shillings
for 1800, much more than double the usual price.[32]

No wonder the government was conscious of the country
members; and the tone of the reply to Bonaparte seemed to
do some good. Huskisson's impression, when he returned to
London on 5 January after visiting the Russian troops from
Holland, was that the reaction to the note was highly favourable; and he hoped that the qualified nature of the commitment to the French monarchy would reassure supporters who
had been showing signs of war-weariness. He thought the
note was a firm and dignified, yet moderate and politic reply
to an insidious and impertinent proposal.[33]

Needless to say, the opposition did not agree, and made
the most of the note's excesses. Charles Fox reappeared in
the House after his long secession to deplore the 'harsh and
unconciliating language, . . . always reprobated by diplomatic
men'. The Foxite lawyer Thomas Erskine denounced the
'lofty, imperious, declamatory, insulting answer to a

[32] Dropmore, VI. 78, 81; *Journal of Elizabeth Lady Holland*, II. 36, 43;
Windham *Diary*, 419; *Parl. Hist.* XXXIV. 1495.
[33] SRO, GD 51/1/529/7.

proposition professing peace and conciliation, . . . in the face of a suffering nation and a desolate world'. In the Lords Grenville's provocative language was attacked by the Duke of Bedford. If their Lordships repaired to the field and woods, 'they would everywhere discover the traces of those miserable wretches whose poverty left them no other resource but depredation . . . the plaintive and unavailing cries of children calling for that food which their parents had not to give them'.[34]

Not all the government's supporters were happy with the note. To make propaganda at home it had presented an uncompromisingly hostile account of the cause and progress of the war, and of Bonaparte's character. This might please the English public but was likely to repel the French; and the Speaker Addington thought the note was 'in some parts too caustic and opprobrious . . . there was a temper in it which takes from its dignity; and it has not quite enough of the character of moderation'. Lord Grenville's elder brother Buckingham warned him that many of the ministry's friends were wilting under the load of war taxes, and would soon clamour for peace in the belief that the French danger had receded. The ministers, he said, would be on firmer political ground at home if they had parleyed with Bonaparte and demonstrated their wish for peace before breaking off the talks. Huskisson too had second thoughts. A couple of weeks later he warned Dundas that unless great care was used in the sequel to the overture, 'you will see *Wilberforce* (already wavering) and many others gradually incline to be troublesome'. For some time indeed Huskisson had felt as Buckingham did about parliamentary feeling, and he had written to Dundas in Scotland before the overture was received to warn him that Pitt was not sufficiently aware how volatile public opinion might become. Like Buckingham he feared that people might soon be thinking that a reasonable security had been achieved against revolutionary France, and that England had won enough success against French sea-power and colonies to negotiate with advantage. 'Without exhausting our resources (for of that I am not afraid) we may exhaust and

[34] *Parl. Hist.* XXXIV. 1224, 1286, 1353.

wear out public spirit, and for all the purposes either of war or of negotiation the one evil is almost as bad as the other.' Prescient words, when one considers the public pressure for peace under which negotiations were to be conducted little more than a year later.[35]

Dundas took notice, and though he approved of rejecting Bonaparte's overture he warned Pitt that support for the war could collapse if the coming military offensives did not achieve rapid success:

We shall not be able to persuade the country, with an honourable and advantageous peace (as they will suppose) in their hands to continue the war upon a speculation which many will think not within our province, and which still more will be disposed to think not at all within our reach but by an expenditure of money and blood, and even that expenditure very doubtful in the issue. I don't pretend to decide when these feelings will begin to operate, or how soon they may force themselves upon our line of conduct, but I think I see with clearness that they will sooner or later press themselves upon us. . . .[36]

This advice lacked the classical precision and balanced phrases of Grenville's letters. But its measured and undogmatic warning echoed what Pitt in his own heart was beginning to fear.

[35] Sidmouth Papers, 9 Jan. 1800, Speaker Addington to Hiley Addington; Dropmore, VI. 95; SRO, GD 51/1/529, 25 Dec. 1799 and 18 Jan. 1800, Huskisson to Dundas.
[36] Rylands Library, Eng. 907, 4 Jan., Dundas to Pitt.

CHAPTER III

Plans and Illusions

1. *Russians*

The political aim for the campaign of 1800 was settled; the shadowy outline of a strategy had been traced; operational plans and preparations did not as yet exist. The strategic aim was to encircle France with concentric attacks from the Alps, the Mediterranean, the Channel and the North Sea, and thus to drive Bonaparte into the arms of the Bourbons or to bring him down. In the west a Russian force would land in the Scheldt, and 60,000 British troops in Brittany. In the Mediterranean 20,000–30,000 British and Russians were to threaten the communications of the French army of Italy, and aid the royalists of Provence while the Austrians advanced across the Alps.

But nothing had yet been done to prepare the forces, and Dundas knew from experience the chasm that lies between planning and execution. Grenville had promised 100,000 men for the western landings; Dundas himself 80,000. Could so many troops be obtained, were they fit for the field, and was there enough shipping to move them and supply them? Dundas, the administrator, was gradually to establish that the Utopian strategies of Grenville outstripped the resources.

About the Russian army Dundas was already a declared sceptic. Lord Grenville's promised 100,000 men must have included the 15,000 Russians who were expected to return from Holland; but little could be expected of these, in the light of their behaviour in the field. It had leaked out that in the Duke of York's second offensive battle in Holland the Russian Jäger had thrown themselves flat on their bellies and refused to advance, a fact that was kept out of parliamentary debate with difficulty. This conduct, however, was exceptional, and the real Russian weakness was not lack of courage but indiscipline and disorganization. Though several regiments had been commended by the Duke, the operations of the Russian force as a whole had been marked by breakdown of tactical order in the attack, straggling in the retreat, and looting everywhere. Grenville hoped that the replacement of their incompetent commander would improve them: 'they required an uncommon degree of attention to their discipline both in the field and out of it'. But in his heart he knew that the trouble lay deeper. The roots of the Russian defects in Holland were the same as in Switzerland: low pay, lack of trained staff and commissariat, and bad officers. It needed more than a new general to make them efficient.[1]

The British public was soon to discover the truth about these barbarians. The Russians returning from Holland were landed at Great Yarmouth, where they stole and drank the oil from the street-lamps; no surprise to those who had seen them butter their bread with the British artillery's axle grease. Sir Charles Grey could scarcely believe his eyes. 'They really are not human', wrote his son, 'and their filth is shocking . . .. Those that are landed to be carried to the hospital are immediately washed from head to foot in a warm sea bath, their heads are shaved, and new clothes are given to them to prevent contagion.' Most of them were dressed in 'rags, squalid and disgusting to the sight, or wrapped up in a large loose white greatcoat of a texture something between a blanket and a cloth, which is tied by a string or a dirty pocket handkerchief round the waist'. 'Thus', Elizabeth, Lady Holland gloated in her journal, 'has this mighty horde of barbarians dwindled to a handful of tattered, ill-disciplined, worse-officered, half-starved savages'. Captain Home Popham warned the War Department that the Russian troops had lost the confidence of the British army: they could not easily be integrated into another British amphibious operation.[2]

Of this Dundas needed no convincing. He had already written off Suvorov's Russians on the eastern front,[3] and he contended that the Russians from Holland were not fit to be included in a British force and should operate separately if at all. In the meantime they had to be accommodated for the

[1] *Journal of Elizabeth Lady Holland*, II. 27; Watkins, *Duke of York*, 384–5; FO 65/44, 15 Oct. 1799, Grenville to Whitworth. For an appraisal of the army of Paul I, see C. Duffy, 200–9.

[2] *GL* vol. III, p. 293 n. 3; *Journal of Elizabeth Lady Holland*, II. 30; WO 1/411, Popham to Huskisson.

[3] Above, pp. 21, 25.

winter. To quarter these dirty, plundering troops in England was out of the question; and Cornwallis objected to their being sent to Ireland, where their presence would allow the opponents of the Union to say that it was being imposed by foreign bayonets.[4] They were therefore to be corralled in the Channel Islands for the winter.

When Dundas departed for Scotland, he left instructions with Huskission to examine the problem of using the Russian force. Its incompetent and ill-disposed commander in Holland, General Essen, had been recalled by the Tsar, and General Kutusov was believed to be on his way to replace him. In the meantime the troops were left under the supervision of the ambassador Vorontsov; but his competent senior officer General Bauer had been summoned to join his regiment in Germany, leaving Major-General Shapseiwitsch in immediate command.[5] Huskisson sent the consular expert William Eton to call on him in London, and the general, whose ill-will towards the British was evident, told Eton that he was in a consumption and could not walk four steps without becoming breathless. After twenty-four hours in command, however, he discovered that he could give his orders and do all his writing in his bedroom. This, as he truly observed, made his task less arduous.

Some of the Russian troops were still in transports at Portsmouth, waiting for smaller vessels to take them to the Channel Islands, and Huskisson went down there with Vorontsov to visit them. He was appalled by what he found. He wrote to Dundas on Christmas day:

No words can describe the sulkiness, filth, torpor and wretchedness that prevail among them. Their officers appear to care much less for them than we do for our sheep; and no exertion by our people can make them observe any of the regulations necessary for the preservation of cleanliness and health. There is not a ship without the seeds of infection on board, and numbers are sent ill every day to the hospitals. In this weather they are more helpless than so many lascars, lying close to one another upon the decks literally like bees in a hive, and never suffering the least change of air, or cleaning the decks, or ventilation of any kind, for they will nether go above nor suffer the port holes to be opened on any account. Never certainly was there such a scene of misery and

---

[4] Cornwallis, II. 431–2.
[5] William Eton's transliteration of the name.

disease witnessed in this country; and by the accounts from Guernsey and Jersey I am afraid, matters are not better managed there.

Huskisson was convinced that the Russian force would be of no use whatever for the next campaign unless all the generals and staff were changed. Even then he doubted that it could ever be made efficient; for all ranks had a horror of service afloat, and wanted only to return to Russia. They certainly could 'never be relied upon or employed with any advantage in any conjunct expedition, for which in every point of view they are a description of force totally unsuitable'.[6]

2. *An Army to Build*

Huskisson's advice confirmed what Dundas expected; and he had not included the Russian force in his promised 80,000 men for the spring. Yet his own calculation was a paper army. It included 3,000 French *émigrés* at Lisbon, who he thought might be spared from the defence of Portugal but in the event were not; and 5,000 Dutch troops evacuated from the Texel, who had never been in action and would not be ready for service till the end of the summer. To this wonderland he added 15,000 supernumerary seamen and marines to replace the Russians: instant soldiers who were to spring armed and trained from a fleet which was fully stretched and chronically short of men.[7]

The only troops on which Dundas could reasonably count for spring operations were the British. 'Bring me back as many good troops as you can', he had urged his friend General Abercromby when the evacuation of Holland was ordered, 'and before next spring I will show you an army the country never saw before.'[8]

But from Holland only 24,000 effective infantry would return, while Dundas needed 80,000 effectives to make up 60,000 present and fit for duty.[9] How could he produce this

[6] WO 1/411, 13 Nov., Whitworth to Popham; FO 65/44, 10 Oct., Whitworth to Grenville; SRO, GD 51/1/529, 17 Dec., Eton to Huskisson, and 18, 25 Dec. 1799, 6 Jan. 1800, Huskisson to Dundas; Dropmore, VI. 37, 47, 71, 72.
[7] Dundas MSS, Duke University MSS, XVIII F, memorandum on disposable force.　　　　　　　　　　　　　　　　　　　　　[8] Dunfermline, 208.
[9] British and French returns distinguished between 'effectives' (men borne on

force? He counted the 15,000 cavalry in the British Isles, though shipping could never be found for more than a few of their horses with their forage. He counted on 6,000 fencible infantry raised for home service who had volunteered to serve in Europe: some of these in the event would be used to relieve regulars in garrison at Gibraltar and Minorca. From the Guards and regiments of foot in England or expected home from the colonies, another 10,000 could be found; but since many of these regiments of foot were grossly under strength Dundas hoped for 25,000 more volunteers from the English and Irish militias to fill their ranks, and to authorize this recruiting from the militia a special session of Parliament had been summoned in September.[10] Seven of the regiments to be completed, however, were still abroad, all of them very weak and one which was due home from the West Indies less than a hundred strong. To judge from the experience of absorbing militiament for the expedition to Holland, regiments which took large drafts from the militia would require drastic and prolonged retraining.[11]

Even if these troops could be collected and trained, would they then be fit to face the French? Reports of the British army's performance in Holland varied widely. 'The English', wrote a Dutchman, 'unless they change their military system, ought to give up making war against the French on land.' Their generals, he said, would not keep on attacking like Suvorov, the Archduke Charles or the French. These brave words, written behind the French lines by an observer who had decided to stay at home in safety till the campaign was decided, no doubt echoed an opinion widely held on the continent and even in England. 'I am sorry', Lady Holland wrote of her friend Lord Granville Leveson who was raising his Staffordshire Volunteers, 'he throws away very excellent abilities upon a profession where so little is required — at least as it is practised in this country.' One might dismiss

the books but including men sick, missing, absent on extra-regimental duties or recruiting, and deserters) and men 'present and fit for duty' (*présent sous les armes*). The distinction was a source of confusion for slipshod political planners.

[10] *Parl. Hist.* XXXIV. 1183; Western, 233. See also *Strategy of Overthrow*, pp. 142-3.

[11] Duke University, loc. cit., which could be compared with Dropmore, VI. 188-9.

Lady Holland's Whiggish sneers; but Dundas had to resist Lord Grenville's contention that British troops lacked enterprise. 'We totally differ in sentiment', he wrote after the Cabinet meeting at which Grenville had let fall this opinion. 'In truth I believe it is their distinguishing characteristic.'[12]

Professional opinion was equally divided about the British force. Accounts reaching Canning from the field reported good conduct, courage and steadiness; while Lord Cornwallis's friends in Holland painted a picture of the greatest confusion and bad behaviour. In fact the conduct of the troops had been as varied as their training and experience. Many of the spearhead battalions with which Abercromby had seized the beach-head were excellent. But the reinforcements had consisted of cadres hastily filled with officers from the half-pay list and volunteers from the militia. When Dundas saw them embarking he thought them 'the most beautiful troops you ever set eyes upon'; and in a sense he was right, for they were excellent material. But the recruits were unsettled in mind and unknown to their officers; their training was basic and their discipline mediocre. They were not ready for war; and some of them were committed to their first battle in the worst conditions for inexperienced troops, to stem the retreat of a flying rabble of Russians. It is no wonder that they were sometimes unsteady.[13]

The new troops were appraised by the wise and experienced Sir Ralph Abercromby. In Holland he had welcomed the militiamen as 'a superior race of men, and a great acquisition to the army', and he was anxious that their training should be completed on their return. 'In the spring you will have a fine army,' he assured Dundas, 'if the brigades are put under major-generals who are capable of instructing young officers and raw troops. They must remain stationary, and must not be allowed to dance all over Great Britain.'[14]

Abercromby himself returned from Holland to his Scottish command in Edinburgh, and took no part in the winter's

---

[12] Algemeen Rijksarchief, G. K. van Hogendorp Collection, N. 39 (for the writer see *Strategy of Overthrow*, 249); *Journal of Elizabeth Lady Holland*, II. 33; Dropmore, V. 494.

[13] Cornwallis, III. 141; Canning MSS, 20 Oct. 1799, Canning to Mornington; Spencer, III. 127. For the militia in Holland see *Strategy of Overthrow*, esp. pp. 268, 296.   [14] SRO, GD 51/1/703/11.

training in England. But he explained his ideas to his brother-in-law Colonel Alexander Hope, who had served on his staff in Holland.

I am most anxious that the troops should be attended to during the winter with prudence and good sense. The Militia men are rather a better species of man, they understand the use of arms, and can move tolerably well, but they have not been accustomed to due subordination, to this they must be led by degrees, they must not be treated with too much harshness and severity. It is well worth while to bestow some time on such men, and rest assured if they are used with judgment and discretion you will have a fine army.'

There spoke one of the creators of the new British army which was to rise from the ashes of the regiments burned out in the early years of the war.[15] It was no fault of his that the winter's training did not fulfil his hopes. The harsh weather and the need to garrison Ireland were to prevent the regiments from receiving the polish they needed.

3. *Plans and Shipping*

Assuming that Dundas's force could be collected by the spring, it was time to begin the complex operational planning to put a large force ashore in western Europe, and in the last days of November Dundas set his experts to work. Sir Charles Grey and Lord St. Vincent were invited to examine the problems; and Huskisson was given charge of the business which was causing Dundas the most anxiety, the provision of shipping for the invasion armies.

He had learned in the course of the war how difficult it would be to collect the tonnage for these large troop movements. Shipping had been a bottleneck in the Dutch expedition, and the scale of the next year's operations would be larger still. It was to economise tonnage that he had thought of transferring Suvorov's force in Germany to the Mediterranean, to avoid shipping Russian troops from England and the Black Sea. Transports, he had warned the Foreign

---

[15] Hope of Luffness, 20 Nov., Abercromby to Alexander Hope.

Secretary on 29 November, would be the main obstacle if large-scale operations were mounted from England.[16]

When Dundas informed Huskisson of the scale of the invasion plans, the Under-Secretary more than confirmed his fears; for he calculated that to transport 50,000–60,000 British troops to the continent and supply them would need 200,000 tons of ordinary merchant shipping in addition to the armed government transports. The total tonnage in British ownership was about 1½ million, and with overseas trade still at a very high level the hiring of transport would be very difficult and would cause severe economic dislocation. If the Russians were to be shipped to the Mediterranean, they would have to be ferried back from the Channel Islands in small ships in the winter to embark in ocean-going transports, and could not sail till about 1 March; and their shipping, which would be needed again for the British expedition, would be tied up for at least three months by the Mediterranean voyage and subsequent refitting. Huskisson doubted whether more Russians could be shipped from the Baltic, remembering the difficulty of doing so before the Helder expedition, and was even more doubtful about bringing a force from the Crimea. He thought that if anything he had underrated the difficulties; and his notes confirmed Dundas's fears.[17]

Before Dundas's departure for Scotland he showed Huskisson's report to Pitt, and insisted that the shipping problem must be assessed before the ministry committed itself more deeply to these great expeditions. He wanted an immediate discussion with Pitt and Grenville at Holwood, Pitt's country villa near Keston in Kent. Pitt however was not much disturbed. He refused to meet till they were all in London again, and thought from past experience that Huskisson had much overrated the expense and difficulty of collecting transports. Dundas was not persuaded. He longed to attack the Combined Fleet in Brest if shipping was available; but it was probably impossible. 'I have my serious doubts if all the maritime resources of this country can be so brought and

---

[16] Dropmore, VI. 51–2.

[17] Add. MSS 38759, 28 Nov. 1799, memo. by Dundas for Huskisson; Grey Papers, 2252, 30 Nov., Huskisson to Dundas (copy); Nat. Library of Scotland, MS 1076, f. 52.

concentred together in the execution of the details necessary on such an occasion as that of sending to sea *at once*, and directed to *one point*, an army of 70 thousand men, with all its necessary accompaniments.'[18]

With that declaration Dundas took another step to distance himself from Grenville's continental strategy. Of all the Cabinet it was he who knew the most about assembling a great amphibious expedition: the immensity of the transport tonnage, and the difficulty of co-ordinating the different elements of the force. He knew what Pitt and Grenville would never learn, that in war execution is everything.

From Scotland he continued to press the shipping question to Pitt, suggesting that the Dutch warships taken at the Helder might be converted to armed transports. But still he feared that the tonnage could not be found: 'After our utmost exertions we will require more than we can by any means collect.' He reminded Grenville of the importance of transferring Suvorov's force in Germany to the Mediterranean, to avoid the notion of finding transports in the Baltic and the Black Sea: 'I hope nothing has occurred to bring back that wild idea.' Suvorov's troops were indeed available, for news reached London on 18 December that the Austrians would not accept Russian troops for the next campaign; but according to Huskisson Lord Grenville had neglected to propose their transfer to the Mediterranean in his dispatch to Petersburg.[19]

While Huskisson grappled with shipping statistics, the fighting men were planning operations. Their progress was discouraging. Dundas had asked Sir Charles Stuart how the enemy could be harassed in the Mediterranean by 20,000 men, or seriously assailed if the force could be raised to 25,000–30,000 by Suvorov's Russians. He had difficulty in extracting a reply, for Stuart, home from Minorca for his health, was having trouble with his arm and could not reply till a confidential aide was available to take his dictation. If

---

[18] Grey Papers, 2252, 2 Dec., Pitt to Dundas; Dropmore, VI. 60.

[19] Spencer, III. 208–10; Rylands Library, Engl. 907, 23 Dec., Dundas to Grenville; Add. MSS 58917, 17 Dec., Dundas to Grenville; SRO, GD 51/1/529, 18 Dec., Huskisson to Dundas. Grenville's 'additional' instruction to Whitworth about Suvorov is undated in Dropmore, VI. 80–1; the draft in FO 65/45 is dated 30 Nov.; and I have only Huskisson's word that it was not sent.

an answer was ever sent, it has disappeared; but Dundas
visited him on 1 December and by one means or another he
established that Stuart was an enthusiastic advocate of a
Mediterranean offensive.[20]

For the western offensive planning of a kind had been
going on since August. The object was an attack on the Combined Fleet in Brest, but for lack of information little progress
had been made. The officers of the Channel Fleet knew little
about the shore defences or the landward approaches to the
port; and General Grey could find no recent plans of the
French works and was offered documents dating from the
American War. Ignorant he must therefore remain, but his
demands on resources were rising alarmingly. In the summer
he had seemed to think that 20,000–30,000 men would be
enough; but in the course of the autumn the figure crept up
to 80,000, and Grey's staff calculated that the force would
need 350,000 tons of shipping, a requisition which soared
far above Huskisson's most pessimistic calculation.[21]

Grey's requirements had risen because he had given up the
idea of a *coup de main* against Brest, and was now thinking
in terms of a regular investment and siege with a covering
force. Were there safer and more limited alternatives to this
ponderous attack? Pitt approached the problem in a more
cautious frame of mind than he had brought to the planning
of the Dutch expedition a few months earlier. He saw how
much depend on the distribution of the enemy's forces, and

[20] Wortley, 322, 324–6; Grey Papers, 2252, 2256. A well-known paper printed
in Wortley and ascribed by the editor to General Stuart proposed a landing on the
Riviera to sever the French communications with Italy. Whatever Stuart's views
may have been, this paper is too grandiloquent to have come from his pen. Its
reference to Masséna's command in Italy probably dates it after the New Year of
1800, and an allusion to Bonaparte's option between offensives in Germany and
Italy suggests that it was written after the assembling of the French Army of
Reserve became known, which cannot have been earlier than March, at least three
months after Stuart received Dundas's enquiry. The tone of the paper relates it
rather to the royalist Rosière's plans for which Stuart expressed only contempt;
see below, p. 65.

Stuart may have been contemplating plans for operations in Italy for some
time: see Moore, II. 330–1. A fellow-veteran of the American War, General
Simcoe, probably made some suggestions of this kind to him, as he certainly did
to Addington, about January 1799 (Sidmouth Papers, 29 Jan. 1799, Simcoe to
Addington).

[21] Spencer, III. 109–28; Grey Papers, 2252, 2253, 2256.

that either Brest must be captured before the enemy could concentrate a superior force, or a defensible beach-head obtained to guarantee a safe re-embarcation.[22] A less risky if less effective alternative was to seize a coastal island, and Belle Île off the bay of Quiberon had been mentioned. When Dundas left for Scotland in the middle of December the immense difficulties of the Brest operation were recognized, and opinion was shifting towards Belle Ile. He left instructions with Huskisson to meet Grey and St. Vincent and review the plans for a major landing. If an invasion of Brittany was considered imprudent, they were to examine the whole coastline from the Channel to Gibraltar for alternative landing places. Dundas himself now favoured Belle Île, as a good place for supporting the Breton insurgents and destroying the French coastal trade which supplied Brest. Moreover it could provide a base for other expeditions. The notion of 'other expeditions' opened a larger field in Dundas's mind than his colleagues suspected; he would soon be thinking of Spanish America.[23]

4. *Pitt and the Royalist Illusion*

Dundas travelled north to relax at Melville Castle under the impression that the Brest plan was ebbing away. He was mistaken; and just before Christmas the Breton schemes were given fresh life at a meeting between Pitt and the future Charles X of France, the comte d'Artois. *Monsieur* came armed with a new plan, and was accompanied by its author, the military engineer de la Rosière. They proposed that a British force should seize and fortify the peninsula of Ruis, the eastern arm of the Morbihan inlet at the back of Quiberon Bay. Rosière believed that 15,000 men could entrench the peninsula at the beginning of March to form a secure base from which to aid the insurgents. Artois suggested that the landing could be combined with an attack on Brest, a hundred miles to the west; for Ruis was sixty miles from the centre of the Breton road network at Rennes, and the royalist army,

[22] Grey Papers, 2252.
[23] Windham *Diary*, 419; Nat. Library of Scotland, MS 1043, f. 42 (11 Dec., Dundas to Huskisson).

assembling at Ruis in full strength, could cut the road from Paris and form a covering army for the siege of Brest. The investment of the port might cause the garrison to mutiny; but in any case Rosière, who had been employed in the maintenance of the fortifications, was positive that the town could be taken easily. All that Artois asked for was a promise that the French fleet would be held in trust for the Bourbons. Pitt gave it, and the parts of the plan slipped into place.[24]

Pitt often reacted to a new idea with elation; and after talking to Artois he saw a clear road ahead: 'The more I consider it, the more I feel impatient to arrange a plan for giving as speedily as the season will admit, effectual succour in troops as well as arms and money.' Studying the latest army returns from the Horse Guards, he basked in visions of 30,000 British troops being brigaded immediately for a spring invasion of Brittany. This was music to the ears of Windham, obsessed as he was with the royalists; but Pitt knew that he must first satisfy Dundas and the military commanders that Ruis was tenable, and asked Rosière to put his plans in writing.

With Dundas Christmassing in Scotland and the Foreign Secretary lurking in the Grenville abodes of Buckinghamshire, Pitt assumed the direction of the Quiberon plan. Now sanguine, now cautious, always flexible, he was tugged between the views of Windham, Dundas and the generals. Rosière's promised paper was a disappointment, neither so full nor so convincing as his verbal exposition. Pitt was struggling to be realistic, and rather than rely on Rosière's 25,000 insurgents to hold the peninsula, he preferred to reinforce the British spearhead rapidly to 30,000–40,000. Yet he was nervous of such high stakes, fearing a public revulsion in the event of a major disaster and apprehensive about Dundas's reaction to the plan. He confided his worries to Windham and received a withering retort. The worst that could result from a great failure, said Windham, was that Britain would be forced to make peace with a republican government; and that would happen anyway if the operation were not attempted. What, he asked, would be the verdict of history, if the British

[24] Stanhope, III. 205-6.

government made peace with the Jacobin republic without having landed a single soldier in France?[25]

Pitt's anxieties were not allayed by the damning reaction of General Grey to Rosière's paper. Grey advised that the Ruis position was too extended to be secure, and the force too small to take the offensive; there was no shelter on the peninsula, and troops housed in tents before May would become sick; the locking up of the force on Ruis would rule out any other expeditions; the fleet and transports would have to remain in constant attendance to supply or re-embark the army. The last point was echoed by Lord Spencer who was anxious about the shortage of warships in home waters; he also disliked combining operations with the royalists. Pitt was rightly unwilling to give way to the first difficulties raised by his advisers. He thought Grey's remarks were loosely written, and that both Grey and Spencer were ignorant and prejudiced about the royalists. It was a relief to learn that Dundas had received the Rosière plan with an open mind and was willing to give it fair consideration; yet Pitt could not resist poking fun at him with Grenville: 'Dundas's geography, you will observe is as accurate as his language.'[26]

The verdict on Rosière's plan had to wait for a fuller report from General Grey, who was ill, and in the meantime Pitt assured Dundas that he would not let himself be 'captivated by any project that is not thoroughly weighed and examined in all its parts': a contrast with his attitude on the eve of the Dutch expedition, when he had blithely reported to Grenville that 'all military difficulties are completely overruled'.[27] Nevertheless Pitt felt more and more strongly that the expedition should go for Brest and not Belle Île; and if the royalists were as strong as be believed and the British army landed in force, 'I really think there is the fairest

---

[25] J. H. Rose, *Pitt and Napoleon*, 288–9; Dropmore, VI. 84–5; Canning MSS, 24 Dec. 1799, Pitt to Canning; Add. MSS 37844, 27 Dec., Windham to Pitt. Pitt's military calculations, based on figures of 20 Dec. in PRO 30/8/197 [1], are in an undated memorandum in PRO 30/8/140 which, from its reference to the Condé corps, must be before 24 Dec.

[26] Grey Papers, 2356, 22 Dec., memo by Rosière with comments; Dropmore, VI. 85, 86, 89; Spencer, III. 282. I have not identified Dundas's letter which is the subject of Pitt's derision.

[27] *Strategy of Overthrow*, 166.

prospect that Brest must in the course of the summer, be in our power.'[28]

It was this day-dream which prompted Dundas's warning from Scotland that the country might tire of the struggle.[29] 'I perfectly count on the assurance you give me', he went on, 'that you will not permit the eagerness or the sanguineness of your temper to carry you beyond the result which an accurate investigation of the subject in detail actually presents you.' Yet though others might refrain from saying so, Dundas felt he had a duty to warn Pitt against his optimistic temperament, 'which although on many occasions it produces the most happy consequences, is to be carefully guarded against in the formation and execution of military plans'.[30]

Dundas's warning was echoed by the generals, who were alarmed by Pitt's reliance on royalist advice. Sir Charles Stuart had been shown a grandiose essay in strategy by Rosière, proposing in addition to the Breton invasion a landing at two points on the Languedoc coast to aid the southern royalists. The scheme found favour with ministers, and was soon to be promoted from Germany by William Wickham; but Stuart dismissed Rosière's ideas contemptuously as being founded on ignorance: 'I have generally perceived in the French memoires delivered to me upon service precisely the same ignorance hidden under extensive and apparently advantageous proposals, which, when critically examined as to their execution dwindle away to nothing.' Grey strongly agreed. 'Beware of the Royalists and Chouans', he wrote a week later to Huskisson, ' . . . it is rotten ground, and Mr. Pitt and Mr. Dundas must not entangle themselves with it.' Stuart's point could have been applied to all exiles. Cut off from direct information, relying on indifferent maps and the eye of memory, clutching at straws and eager to lure the British into supporting them, neither the Bourbons nor the House of Orange were reliable sources of political or military advice. Rosière was claiming with one breath that the royalists could put 150,000 men in the field, and with the next that they could not hold the two small towns of

---

[28] Cornwallis, III. 154–5. [29] Above, p. 51.
[30] Rylands Library, Engl. 907, no. 26, 4 Jan., Dundas to Pitt.

Auray and Vannes which commanded the exit from the Ruis peninsula.[31]

When Grey's delayed final report on the Rosière plan arrived on 16 January, it vindicated his distrust of the royalists. When questioned Rosière had admitted that there were no provisions on the peninsula and was silent even about fresh water. The exists from Ruis could not be held by the insurgents; and more time would be needed merely to land the fascines, gabions and other engineers' stores for building the proposed redoubts than Rosière allowed for completing the entire system of defences. Nor would his redoubts at four hundred yard intervals give much trouble to an enemy forcing the line of entrenchments. Many queries remained unanswered, and the account of royalist and republican numbers was highly dubious. 'I earnestly hope you will not embarrass yourself with this enterprise,' Grey concluded.[32]

Grey's advice came by now as no surprise, and Pitt had already resolved to keep the decision about a western landing in suspense till Dundas's return. But if the Ruis operation was abandoned, he found it hard to see how a large British force could be used decisively. And decisive the operation must be. 'I feel, as you do', he told Dundas, 'that we must make our impression in the course of the ensuing campaign, or we shall find our means fail us.' An attack on Belle Île would be useful; but beyond that Pitt could think of nothing better than demonstrations and raids, unless they were prepared to take a great risk and either attack Brest or land between the Seine and the Somme to threaten Paris. Either of these operations could win the war — or lose it. The risks would be unacceptable unless military advice showed that the odds were strongly in favour of success. This cautious attitude drew Pitt further apart from Windham and Grenville, and closer to the views of Dundas.[33]

The truth was that though Pitt was indulging himself with speculations about a direct assault on Brest, Grey had virtually

[31] PRO 30/8/181, 3 Jan., Stuart to Pitt; Add. MSS 38736, 9 Jan., Grey to Huskisson. Sir John Moore's diary infers that the scheme to aid the Provençal royalists, as distinct from the plan to attack Masséna's communications on the Riviera, found favour with the ministers but not with Stuart. (Moore I. 363-4). A set of Rosière's plans is in the Pretyman MSS T 108/43.

[32] Dropmore, VI. 98-9.   [33] Stanhope, III. 208.

killed the Brest operation as well as the Ruis scheme, by raising his latest requirement for the siege and covering force to
120,000 men: 'a visionary force', said Huskisson. As for
alternative projects, Grey and St. Vincent had obeyed their
instructions to consider other points of attack between the
Channel and Gibraltar, but in the absence of proper data
refused to recommend any mainland attack. All their information came from commercial charts, or from plans in the
Tower collection which were neither dated nor authenticated.
They had no information about the state of the country, the
garrisons near the ports, or the number of troops which the
enemy could concentrate in a given time. Without better
intelligence island attacks were more likely to succeed; and
they suggested Belle Île, Oléron or Rhé. Belle Île it was now
likely to be; and on 18 January Colonel Thomas Maitland
sailed in the frigate *Alcmene* to reconnoitre the island.[34]

But what of the royalist insurgents, whose co-operation
was the basis of every plan for a western offensive? Their
autumn operations had begun badly, for the republican
commander General Hédouville had served in the Vendée
under Hoche. He was familiar with counter-insurgent tactics,
and quickly formed *colonnes mobiles* to deal with the guerrilla
bands. The coming of the Consulate disconcerted the insurgents still further and, unable to guess Bonaparte's intentions,
most of the bands accepted an armistice. The truce was due
to expire on 21 January, and in Quiberon Bay Captain Pellew
feared that some of the royalists would succumb to Bonaparte's
tempting offers of peace. And many of them did so. Only
three leaders remained in arms; and General Brune, the victorious commander in Holland, was following his demi-brigades
south to command the Army of the West. Brune left Paris for
Brittany with orders which Bonaparte had issued on 14 January on receiving the British rejection of his overture. He was
to march rapidly and crush the remaining insurgents with
such speed that as soon as possible after 21 January the
British would know that their friends' overthrow was inevitable. A fortnight was enough for Brune. Georges Cadoudal
and Bourmont submitted with their bands. The remaining

[34] SRO, GD 51/1/768, 14 Jan., Huskisson to Dundas; Grey Papers, 2253,
2254, 2256; Add. MSS 38736, 18 Jan., T. Maitland to Huskisson.

leader, Frotté, asked for an armistice in mid-February, but in spite of a safe-conduct he was seized, tried and shot with his principal officers. The insurrection was dead.

By late January reports of the royalist disintegration were reaching England. On the 25th newspapers from Paris recorded Brune's assumption of command; on the 27th they claimed that a great part of the insurgent departments had accepted offers of peace. This was denied by the *émigrés*; but on 7 February Captain Lukin returned with Colonel Maitland from their reconnaissance of Belle Île and reported a general crumbling of the insurgents. The movement was sinking back from open insurrection to the old sporadic *chouannerie*.[35]

Bonaparte had won his war in the west. He was after all to be the conciliator of royalist France, but not in the manner of General Monk as Grenville had hoped. Captain Pellew was to voice in anger what the royalist exiles in London dared not recognize. The insurgents, he wrote, were 'rascals who care not one curse for all the Princes on earth, and who provided Mass be sung, care not a rush who governs France'.[36]

---

[35] Add. MSS 5744, ff. 19–20 (Herries' journal); Dropmore, VI. 114; Windham *Papers*, II. 151.   [36] Parkinson, *Pellew*, 243 (written in July 1800).

CHAPTER IV

The Challenge to Grenville's Strategy

1. 'Into the arms of the House of Austria'

Pellew's royalist 'rascals' were but one arm of a concentric onslaught against the French republic; for the western plans with which Pitt was busying himself in December and January had no chance of success except as part of a general offensive of which the main force was to be the Austrian army. Yet while the ministers and their advisers fumbled with plans for Brest and Quiberon, the situation in Europe on which their hopes depended was shrouded in the darkness of another iron winter. The weather through which Dundas struggled when he returned from Scotland in late January was a symbol of the confusion he would find on reaching London. Skirting the Lammermuirs, he broke his journey for a night on the Lothian coast at Tyninghame; but as he settled in his coach for the next stage a hurricane of wind and snow swept down, the post-boys refused to drive on, and he was forced to return to the house. By now the German rivers had frozen, and the couriers were trapped with their dispatches at Heligoland or Cuxhaven waiting for a passage through the ice. Remembering the difficulties of the preceding winter, Grenville had set up emergency arrangements to send summaries of his instructions in invisible ink through the ice-free enemy ports of France and Holland, and this traffic was used to some extent.[1] But the incoming dispatches from foreign courts continued to depend on the weather in the Elbe. Throughout January Grenville remained in dark ignorance of events in Vienna and Petersburg. What did the unpredictable Tsar Paul intend? Were there to be more Russian troops in Germany and the Mediterranean, or would he withdraw those that were there? Would more Russians be sent from the Baltic to strengthen the western offensives? What were Austria's military plans, and where did they want the British army's support? For

[1] Dropmore, VI. 81, 107; Add. MSS 41855, f. 275; FO 7/57, 24 Dec. 1799, Grenville to Minto; FO 7/58, Minto's of 29 Jan. 1800.

weeks nothing was known, till on 7 February a temporary thaw in the Elbe released twelve batches of mails, shedding blinding flashes of illumination. They came at the very moment when the royalist insurrection in western France was collapsing

One thing which the mails made clear was that the Russian army's role in Germany was finished. At one moment the Tsar had countermanded the withdrawal of Suvorov's force, but only to fall into a fresh rage in January over the conduct of the Austrian generals besieging Ancona. When the Adriatic port surrendered, the Austrians had excluded the Russian admiral from signing the capitulation and prevented him from seizing the enemy ships in the harbour. This was the end of Paul's co-operation with the Austrians. His troops were recalled, and Suvorov came home to die in disgrace.

Grenville, however, already knew that the Austrians would accept no direct help from the ill-found Russians, and believed that they had force enough to win without a Russian infusion.[2] To balance the Russian withdrawal, the dispatches brought news of unexpected diplomatic progress in Vienna. When Lord Minto had been appointed to Vienna in the summer, Grenville had not credited the new ambassador with much perception. He had described him as 'ten times more enamoured' of Thugut than his predecessor Morton Eden had been: 'Lord Minto has not yet learned to receive Thugut's promises with the distrust with which seven years of painful experience has inspired me.'[3] But Grenville was now to change his tune, about both Minto and Thugut. For by the end of the year Minto had been achieving results, aided by the Austrian breach with Russia. Thugut was always constrained by the coolness of the Austrian army and public towards a British alliance; but with much bargaining and raising of his demands, he at last agreed to ratify the loan agreement of 1797 which had kept the British and Austrian governments apart. To Starhemberg, the Austrian ambassador in London, the effect of the news on the English ministry seemed 'truly miraculous'. For Grenville the news heralded victory in the war, with Austria at last a true ally. If the Austrians could

[2] FO 7/57, Minto's of 1 Dec.; SRO, GD 51/1/529/4, 18 Dec., Huskisson to Dundas.   [3] Dropmore, V. 431, 433.

resist the temptation to make a separate peace, 'I should really think our success assured, so far as human calculations can ensure it'. On 13 February he learned that Starhemberg had received the ratification; and that very day a royal message to both Houses of Parliament asked for financial advances to Vienna. In the next four days Parliament voted an advance of half a million, in anticipation of a treaty subsidy of £2.5 million; and after nearly three years of suspicion, scepticism and hostility Grenville threw himself into the arms of Thugut.[4]

The parliamentary debate reopened the question why the British were fighting the war. The times were dark, the weather was cruel, and the price of food and fuel was soaring; but ministers were denying that war and scarcity were connected. George Tierney took the bull by the horns. The Austrian loan was wrong, he declared, because the purpose of the war had been achieved by Bonaparte's destruction of the Jacobin menace. He demanded that Pitt should state his war aims in one sentence; and Pitt replied with a famous declaration. 'Sir,' he said, 'I will do so in a single word. The object, I tell him, is security.' Was Britain's security to be Bonaparte, asked Pitt in words which echoed Grenville. Jacobinism was not dead but was centred in this one individual, 'who was reared and nursed in its bosom; whose celebrity was gained under its auspices, and who was at once the child and the champion of all its atrocities'.[5]

Pitt's words are more often quoted than Tierney's reply, which deserves to be recorded. 'Security', Tierney retorted, 'may be urged by every nation with equal propriety, as the pretext for continuing expensive and ruinous wars. The Chancellor of the Exchequer has availed himself of a phrase which undoubtedly sounds well, and is in itself grateful to mankind; but . . . it is only using an indirect mode of evading a distinct answer to a most important question.' Pitt might deny that his aim was to restore the Bourbon monarchy; but Lord Hawkesbury's language did not suggest that the ministry

---

[4] FO 7/58, 8 and 14 Feb., Grenville to Minto; Dropmore, VI. 123; Helleiner, 122, 124; Buckingham, *Courts and Cabinets*, III. 38, 17 Feb., Grenville to Buckingham; *Parl. Hist.* XXXIV. 1438-9.
[5] Stanhope, III. 215-17; *Parl. Hist.* XXXIV. 1442-6.

would ever make peace with Bonaparte, that 'artful and daring Corsican adventurer' who had set the stage for the latest of France's 'successive scenic changes in their farce of government'.[6]

Grenville's elation at the ratifying of the Austrian treaty is at first sight surprising. Four months earlier after the battle of Zurich he had written off the Austrians as too untrustworthy to be weighed in the military balance, and had declared the Russians to be England's only true allies. It was now clear that Suvorov's plundering Russians were not to be the saviours of Europe; but why should Grenville rest his entire hopes of a victorious war on those 'perverse and crooked' statesmen in Vienna on whom he had so disastrously relied in the previous campaign? Even now Thugut was demanding larger advances, and blackmailing him with threats to accept Talleyrand's offers of a free hand in Italy.[7]

The key to Grenville's changing attitude was his old friend William Wickham, and the reports he had been sending from the Austrian headquarters in southern Germany. Grenville was effusive in his gratitude to Wickham for revealing the true character of the Russian army, and rescuing him from the illusion that Suvorov was the instrument of Providence.[8] For some time Wickham, in his disillusionment with the Russians, had been falling into headlong admiration for the Austrian army. He enthused at its bold offensive spirit, its staff officers unequalled in Europe; and he believed its force was sufficient to win the war without Russian aid. By his reckoning the Austrian army, with German auxiliaries to be subsidized by England, could put 230,000 men in the field between Mainz and the Mediterranean, while the French could not maintain more than 150,000–180,000 in the line. But this decisive superiority would throw strategic decisions into the hands of the Austrians, and Britain would have no means of controlling their great military machine; for experience showed 'the impossibility of forcing either the Court of Vienna or the Austrian Generals to do what they do not like

---

[6] *Parl. Hist.* XXXIV. 1519ff, 1528-9.   [7] Sherwig, 130-1; Duffy, 404-8.
[8] Dropmore, VI. 52. For Wickham see *Strategy of Overthrow*, esp. pp. 73-4.

excepting at the risk of some mischief to the ... common cause'. In a private letter Wickham urged Grenville to accept this truth. 'Are you prepared to throw yourself into the arms of the House of Austria, or no? If not, renounce at once every idea of a continental war against France; for you can neither carry it on without Austria, nor force her to carry it on in any other than her own way.'[9]

These views Lord Grenville accepted, for Wickham was one of the few men outside his own family whose advice he respected. 'The value of your suggestions has been inestimable to me', he wrote to him on 8 February, 'and ... I shall never forget the obligations I owe to you for them.'[10]

The Austrian war plan, so far as Thugut allowed Lord Minto to discover it, seemed to be to deploy 230,000 Austrian and German troops on France's eastern frontier. Of these, 80,000 would clear Savoy and Nice, and invade France by the south. The French salient in Switzerland would be cleared by a major offensive against its northern hinge at Basle with 65,000 men, while a secondary force of 20,000 advanced into the Valais from Italy.[11]

Wickham's military task was to co-ordinate the French forces of the interior with these Austrian operations. In the north in Franche Comté, which the Austrians would enter from Basle, his channels of communication with the insurgents had been destroyed by the French victory at Zurich; and being a country traversed by main roads and heavily occupied by troops, it was unsuitable for irregular operations. Wickham therefore planned that the insurgents on that front should assemble under General Pichegru behind the Austrian lines instead of in the interior of France. But Thugut vetoed the scheme. He no more wanted French deserters and irregulars assembling in the rear of his army than he wanted Suvorov's Russians or the *émigré* rabble of the Prince of Condé. Wickham was forced to abandon the plan, and began to improvise an insurgent assembly inside France in the Vosges.[12]

---

[9] Wickham, II. 320, 320, 338, 369–79; Dropmore, VI. 73.
[10] Dropmore, VI. 120.   [11] Wickham, II. 350–2.
[12] Wickham II. 353 ff., 400, 404; Mitchell, 237 ff.

Further south in Dauphiné strict surveillance in the Lyon area would force the royalist bands under General Précy to form to the westward in the hills of the Vivarais and Forez. But the vital area for British planning was the Mediterranean coast of Provence. Here General Willot was to form companies of French deserters in the frontier mountains to harass the communications of the Army of Italy. As the situation ripened these forces would unite and descend into the Rhône valley, to seize and fortify the bridge at Pont Saint-Esprit on the main road between Piedmont and the guerrilla areas of the Vivarais. From there they would spread tentacles west and south, occupying at least one coastal town to assist a British landing. Willot was to leave Germany for Turin in early February to assume command, and he asked for the aid of the British Mediterranean fleet, particularly for landing arms and ammunition.[13]

2. *The Plan for the Mediterranean*

Wickham's plans in those mails of early February made it seem that the Mediterranean was the most fruitful area for British co-operation with the Austrians. Here the main weight of the Austrian offensive was to fall; here the best-matured insurgent operations were planned; and here alone could the British army directly aid its ally.

In contrast, the major western offensive was withering. The royalist had collapsed, and the onslaught against Brest and Quiberon had shrivelled to an island landing on Belle Île. There was still hope of a separate Russian operation, for in spite of the Ancona affair the Tsar seemed willing to raise his force in the west to 25,000, and yet another new commander was on the way. This was the French *émigré* Comte de Viomesnil, armed with a new plan inspired by Dumouriez to land at the Sables d'Olonne near Rochelle, about a hundred

---

[13] Wickham, II. 402-4; Mitchell, 238 ff. Though Gwynne Lewis's *The Second Vendeé* has nothing to say about Wickham's plans for a southern rising in 1800, it describes the continuity and violence of Catholic royalism in the department of the Gard, on whose boundary Pont Saint-Esprit lies. Wickham had tried to organize risings in the Rhône valley in 1795.

miles south of Belle Île. But whether this attack would materialize depended on the whim of the Tsar, and of that no more could be discovered, for the Elbe froze again and as late as 14 March not a drop of open water could be seen from Cuxhaven. 'This frost is cruel,' Grenville lamented. 'We know nothing whether we are to have more Russians here, or lose those we have. Of course all our plans (or nearly all) are at a standstill.' Minto echoed him from Vienna. 'If anything amiss happens it will be entirely the work of Jack Frost and the frozen Elbe.'[14]

Yet even the Mediterranean offensive was stricken by the lack of Russian troops. No Russians would be available to reinforce General Stuart's British, for there was neither time nor shipping to fetch them from the Black Sea, and Thugut refused to allow Suvorov's force to march down to the Mediterranean through Italy.[15] Without them the existing British force in the Mediterranean would be too weak to aid the insurgents of Provence or sever Masséna's communications on the Riviera. Was it right in these circumstances to commit virtually the whole of Britain's invasion force at home to the offshore landing at Belle Île? The British government agreed that it was not, and resolved to switch its priorities. The missing Russians in the Mediterranean should be made good with 15,000 British troops from England, to give Stuart a striking force of 20,000. Stuart himself was to leave as soon as possible without waiting for his troops, and travel overland through Germany to concert his plans with Wickham and the Austrians.[16]

Thus was the plan arranged which, it has been alleged, could have saved the day four months later at Marengo.

Sir Charles Stuart, the soldier who had seized Minorca eighteen

[14] FO 65/46, Whitworth's of 14 Jan. 1800, Grenville's of 8 Feb.; Saul, 137–8; Dropmore, VI. 109–10, 151; Minto, III. 114.
[15] FO 7/58, Minto's of 29 Jan.; FO 65/46, 8 Feb., Grenville to Whitworth.
[16] FO 7/58, 8 Feb., Grenville to Minto; FO 74/29, 11 Feb., Grenville to Wickham; Mitchell, 240; Add. MSS 58916, 21 Feb., Dundas to Grenville. The entry in Moore's diary under the date 12 December 1799 might suggest that the expedition had been planned in December, but a careful reading shows that it does not bear this interpretation.

months earlier in a swift and daring combined operation, was
a younger son of the former Prime Minister Lord Bute. The
ministers and the navy admired his enterprising spirit, of
which some thought there was too little in the British army.
The army's historian Sir John Fortescue judged him to have
been the one soldier of his generation who was capable of
undertaking the task later accomplished by Wellington in the
Peninsula; but he had two defects which make this unlikely.
His health and his temper were uncertain. 'He has certainly
got a most untoward temper', said Dundas; and twenty years
earlier his father had warned him not to 'think your honour
every minute concerned because this or that desire is not
complied with'. Faced with the constraints of political
considerations and limited resources, Stuart would not be
patient.[17]

During the next month Sir Charles Stuart busied himself
with military preparations. By 10 March Admiralty troopships would be ready in the Downs to embark his first four
battalions for Minorca, but there were the usual complications
of assembling a maritime expedition. The Admiralty objected
to sending transports into the North Sea to embark three
battalions in Norfolk, for fear that the westerly winds of the
early spring would prevent the ships from returning through
the Straits of Dover. Battalions in Essex were substituted,
because they could be ferried across the Thames at Tilbury
for a short march across Kent to the Downs. Battalions
stationed in Ireland had to be relieved by Foot Guards from
London, and these were marched to Portsmouth, where they
picked up shipping which would later take the Irish battalions
on to Minorca. Stuart wisely asked that if his troops were to
sail in separate convoys as shipping became available, each
convoy should form a complete force with its own supplies,
medical services, artillery, engineers and staff so that it could
take the field as soon as it arrived in the Mediterranean.[18]

There was the usual indenting for stores and staff. The
Treasury ordered provisions and spirits for 20,000 men for
three months, and Stuart applied to the Ordnance for cannon.
He wanted thirty light battalion guns (twelve of them to be

[17] Add. MSS 37877, 4 June 1798, Dundas to Windham; Wortley, 180.
[18] Add. MSS 38736, ff. 22, 35-7, 39-40.

harnessed abreast for 'a particular purpose'), six light and six heavy 12-pounders, six 5½-inch mortars and six 5½-inch howitzers; a demand which the Master-General Lord Cornwallis regarded as unreasonable. For himself Stuart wanted a commission as Commander-in-Chief in the Mediterranean; as second in command he asked for Major-General Simcoe with the rank of lieutenant-general; and he invited Moore to command a brigade. The appointment of staff, however, brought out the worst side of Stuart's character, and his preparations were punctuated by truculent protests about the Duke of York. The Duke's offences were that he had refused a permanent commission to Colonel Graham, who had distinguished himself at Malta, and would allow only a Deputy Quartermaster-General and Deputy Adjutant-General on Stuart's staff. 'Where I am concerned', Stuart warned Huskisson, 'I can not be answerable for the product of an army without I select competent officers and appoint a customary staff.' The predictable explosion was detonated by the medical appointments. The Army Medical Board had suggested some changes to Stuart's list of medical staff, pointing out that some of the surgeons he named were very junior, or lacked evidence of training in surgery, or indeed were not on the Board's list at all. Stuart replied with observations on the men he had named, all of whom had served with him. 'However unskilled I may be in the medical art', he concluded, 'six years continued service abroad with most of the gentlemen . . . give me some right to decide whether or not they are competent.' The Duke replied courteously; but he was struggling to impose administrative regularity on the army, and had to support the Medical Board or allow a horse and cart to be driven through his own regulations. Stuart retorted by citing some irregular appointments which he maintained showed that no such regulations existed, and demanded to be superseded by 'some officer more suitable to his [the Duke's] wishes and more adequate to the command'. The echoes of this tantrum reverberated through the corridors of power. But Stuart's resignation was not pressed or accepted — as yet.[19]

[19] Wortley, 328-9; Moore I. 363; Dropmore, VI. 140-1; Add. MSS 38736, ff. 20, 51-6, 62-9; Cornwallis, III. 218.

The most serious threat to the expedition, however, did not come from the temperament of its commander, but from the doubts of the Secretary of State himself. For some time Dundas had been questioning the country's capacity to mount a major maritime expedition.[20] Those doubts may have been strengthened by a memorandum from the Quartermaster-General Sir David Dundas (who was no relation) on the resources needed to maintain an army of 100,000 men in the field in Germany. The figures were alarming: 60,000 horses, and 4,200 waggons.[21] If one extrapolated the figure for a British force landing from the sea, the shipping requirement for horses and waggons was terrifying. It was simply impossible to ship them.

Even troops would be difficult to find as the King had been the first to suspect. As soon as he heard of the expedition he uttered a warning, drawn from his long experience of military planning, against relying on fallacious paper figures, and he was right. When the Duke of York was asked to name the regiments for the expedition, his reply was full, careful, and shocking.[22]

The Duke divided the regiments at home into those which could serve anywhere in the world, and those which were limited to Europe because they were filled with militiamen who had volunteered on that condition. There were at home 9,000 infantry in fourteen battalions whose service was unlimited, and the Duke argued that these should not be sent to the Mediterranean, which was a European theatre, because it would leave no reserves available to attack enemy colonies or meet a sudden emergency outside Europe. Nor could the Duke proceed with his plans to train riflemen and form a light brigade if these troops were sent.

He proposed, therefore, that only troops whose service was limited to Europe should be sent to the Mediterranean; but these were not yet fit for the field. Why this should have been so was a question on which opinions varied. The battalions had been filled with volunteers from the militia in the previous summer and sent straight into action in Holland without

[20] Above, pp. 59-60.
[21] Dundas of Beechwood Papers, memo. of Feb. 1800.
[22] *GL* 2112, 2113.

adequate equipment or training. Though they had been re-equipped since their return at the end of November, many of the regiments had been diluted again with further drafts from the militia; and ten of the strongest had been shipped off to take over security duties in Ireland, instead of remaining in England to train. It had been unavoidable to reinforce Ireland, where the militia were being depleted by volunteering for the line; but even the troops in England made disappointing progress with their training. The Duke of York attributed the failure to the harsh winter weather, which was no doubt the most important reason; but the Duke himself had shown a deficient sense of urgency when he gave the officers the normal generous winter leave. Half the staff officers and captains, and a third of the subalterns, were allowed to be absent at any one time. General Moore complained of this absence and the consequent neglect of discipline; and frequent changes of quarters had interrupted such training as had been possible.[23] The troops had been re-brigaded to mix the 'militia' battalions with better trained regular units; yet Lord St. Vincent formed the opinion that this brigading was premature and was itself a hindrance to battalion training. Whatever the reasons for the retarded training may have been, the Duke warned Dundas that none of the twenty battalions he named for the Mediterranean were yet fit for service. They needed two more months of uninterrupted training, and he earnestly hoped that they would not be thrown into active service again before they were ready.

General Stuart's reaction to the Duke's report was predictable. The 15,000 'effectives' meant only 12,000 'in their shoes'; and of these a hundred militia recruits in every battalion ought to be discharged as unfit. Stuart demanded authority to appoint a general to inspect the regiments and discharge useless soldiers; and to replace the weeded men with several additional battalions.[24] To Dundas the Duke's report was confirmation of his doubts. 'I am becoming truly uneasy in the backwardness . . . with regard to the chance of acting offensively in any quarter of the world', he confided to Lord Spencer, asking him for information about shipping.

[23] Cornwallis, III. 165, 167–8, 202; Glover, 169; Moore, I. 364.
[24] Add. MSS 38736, f. 33.

On that score at least Spencer was reassuring; for enough transports would be ready in the course of March to embark the whole force in three contingents.[25] The state of the troops, however, was spreading increasing alarm among the ministers as the Duke of York's paper was circulated. Before the middle of March Windham remonstrated with Pitt, who agreed to stop the embarcations and summon the Cabinet. But having soothed the placable Windham Pitt characteristically did nothing, until his brother Lord Chatham raised the question again at an evening meeting on the 19th and demanded a special Cabinet meeting on the subject.

Dundas had left before the matter was raised; but on hearing what had been said he summoned the Cabinet for noon on the 21st, and asked Grenville to meet him beforehand at Pitt's for some 'serious conversation . . . I feel very unpleasant in the prospect of the next campaign so far as our force may be concerned.'[26] This was the opening of a decisive battle for ascendancy between Grenville and Dundas: a battle between Foreign Office intelligence and the War Department's administrative realism; between an unlimited continental strategy and a limited maritime one. Underlying the calculations and the strategy was a clash about the purpose of the war.

3. 'We calculated beyond our means'

The Cabinet meeting of 21 March was a contentious one. Some of the members argued warmly that the Mediterranean expedition should go on in spite of the Duke of York's paper; but it was finally agreed to suspend the embarcation of the second and third convoys.[27]

Dundas was by now deeply agitated about the state of British planning. Had there been agreement in the Cabinet about strategic principles, he felt that it would have been his clear duty to execute the plans with energy. But there was no such agreement, he wrote to Chatham after the meeting. No two ministers seemed to share the same ideas, and his own

[25] Spencer, III. 323–4.   [26] Windham *Diary*, 422; Dropmore, VI. 170.
[27] Windham *Diary*, 422.

views probably placed him in a minority of one. He was convinced that in the whole course of the war the only useful
military efforts had been those mounted for strictly British
interests. It was because the enemy's colonies had been
annihilated early in the war that Britain had the flourishing
resources to continue the struggle. Now the country was
committed to continental operations whose success was
doubtful; yet not a man was allotted to overseas operations
which favoured the permanent interests of Britain. If a small
part of the army was devoted to securing Britain's own
interests overseas, the rest would be enough to aid the continental allies by demonstrations, which Dundas believed
were the only feasible form of co-operation.

This letter was more than a plea to abandon the major
offensive in the Mediterranean. Dundas was asserting in
effect that no major landing should take place in Europe
at all; that even the Belle Île operation should be no more
than a demonstration, and not the prelude to a mainland
offensive. He told Chatham that he intended to compose a
detailed paper, arguing the case for securing England's permanent advantages 'in its essential interests of commerce and
navigation'.[28]

Four days later, however, in spite of Dundas's doubts, the
Mediterranean expedition was restored to its full scale. A
thaw and an east wind brought another batch of mails in
from the Elbe, and ministers who bothered to call at the
Cabinet reading room and read the dispatches found that the
Austrians had lifted a corner of the curtain which concealed
their plans. They confirmed that they would launch an offensive on the Riviera as soon as the weather allowed; and Thugut,
who had revealed nothing while he was dickering with Minto
about the loan and parleying with Talleyrand, was now impatient to know how the British army would be used. The
British government could only reply that its plans for the
west were at a standstill, awaiting Paul's decision whether to
send more Russian troops. The plans for the British force
were in truth too trivial to be revealed. Colonel Maitland's
reconnaissance of Belle Île had resulted in a plan to occupy

[28] Add. MSS 40102, f. 40.

the islets of Houat and Hédic on the skirts of Belle Île, and gradually to build up the force till Belle Île could be surprised. Quite what the force could then achieve was uncertain; the only ray of promise was that the pacification of the Vendée still seemed 'very imperfect and precarious'.[29]

Grenville promised Thugut that the British would do what they could in the west to annoy the enemy, but could admit no more. But there was still the Mediterranean; and the Cabinet agreed to press ahead with the full reinforcement of 15,000 men, and to send General Stuart off as soon as possible to confer with the Austrian commanders.[30]

The Mediterranean expedition was thus, like the naval re-entry two years earlier in the spring of 1798, decided by the supposed wishes of the Austrian government. In 1798 the British ministry had hoped to lure the Austrians into the war; now they hoped to deflect them from making a separate peace. But Dundas's uneasiness about the expedition was not abated. He saw in the Cabinet's proceedings the old fault of piecemeal planning of which Windham had complained at the time of the Dutch expedition: 'the taking up only one point at a time', said Dundas, 'whereas in deciding on the appropriation of any part of our force, we ought to take the whole under our view'. He had spent a couple of mornings composing his promised paper on strategy; and he guessed that it would not please those of his colleagues who wanted to hold the army in one inactive mass waiting for an improbable chance of acting together. No longer did he believe in a major invasion in the west. 'I have been for a long time', he warned Lord Spencer, 'perfectly satisfied that we calculated beyond our means when we supposed that with the sea in our rear it was advisable to undertake any very extensive and detailed military operations in an enemy's country, where there were great armies and internal resources to oppose us.'[31]

[29] Windham *Papers*, II. 153-4; Spencer, III. 322; FO 65/46, 14 March 1800, Grenville to Whitworth.

[30] Add. MSS 39879, 23 March, summons to Cabinet on 24th; FO 7/58, Minto's of 23 Feb. and 9 March; Stowe Papers, 22 March, T. Grenville to Buckingham; FO 7/58, n.d., Grenville's no. 12 to Minto; Dropmore, VI. 185-6; Spencer, IV. 113; Windham *Diary*, 422.

[31] Spencer, III. 324-5. For Windham's earlier criticisms of Cabinet procedure, see *Strategy of Overthrow*, 178.

Map 4. The Atlantic and the Americas.

Cabinet procedure was the starting-point of Dundas's memorandum, which he circulated to the Cabinet on 31 March. Strategic discussions had been 'desultory, unconnected and partial', making no attempt to assess the relative importance of the various objectives. For some time past only the continental war had been considered, and commerce and naval power had been forgotten. Yet it was these which were 'essential to the permanent interests and prosperity of the British Empire'. To protect them, new markets must be won and defended. 'The prosperity of this country knows no bounds, unless . . . its industry and commercial enterprise shall outrun the extension of its foreign markets.'[32]

Dundas viewed Britain's existing overseas markets with pessimism. European markets were precarious; the commerical tie with the United States was slender and uncertain; and the West Indies were already at the summit of their prosperity and likely to decline. Though the Indian market was safe and likely to grow, its needs were limited and competition from local manufactures was severe: India was more valuable for its remittances than its trade. England must find new markets, for 'the more they are multiplied the safer they are'. And the great markets still waiting to be opened were in Spanish America. If Britain did not act, France would use the weapon of revolution against the weak Spanish colonial governments and seize the markets for herself.

Dundas did not advocate the occupation of the vast Spanish Empire or the replacement of Spanish rule by rule from London. Against that sort of colonialism the lessons of the American War and the gospel of Adam Smith cried out decisively. The penetration of the Spanish colonies must be purely commercial: 'no other connexion with them can be either attainable or durable'. But commercial penetration needed bases and trading stations; and these key positions must be seized from Spain. There was Tenerife, an ocean base on the routes to the Far East and to the whole of Central and South America and the Caribbean. In the Americas 'an unbounded market' would be opened by controlling New

---

[32] Dundas's 'memorandum for the consideration of his Majesty's ministers', dated 31 March, is in PRO 30/8/243. There is a copy in Duke University Library, MS XVIII F, bound volume of Dundas papers, no. 39.

Orleans, the mouths of the Orinoco and the River Plate, and La Concepción on the coast of Chile.

Dundas asserted that these operations were not incompatible with operations in Europe. He could advance this argument because he was convinced that military intervention in Europe must take a limited form: 'we cannot take a direct part in the military operations on the continent, and can only act collaterally and indirectly with our continental allies'. Underlying this military argument were his deeper beliefs about the future of the war: that decisive victory was unattainable, that Britain could not afford for much longer to subsidize continental warfare, and that republican France no longer presented an ideological threat.

How, then, could Britain find the forces for both overseas expansion and European war? Dundas proposed to occupy the Chilean post with a force from the Cape and India; and all the others could be taken by 12,000–15,000 men. Some of these would be West Indian Blacks; but where could the white troops be found? He was too artful to suggest that it should be done by cancelling the Mediterranean expedition. But suppose that the force in the Mediterranean proved to be unable to do much for the allies and the royalists. If it turned out that only 5,000 could be used in the Mediterranean, the other 10,000 should be diverted to seize Tenerife, and go on by way of Jamaica to attack New Orleans. If it turned out that no offensive force at all could be used in the Mediterranean, a further 3,000–4,000 men should be sent to occupy the Orinoco; and then 4,000 from England would be enough for the River Plate.

This plan showed little faith in the Mediterranean offensive; there was even a latent hope that it would be abortive. And what of the western attacks? Dundas's calculations were rather loose, but clear in their implications. He rightly assumed that no Russians would be available; but he believed that by early June 23,500 British infantry at home would be ready for service. He proposed that 9,000 of these should seize Belle Île, and 5,000 attack Walcheren supported by 4,000 Dutch. That left 9,500 for the security of Ireland and any other purpose, with another 10,000–12,000 coming forward later for foreign service when regiments returned from overseas and completed their recruiting. If unforeseen opportunities were created by Austrian victories or risings in France or Holland, 20,000 infantry and 10,000 cavalry could be concentrated from Belle Île, Walcheren and the home forces.

'I cannot expect', Dundas repeated, 'the full approbation of those who may think that the whole or the greatest part of our force should be kept entire and in reserve to wait for such occurrences as the chance of events may cast up.' No, indeed. For what he had proposed was the diversion of the Mediterranean force to the far side of the globe, and the dispersal of the offensive force at home to occupy widely separated islands.

If anything, Dundas had overestimated the force for the western expeditions. A list of the infantry in the British Isles on 2 April, excluding those under orders for the Mediterranean, showed that only 8,000 were ready for immediate service; that only 16,500 would be ready by June; and in the whole course of the campaigning season only 27,000. As for their quality, Cornwallis warned that after allocating the best regiments in Ireland to the Mediterranean expedition, it was unlikely that he could provide the sort of troops Colonel Maitland would like for Belle Île. The British forces at home were too few to invade western France; and it was far from clear that if the Russians made a landing there was enough shipping to supply them. In any case news arrived on 31 March that the Tsar had demanded the recall of the British ambassador, Sir Charles Whitworth, which made it even less likely that a Russian force would be available.[33]

Yet while the forces for a western offensive evaporated and the Cabinet reiterated its determination to build up an army in the Mediterranean, news was on the way from Wickham which totally reversed the picture of what the Austrians wanted of the British army. On 4 April an outline

---

[33] Dropmore, VI. 147-9, 155-6, 188-9; Cornwallis, III. 236; Add. MSS 58861, 31 March, Grenville to King. I have not discovered when it was known that the Russian troops were to be recalled. Whitworth's dispatch of 25 March announcing the fact was received on 23 April, but he believed Vorontsov had been informed some time earlier.

of the French order of battle arrived from him which showed that the Austrians had allowed their obsession with Italy to unbalance their forces. There they had an overwhelming superiority of 100,000 against 30,000 French, while in Germany General Kray had only equal numbers; and in a central position at Dijon Bonaparte was assembling an Army of Reserve from the interior of France. All Wickham could say of this Dijon force was that its position was admirably chosen to give it a choice of options between the German and Italian fronts, and it could tilt the balance dangerously against Kray in Germany. The Austrians were now showing little interest in the British plans for the Mediterranean, but were desperately anxious to prevent the enemy from detaching 20,000 men to Germany from the west. What they now emphasized was not the Mediterranean front, but diversions on the coasts of western France and Holland. The implications for the Mediterranean expedition were grave. None of the British force had yet sailed, and to send a large force to the Mediterranean now would show the enemy that no serious landing was intended in the west and allow him to transfer troops to the German front. Lord Camden urged Pitt to cancel the Mediterranean expedition, and use the 15,000 troops thus released to hold the French army to its ground in the west.[34]

To this argument Dundas was indifferent. He no longer believed in a major effort in the west, and as General Stuart's departure for Germany was delayed by the death of an uncle, he saw no hurry to decide the fate of the expedition. He preferred to ride in the spring sunshine at Wimbledon, and even cancelled a Cabinet meeting. For him a much more alarming piece of news arrived on 8 April: a warning from Lord Minto in Vienna of Thugut's indifference and even positive hostility to Britain's Mediterranean plans. Thugut had refused absolutely to provide any Austrian troops for the Mediterranean as substitutes for Suvorov's Russians, and had refused to discuss the Provençal insurrection even in outline till General Willot arrived in Vienna. This absence of goodwill to the British

[34] Windham *Diary*, 423; Cambridge University Library, Add. 6958/13, copy of Camden's of 6 April 1800 to Pitt, wrongly dated 1799; FO 74/29, Wickham's of 24 March.

expedition was disturbing, for it depended on Austrian aid. Stuart counted on the Austrian commanders' permission to buy horses, stores and provisions in Italy, for they could not be brought from home. And he needed Austrian cavalry. To ship a large mounted force from England was impossible; and though the British cavalry in Portugal could be shipped a little more easily, they could not be assembled at Stuart's base in Minorca where there was neither accommodation nor forage. Stuart was 'astonished and staggered' at Dundas's doubt whether the Austrians would give him cavalry, of which they had more than enough; and if they would not do this, how could they be trusted to provide for his other needs?[35] Without Austrian co-operation his force would be crippled.

4. *Dundas the Obstructor*

That morning Dundas was visited by Pitt at Wimbledon, and he persuaded the Prime Minister that only the first Mediter-ranean convoy of 5,000 troops already embarked should sail. The other 10,000 were to be held back at home till General Stuart reached Germany and discovered what help he could expect from the Austrians. Dundas saw that in the Mediter-ranean plan two crippling constraints on British amphibious strategy had converged: the shipping bottle-neck which made it impossible to send a large force abroad equipped with transport and cavalry for mobile warfare; and the difficulty of concerting military plans with continental allies. He explained the dilemma to Grenville. If the Austrians would allow Stuart to buy horses, waggons, and provisions for an army of 15,000 men, his force would be capable of advancing inland. If they refused, the army could not survive more than two days' march from its ships. 'Is there any thing in the con-duct of Austria . . . to justify us in the belief that these essen-tial requisites will be supplied by Austria?'

Dundas's conclusion was clear. The Cabinet was about to send a huge proportion of its trained troops to a distant theatre; not to execute a plan but to look for an opportunity,

[35] Dropmore, VI. 190, 194; FO 7/58, Minto's of 23 March; Add. MSS 38736, f. 86.

relying on the unlikely co-operation of the Austrians and the uncertain efforts of the French royalists. If a landing was made, the force would probably lack the means to advance from its beach-head. To commit half the country's offensive force to a distant theatre in these conditions would be madness; and Dundas insisted that until the Austrians undertook to provide transport, supplies and cavalry, only a small raiding force of 5,000 men should be committed to the Mediterranean. In the meantime the remaining 10,000 could be used to seize Belle Île.[36]

Dundas's reasoning was based on logistics, and in operational terms it was unassailable. But it also fitted his strategic preconceptions. If the Mediterranean force was reduced by two-thirds, it would be too weak to open a front in southern Europe; yet the 10,000 held back waiting for news from Stuart would not be committed to an invasion in the west. There would be no second front in Europe in 1800; but 10,000 good infantry in Belle Île would be available for colonial offensives. This, we shall see, was what Dundas intended.

To Lord Grenville it was clear that the European offensive was at stake, and that Britain's coalition strategy would fall between two stools: by waiting for news from Germany which would come too late, the ministry would ensure that no attack took place either in the Mediterranean or in the west. He believed that the Mediterranean plan, with the Provençal insurgents organized by Wickham, offered the best and the last hope of striking an effective blow for the Coalition; and he was confident that Thugut would allow Stuart to purchase what he needed. But if the British force was to linger at home while Stuart visited General Kray at Augsburg, and was referred by Kray to General Melas at Turin, and was then referred back by Melas to Vienna, it would be the middle of July before word came that the troops could sail, and the middle of August before they arrived in the Mediterranean. By then the fate of the Provençal royalists would have been settled. The Cabinet must decide now, said Grenville. Either the 10,000 additional troops for the Mediterranean must sail

[36] Dropmore, VI. 193-4.

immediately, or the Mediterranean plan should be abandoned
and the force released. Plans could then be made for a real
offensive in the west, instead of fiddling about on the skirts
of Belle Île; the force released from the Mediterranean would
provide enough troops to invade Walcheren or try Dumouriez's
plan at Bordeaux. 'Do this or anything else you prefer', he
implored Dundas, 'but for God's sake, for your own honour,
and for the cause in which we are engaged, do not let us, after
having by immense exertions collected a fine army, leave it
unemployed, gaping after messengers from Genoa, Augsburg
and Vienna till the moment for acting is irrecoverably past.
For this can lead to nothing but disgrace.'[37]

Grenville would have liked to say this to Dundas's face,
but instead of riding over from Dropmore to find perhaps
that Dundas was out, he wrote his acrimonious letter. His
next communication was downright offensive, and it was
characteristic of Grenville that he was surprised when Dundas
was offended. He told Dundas that if he wanted a letter sent
to Vienna seeking categorical assurances about supplies,
transport and even Austrian troops to be put under British
orders (of the latter he saw no hope), Dundas had better
draft the dispatch himself and state the plan, numbers and
timing. For, said Grenville, he did not really understand
Dundas's plan, and if it depended on a negotiation with
Vienna it was ruled out by the most obvious calculations of
time and space. Dundas replied with unusual asperity that
Grenville had known from the beginning that he had no fixed
plan, and that Stuart's operations were to depend on the
circumstances he found in the theatre of war. But there could
be no extended operations without Austrian help; and all
that Grenville wrote confirmed that the Austrians could not
be relied on. The British force should therefore be reduced
to 5,000-6,000, which would be enough to take Malta and
make demonstrations on the coasts of Provence. For good
measure he slammed a plan of Grenville's to march Condé's
émigré force in Germany to Leghorn where Lord Keith would
ship it to Minorca: 'It is very easy for an ambassador residing
in Vienna to write such a letter to a commander-in-chief of

[37] J. H. Rose, *Pitt and Napoleon*, 266-8.

the fleet in the Mediterranean, but it is not so easy for him to comply with it.' Dundas sent copies of this angry exchange to Pitt, complaining that Grenville could never distinguish between the desirable and the possible. 'I wish he would exercise his genius for two months in executing as well as planning, and then he would learn that however desirable the *end* might be, it was necessary there should likewise be the means.'[38]

In spite of their anger, the two Secretaries of State had arrived at the same plan from different directions. Only the force already embarked for the Mediterranean should sail, the remaining 10,000 to be retained for an assault in the west as the Austrians apparently wished. Grenville still insisted that the Mediterranean offensive could have achieved a brilliant success; but only with the whole-hearted co-operation of the military departments, which was not forthcoming. Rather than keep the expedition in suspense between the west and the Mediterranean, the Mediterranean plan must be killed at once and not be kept waiting for 'the farce of an illusory negotiation at Vienna'.[39]

Still Grenville asserted that the Austrians would have co-operated with Stuart's expedition; yet he must have known in his heart that Dundas had ample reasons to doubt their reliability. They were negotiating with the enemy, demurring about the need to invade France while pressing for acquisitions in Italy; they had delayed the ratification of the loan agreement, and were still delaying the drafting of a treaty of alliance; they were secretive about their military plans. It was only a fortnight since Grenville himself had confessed to Wickham that he saw no grounds to confide that the Austrian campaign would begin in earnest, or would last longer than the moment when Bonaparte offered the Austrians what they wanted in Italy. But to admit this to Dundas would have demolished his own position.[40]

[38] Rose, *Pitt and Napoleon*, 268-9; PRO 30/8/140, 11 April 1800, Dundas to Grenville; PRO 30/8/157, 11 April, Dundas to Pitt. Fifteen months later the victim of Dundas's backbiting was saying much the same about the military judgement of Pitt: 'his sanguine temper is very apt to make him think a thing *done* in that line when it has been shown that it *may be done* — whereas unfortunately the difference is infinite' (Buckinghamshire R.O., 3 Aug. 1801 to Thomas Grenville).
[39] Rose, *Pitt and Napoleon*, 269-70.   [40] Dropmore, VI. 209.

Grenville saw, however, that the decision must be taken and adhered to without further debate: 'before we summon our numerous Cabinet, it is much better that those who are to execute should understand each other on the subject'. When the Cabinet formally agreed a week later to reduce the Mediterranean expedition to the 5,000 already embarked, it was merely ratifying what the three 'efficient ministers' had already decided.[41] Dundas was the victor of the debate; but was he fit to take the decision? He was a tired man in poor health, and at the very moment of his triumph over Grenville he was making a fresh effort to escape from the War Department. His excuse was the death of General Stuart's uncle James Stuart Mackenzie, which vacated the Privy Seal of Scotland. If Dundas could have the office with its salary of £3,000 for life, he could afford to resign the £4,000 Treasurership of the Navy, the sinecure which supported him as Secretary of State, and could then retire with credit. In vain he proposed the move to Pitt. The conversation ended as usual, with Dundas promising to remain at the War Department till the Prime Minister could release him.[42]

When Pitt departed, however, and Dundas reported the conversation to his wife, she gave vent to a tearful outburst which left him agitated and distressed. He assured her he had made arrangements with Pitt for her financial security if he died. A thousand or two a year was not the point, she replied; and for the first time this sad grey woman opened her heart to him on the subject. Lady Jane was his second wife; they had been married for seven years and she was twenty years younger than he. She told him of her unhappiness after the death of her father Lord Hopetoun; and now she had no joy in life nor ever would have which was not connected with Dundas and his existence. His health and spirits were undermined by work. She never saw him except for ten minutes at bedtime, and he had lost the habit of sound sleep. In the past two or three years her only happy times with him had been a fortnight at Walmer and a month at their Perthshire home on the Earn. Dundas was moved, for he was an affectionate man, and could only reply that if she had told him

---

[41] Rose, *Pitt and Napoleon*, 270; Windham *Diary*, 423.
[42] *GL* vol. III, p. 343, n. 5; Add. MSS 40102, ff. 44–5.

sooner how she felt, he would have given up the War Department. At this Lady Jane climbed down. She admitted that he could not resign without great public inconvenience, and she did not ask him to do so. But she implored him to look after his health and not to socialize so indiscriminately.

Immediately after this scene Dundas sent an agitated letter to Pitt, begging to be released from the War Department as soon as he could be spared. One cannot fully understand the crumbling of the ministry in the next nine months if one forgets the feelings of Lady Jane.[43]

It would be fashionable to attribute the abandonment of the Mediterranean offensive to the fears of a sick man. This would be misleading, for Dundas's appraisal of the risks was sound; yet it must be conceded that the management of the plans could have been better. From the first Grenville had forseen the expedition's need for transport and supplies, and had repeatedly pressed Pitt and Dundas to send a commissary ahead of Stuart to obtain these from the Austrians.[44] To leave the matter till the troops were on the point of sailing was a signal neglect on the part of the tired Dundas and the quarrelsome and probably ailing General Stuart.

Yet failing health was not the whole story; for Dundas's heart had never been in the plan. He had progressively lost faith in the aims for which Grenville was fighting the war and his way of fighting it. He questioned the need to overthrow the French government in Paris; he feared the continuing French presence in Malta and Egypt while the British army hung about the seaboard of Europe; he wanted security for Britain's naval power and new markets for her commerce. As for operations in Europe, he was sceptical of basing military plans on insurgency, and was by now educated in the problems of supply and shipping. And he feared that public support for the war was too fragile to survive a disaster. In Grenville's mind the decision to abandon the Mediterranean

---

[43] PRO 30/8/157, 14 Apr., Dundas to Pitt. Glenbervie (I. 81) describes Dundas as having 'an affectionate heart as a parent, a husband and a friend, and an unparalleled good temper'.

[44] Grenville made the claim in his letter of 10 April to Dundas (Rose, *Pitt and Napoleon*, 266–8). It is supported by his dispatch of 11 Feb. to Wickham, saying that an officer of confidence would probably be sent to the continent immediately (FO 74/29).

expedition had been a choice between a second front in the Mediterranean and one in the west. For Dundas it was a choice of a Mediterranean front or none. This was to be apparent in his next plan of campaign.

CHAPTER V

The Road to Disaster

1. *The Replacement of General Stuart*

The Mediterranean expedition, the one firm element in military planning, was now reduced from 15,000 to 5,000 men; and if anything still remained clear about British plans, it was that to make any contribution to Austrian operations they must be sent off with all speed. But though they were already embarked in the Downs, they were a month behind their original sailing date and still awaited their sailing orders. Nor had their commander Sir Charles Stuart yet set out for the Austrian headquarters in Germany. As if these delays were not enough, the force was about to be deprived of its leader.

The cause of the trouble was Malta, which provoked a further outburst of Sir Charles Stuart's temper when he learned that on the surrender of Valletta he was to admit a Russian garrison, and that the island would eventually be handed back to the Knights of St. John under the Grand Mastership of the Tsar. Behind this decision lay one of Grenville's disagreements with Dundas. To placate the Tsar the British government had swallowed his irregular acceptance of the Grand Mastership; but Paul's growing hostility now convinced Dundas that Russian troops must not be admitted to Valletta. Paul had recently demanded the recall of the British ambassador Whitworth, apparently on personal grounds, and had followed this by refusing Whitworth's courier a passport to leave Petersburg with his dispatches. Dundas related these signs to the activities of the Russian forces in the Mediterranean. They had given no help at Naples or Malta, but instead had occupied the Ionian Islands, suggesting a sinister interest in the Ottoman Empire. If they regarded the Turks as their future prey, they must not have Malta as well as Corfu: 'they should not be permitted to seize upon the whole Watch Towers of the Levant and the Adriatic'. Dundas was determined that Malta should remain under British control, for with bases at Malta and Gibraltar the navy could control the whole of the Mediterranean. Nor must the island be allowed to fall into French hands again: 'To France its value is incalculable.'

With these arguments the Foreign Secretary disagreed. Maritime power did not excite him; nor did be believe in Malta's strategic importance, or in the probability of Britain ever again fighting France in the eastern Mediterranean. He declared that the island was not worth a quarrel with Russia, and refused to reopen the question.[1] There the matter would have rested, but for the orders which Dundas had to give the military commander. Sir Charles Stuart was revolted by the thought of a Russian occupation. He told Dundas that he could not stomach 'the disgrace and misery of Russian interference' and could not obey these orders; and for the second time he resigned his command.

Dundas sympathized with his feelings, but could not condone his defiance of a political directive: 'there is an end of all government'.[2] Stuart's resignation had to be accepted, though with regret, for he was an able soldier; but in the Duke of York's words, his 'jealousy of temper and impatience of control from any superior authority' made it impossible to use his talents. Stuart's temper had always been treacherous, but by now his health may have undermined his power to control it, for he died a year later 'of gout in his stomach'. However that may be, his resignation left the Mediterranean theatre without a commander. The 5,000 troops sailed on 24 April with no instructions except that the garrison commander at Minorca, General Fox, should keep his whole disposable force in constant readiness. Until a new Commander-in-Chief arrived, the expedition would be frozen.[3]

In choosing a successor Dundas did not hesitate. His friend Sir Ralph Abercromby was already on his way south from Edinburgh on a mission to report on the defence of Portugal, and to him the Mediterranean command was offered. He and

---

[1] FO 65/46, Whitworth's of 18 March 1800; Add. MSS 40101, ff. 77-8, 80; Dropmore, VI. 199, 200.

[2] Add. MSS 38736, f. 95; Dropmore, VI. 207.

[3] *GL* 2136; *Gentleman's Magazine* 1801, i. 374; WO 6/55, 26 April, Dundas to Fox.

Dundas were old allies. Abercromby's mother was a Dundas, and his eldest son had recently married one of Henry Dundas's daughters. During his Christmas visit to Scotland Dundas had had some candid talk with Sir Ralph about his Cabinet colleagues, and had heard some bitter comments from the old soldier about his treatment by Pitt and Camden when he commanded in Ireland. The appointment of Sir Ralph did not please the Grenville clan, who had not forgiven him for entrenching instead of advancing after his landing in Holland in the previous autumn. 'Most violently am I indignant', exclaimed Lord Buckingham on hearing of Sir Ralph's appointment. Lord Grenville guessed 'that the Dutch business does not sit very easy upon him, and that he would not be sorry to do something brilliant; but I doubt whether his character is naturally enterprising enough to give fair chance to royalist plans.'[4] Abercromby's career and character have been discussed in the previous volume. He was not without limitations, but among his virtues was an indispensable one in a commander of combined operations: the quality which Dundas called his 'accommodating disposition'. Sir Charles Stuart would certainly have quarrelled with his naval colleague, as he had done when he seized Minorca in 1798; but Abercromby had dedicated himself many years earlier to maintaining good relations with the navy, and would do all he could to avoid disputes. At Gibraltar General O'Hara rejoiced at the change of commanders, and told the naval Commander-in-Chief, Lord Keith, that Stuart would never have got on with him: 'he cannot possibly bear any difference of opinion from his own, and [is] certainly the least accommodating of any man upon earth. Sir Ralph, on the contrary, I hold to be a reasonable, considerate good officer, and listens with temper and patience to every proposal made to him.'[5] Whether Abercromby possessed the other qualities needed for his new command remained a matter of dispute.

Arriving in Jermyn Street, Abercromby studied his task and made his plans. An experienced commander of amphibious

---

[4] Dropmore, VI. 221, 233.   [5] Keith, II. 110-11.

forces, he asked to retain his best transports in the Mediterranean as his force would be almost continually embarked, and
he sent a messenger overland to Leghorn to ask Lord Keith
for a naval force to be waiting at Minorca on his arrival. On
13 May he embarked at Portsmouth, and sailed that evening.
His frigate was to escort a convoy, touching at Lisbon and
Gibraltar on the voyage; an unnecessary economy of warships
when the general was so urgently needed in the Mediterranean.[6]

2. *Standstill in the West*

Dundas's Cabinet victory which overthrew the Mediterranean
expedition did not spell Britain's disengagement from the
Coalition. Far from it: for the next two months and more the
focus of British strategy was to be the news coming in from
Augsburg and Vienna. Wickham's reports were reassuring,
and he asserted confidently that the enemy's plans would fail.
Bonaparte evidently intended to push his Army of Reserve
forward into the Swiss salient from its assembly area at Dijon,
in order to fall on the Austrian rear either in Italy or Germany.
But he lacked the resources for this manœuvre, and if his
army attempted it the Austrians would cut if off and force
its surrender. Bonaparte himself no longer intended to join
the Army of Reserve in person, and would remain in Paris;
and Wickham was convinced that he would be forced to give
up his offensive plans and conform to the Austrian initiatives.
He gave a heartening account of the Austrian army's high
morale and promising plans. Its offensive would be opened
by General Melas in Italy, while in South Germany General
Kray's attack was to wait till he received a large reinforcement from the victorious Melas, or till the enemy were
weakened by detaching troops from the Rhine to Italy.[7]
    This reading of the situation made it impossible for Dundas
to disengage the British army from a continental strategy: it
had to support the Austrian offensive. But since he had no

---

[6] SRO, GD 51/1/774, Abercromby's of 7, 8, 12 May.
[7] FO 74/30, Wickham's of 15 March and 8 April 1800, received 18 and 28
April.

confidence that the Coalition would win, he made it his business to maintain his forces in a balanced stance, so that when the edifice collapsed, Britain would not be buried in the ruins but could make the leap to safety. By safety Dundas meant the capacity to hold the oceans, to defend the country's overseas trade and possessions, and to present the strong defensive front which would win an acceptable peace.

These intentions are clear in his orders for the Mediterranean. The reduction of Abercromby's expedition to 5,000 men ruled out a permanent British front in southern Europe and reduced the force's scope to raiding and demonstrations. But anyone who assumed that within these limits its primary task was to aid the Austrians, would have been surprised by Dundas's orders. His first and longest instruction to Abercromby was to detach 2,500 or 3,000 men to Malta to finish the siege, a British concern of no interest to Austria. Dundas even declared that he would have ordered the whole available force to Malta if a regular siege of Valletta had been practicable.

So much for the priority of aiding the continental ally! For that task about 6,000 men could still be collected by borrowing troops from the Minorca garrison. Being too few to hold a beach-head, the force was to act in a mobile role, assisting the Austrians by demonstrations, raids and occasional co-operation with the Austrian army. Wickham's plan to raise the royalists of Provence was mentioned in an offhand paragraph: 'some progress, I understand, has actually been made towards preparing them to take up arms'.

Even these limited operations, however, were to depend on the local situation when the expedition arrived; and if no useful aid could be given to the Austrians and the royalists, Abercromby should consider an attack on Tenerife in the Canary Islands. This leap of fifteen hundred miles into the Atlantic is astonishing till one remembers Dundas's last strategic paper, with its emphasis on British colonies and overseas markets.[8] In that paper the capture of Tenerife had been assigned to part of the Mediterranean expedition, at that time still assumed to be 15,000 strong. As the orders to

[8] Above, pp. 84–6.

Abercromby explained, Tenerife was an island where no ship could avoid calling on passage to Africa, the eastern seas, the Caribbean, or the American continent south of the United States. It could be used as a secret assembly point for overseas expeditions. And its possession would enable the navy to root out the nests of privateers in the neighbouring islands.[9]

The capture of Tenerife was a contingency plan to be launched if the Coalition collapsed; and there is further evidence of Dundas's determination not to let British forces be tied up in Europe in his attitude to the Portuguese, who chose this moment to raise their perennial cry for help against a Spanish threat of invasion. Dundas suspected that their fears were imaginary: they were allowing themselves to be 'the tools to distract us'. Lord Grenville regarded this interpretation as 'certainly too refined'; but Dundas would allow no more troops to be sucked into Lisbon; and far from reinforcing the troops already in Portugal, he authorized Abercromby to take them under his command, and transfer any that he needed into the Mediterranean.[10]

Thus were the forces in the Mediterranean and Portugal disposed to meet Dundas's new priorities. Malta received a higher priority than any continental operation; and if the continental war collapsed, the whole force assembling at Minorca could be switched smoothly into colonial warfare. It only remained to place the forces at home in a similar stance. Dundas reckoned to have 25,000 British infantry ready for service at home by early June; and he did not intend to lock them into a continental beach-head from which he could not quickly extract them.

The existing plans for the home forces were to attack Belle Île and Walcheren. Dundas could not brazenly cancel these plans and order a standstill, for the Austrian offensive was about to open, and it was, after all, partly in response to Wickham's appeal for pressure in the west that the Mediterranean expedition had been reduced. Dundas could, however, confine the home forces to demonstrations, as he had arranged for the Mediterranean; and it was the more easy to do so

---

[9] Keith, II. 87–91; WO 6/21, p. 48 ff.
[10] Add. MSS 40101, ff. 76, 79–81; SRO, GD 51/1/774, 19 April, Dundas to Abercromby; WO 6/21, p. 60.

because, surprisingly, both Pitt and Grenville seemed to have lost faith in the idea of a major front in the west. 'Harassing and distracting' was all that Pitt thought likely to be achieved: a notion possibly implanted by Dundas himself over their evening bottle. Grenville's doubts are harder to explain, after his fight for a major Mediterranean landing. But his hopes of a large Russian force had been dashed, and the backward state of the British home forces left him little hope of a spectacular blow in the west.[11]

The pessimism of Pitt and Grenville opened the way for Dundas to modify his western strategy in a fashion which would leave his options open. He unveiled his plan the moment he had won his battle to reduce the Mediterranean force.[12] The points of pressure were still to be Holland and Brittany. He proposed to maintain a threat to Walcheren by moving the Dutch brigade from the Isle of Wight into Kent; and to concentrate the whole of the British field force in the Southampton area pointing towards Quiberon. Four thousand British infantry would embark immediately to seize Belle Île; and as soon as the landing had been secured the rest of the British force would be shipped out as fast as possible, till 25,000 infantry were assembled there by early June. In the meantime their concentration on the south coast of England would, he supposed, hold the French troops to their ground along the whole western coasts of France and Holland.

What, asked Grenville, was the point of this enormous build-up in an island in the Bay of Biscay? The force would probably be unusable there, having regard to past experience of landing troops in France where they could not depend on native co-operation and where their only line of retreat was the sea.[13] Dundas agreed with him to this extent, that he had already declared his opposition to a major landing, and his conviction that only demonstrations and island attacks should be attempted.[14] The aim of his new proposals, his memorandum explained, was not to form clear-cut plans but to put

[11] Add. MSS 40101, f. 73-4; FO 74/30, 11 April, Grenville to Wickham; Dropmore, VI. 197.
[12] Copies of these proposals are in PRO 30/8/368, f. 34, dated 12 April; PRO 30/8/243; SRO, GD 51/1/718; Duke University Library, MS XVIII-F.
[13] Add. MSS 40101, f. 73.   [14] Above, pp. 82, 85.

the army in a position to exploit opportunities. This was opportunism on the grand scale; and he explained the advantages of Belle Île for the purpose. The Channel fleet could cover the army without being distracted from the blockade of Brest. The army would be better placed to cover Ireland than if it were operating in the North Sea, which meant that it was safe to use troops from the Irish garrison. Belle Île was the best place to support the royalists, and an excellent base for attacks and diversions along the French coast.

But the sting was in the tail of the paper. Fifteen thousand of the troops assembling at Southampton were regiments available for general service outside Europe. By moving them to Belle Île, away from the Channel with its contrary winds and from the dilatory government departments at home, they could be switched into other operations at a moment's notice: especially, added Dundas, 'if, as may be the case, you should find it necessary to detach expeditions to South America or to distant objects'.

To what distant objects? They had been disclosed in Dundas's earlier memorandum, and were (besides Tenerife) the Orinoco, the River Plate and New Orleans.[15] What had all this to do with victory in Europe? A very limited amount. Dundas's plan went as far as he believed was safe towards providing the pressure in the west which Austria was said to want. Yet if the Coalition collapsed as he feared it would, the army would be ready for another sort of warfare. Without a moment's delay it could be switched into global expeditions for trade and colonies.

3. *The Loss of the Initiative*

Lord Grenville resigned himself to the latest plan as a means of aiding the Coalition, but made no comment on Dundas's ulterior designs;[16] and Dundas himself was now firmly balanced for his leap to safety if the Coalition collapsed. But the time had not yet come, and attention was still fixed on the movements of Bonaparte and Melas. Wickham's news

---

[15] Above pp. 84–5.   [16] Add. MSS 40101, ff. 73–9.

remained encouraging. Bonaparte was now said to be leaving Paris to join the Army of Reserve; but he had been warned to expect British landings in western France and Holland, and had ordered that all the troops on the coast should remain there, and be reinforced as necessary from the interior.[17] Evidently the British amphibious threat was holding the French troops to their ground in the west; and the plans to increase this pressure proceeded. On the day when Wickham's report arrived, the Chouan leader 'Georges' arrived in London from Paris. This was the *nom de guerre* of Georges Cadoudal, who had refused to become a pensioner of Bonaparte like the other insurgent leaders, and had slipped away from Paris to cross the Channel at Boulogne. The son of a Breton farmer, he had seen much service and danger in his thirty years. He was now to join General Maitland in Quiberon Bay, where the assault force for Belle Île was about to assemble. Colonel Nightingall left for Ireland to take command of three good battalions, with which he was to land in the undefended islets of Houat and Hédic near Belle Île and mark out camps for reinforcements, letting it be known that a large force was on the way. In the meantime the main body of the British field force was encamped at Bagshot in Windsor Forest, the only ground in the south of England where a large force could assemble and train.[18]

The assault was not due till the beginning of June, which was later than Dundas had intended. Soon reports began to come in of the opening of the Austrian offensive. Melas had launched his attacks against the thin French cordon in the Ligurian mountains. Sweeping down to the coast at Vado, he had cut off Masséna with the French right wing in Genoa, while the left under Suchet was being pushed back towards the Var.[19] Wickham also reported that 3,000 French troops in the west had been summoned to join the Army of the Rhine, and the time had clearly come for British action to contain them. Maitland was ordered to attempt a landing on Belle Île as soon as possible. Three more battalions were to

[17] FO 74/30, Wickham's 29 March 1800, encl.

[18] Hall, *Pichegru*, 278; WO 6/21, pp. 1-12; *GL* 2136; Add. MSS 37924, f. 27.

[19] FO 70/30, Wickham of 18 April, received 5 May; FO 7/58, Minto's of 10 and 17 April, received 25 and 28 April.

sail from England, to join Nightingall's Irish brigade in Quiberon Bay by 1 June; and the landing was to be made as soon as a plan had been agreed with Lord St. Vincent.[20]

Thus the cumbrous machinery of amphibious warfare had begun to churn when, on 19 May, a new picture of events arrived from Wickham which signalled the total overthrow of the allies' plans.

There are dangers in viewing war from on high, like a god or a historian, and watching the plans of both sides unroll. With such all-embracing knowledge hindsight rushes in. One loses touch with the anxious and uncertain atmosphere which statesmen and commanders breathed; and judgement outpaces understanding. Yet when a great strategic surprise is unfolding, it becomes necessary to see the enemy's moves in order to understand how the initiative is slipping unseen from one commander into the grasp of his opponent. Such a surprise had been the convergence of French and American forces at Yorktown; another was the Napoleonic masterpiece which led to Marengo. From this moment the British government would dance to Napoleon's music.

The first phase of the Napoleonic plan had been completed in January, when Bonaparte launched Brune into the Vendée to free his hands in the west by pre-empting a British attack. The aim was to subdue the insurgents on whom a British landing must depend, and it succeeded by a brilliant combination of force with politics. The armed bands were dispersed, and Brune was warned that the leaders must never again be allowed to call out their followers when the French army was fighting its external enemies in the east. The shooting of Frotté was a salutary warning, and the other leaders who submitted were required to reside outside the Chouan departments as long as the war should last, if necessary on a pension.

By early March the task was done, and Bonaparte's rear was secured. 'The Vendée is pacified,' he reported to General Augereau in Holland, 'all is in train to wage a war which is worthy of us.'[21] Wickham's information that the French

[20] WO 6/21, pp. 12-20; Spencer, III. 330-1.
[21] Lecestre, 4, 9, 11-13.

troops in the west were to stand fast was wrong, for as early as the middle of February Bonaparte had begun to pull troops back from the Vendée. To be fair to Wickham, he had given the government some warning of what was to come, before he fell into the delusion that Bonaparte had lost the initiative.[22] He had reported the new army assembling round Dijon; nor had he derided its quality as recklessly as the Austrians were doing. But about its composition he was mistaken. Some of its units certainly needed further organization and training. There was a dubious Italian legion, and from the home depots of the demi-brigades in Egypt fourteen battalion cadres were organized and brought up to strength with conscripts. But the core of the infantry in the Army of Reserve was formed by seventeen well organized demi-brigades, 35,000 strong and almost all of them from the Army of the West and its strategic pool in the Paris region. From the Vendée came 20,000 infantry, from Paris 14,000. Twelve mounted regiments came in whole or part from Paris, and three from the Vendée, a total of 6,600 cavalry from the west. Of the twelve companies of artillery and artificers in the Artillery Park of the Army of Reserve, ten came from the Vendée, Paris, and western Holland. The assembly of these troops at Dijon was made under a smokescreen of secrecy and deception. In the west Bernadotte was left with only 16,000 men to guard thirteen departments and a hundred leagues of coast.[23]

Of one thing Wickham was rightly convinced: that Bonaparte desperately needed a resounding victory to consolidate his hold on France and ward off the British. 'All however will probably depend on the fate of the first battle, the consequences of which no man living can presume to calculate.' Wickham guessed that Bonaparte would strike his main blow in Germany, and this was indeed his first intention.[24] The Army of Reserve was to use the Swiss salient to fall on Kray's flank and rear in Swabia. But the obstructiveness of Moreau, commanding the Army of the Rhine, caused Bonaparte to revise his plan. With an interior position and a reserve under

---

[22] Above, pp. 86–7.
[23] Analysis of returns in Cugnac, I. 59 *et seq.*, 608–9, 635; Hall, *Pichegru*, 283.
[24] FO 74/29, Wickham's of 26 March, received 8 April; FO 74/30, Wickham's of 29 March, encl., received 18 April.

his direct command, he had the choice of options which suited his temperament so well and brought him his most brilliant victories. On 25 March he issued new orders, which gave the Army of the Rhine a secondary role and transferred the decisive blow to Italy. Moreau was to launch a containing offensive against Kray in the middle of April and push him north-eastwards into Bavaria. This would secure the communications of the Army of Reserve through Switzerland, and sever Kray's lateral communications with Milan. In the meantime the Army of Reserve would move forward 60,000 strong into Switzerland, where half of it would march for the Alpine passes to Italy, leaving the remainder to hold the Swiss communications; and from the Army of the Rhine Lecourbe's experienced corps of 30,000 would follow them into Italy. With these forces Bonaparte would fall on Melas's communications in the Po Valley.

It was on 19 May that the British government learned of Bonaparte's opening moves. A fortnight earlier Moreau had crossed the Rhine and advanced against the Austrians. Kray was caught off balance. His forces were dispersed in defensive positions covering south Germany, while he waited for the news of Masséna's surrender in Genoa which was to signal the start of his own offensive. But deceived by false intelligence that Masséna had been defeated and killed, he had brought forward his magazines, pontoons and reserve artillery in readiness to cross the Rhine; and thus when he learned of Moreau's concentration he was unable to fall back. Standing to fight at Stockach, he was defeated and driven back in disorder towards Ulm, losing a succession of adverse combats and abandoning his magazines and bridging train. The French who attacked him were well clothed, fully paid and dangerously impetuous, by no means the 'ragamuffins' Grenville had expected; and they had been skilfully commanded.[25]

Once again Wickham's interpretation was wrong. He believed that Bonaparte had written Italy off as irrevocably lost and was staking everything in Germany. Yet for the wrong

[25] FO 74/30, Wickham's of 8 May, received 19 May. Cf. Buckingham, *Courts and Cabinets*, III. 38.

reasons he gave Lord Grenville what may have been the right advice. The French advance into Bavaria threatened the Tyrol and the communications of the Austrian army in Italy: and Wickham urged that every soldier Britain could spare should be sent to the Mediterranean to aid the Austrians in Italy.[26]

Thus Wickham reversed his earlier advice that the British army should strike its main blow in the west. What did he mean, Dundas wondered. Not a month ago Wickham had been urging an attack in the west to stop the enemy from re-inforcing the Rhine; and with that aim the Belle Île attack was being mounted. It was now impossible to ship a force of any size to the Mediterranean without dropping the Belle Île operation. 'I don't think our friend Wickham always recollects that it is not so easy to move an army as it is to write a dis-patch', wrote Dundas: a neat thrust at Foreign Office strat-egists. Grenville did not dissent, but explained mildly in defence of his protégé that Wickham had reason to assume that little would now be achieved in the west.[27]

It was therefore agreed to send no more troops to the Mediterranean, except for two additional battalions for which General Abercromby was asking. For Sir Ralph, alas, was still in reach. Instead of being far out in the Bay of Biscay on his way to Minorca, he had been forced back into Portland Roads by a gale which had dispersed and disabled the convoy to which the Admiralty had tied him. Grenville groaned at the news. 'Abercromby and his convoy are as usual blown back. If I were a seaman, with half the supersitition which belongs to them, I should certainly throw him overboard as a second Jonas.' If Abercromby were already on the Riviera, Grenville thought his force would be of great value to the hard-pressed Austrians; but by the time he arrived, the oppor-tunity would probably have vanished.[28]

Without a commander it was unlikely that the Mediter-ranean expedition would avert the growing crisis, but in the west preparations to strike at Belle Île were plodding on. Three battalions were on their way from England by the end

[26] Ibid.; Dropmore, VI. 213.
[27] Dropmore, VI. 236; Add. MSS 40101, f. 83.
[28] SRO, GD 51/1/774, Abercromby's of 19 and 21 May; Dropmore, VI. 233, 236.

of May, and three more embarked tardily at Cobh in early June. Pitt had a little scare on 1 June about reinforcing the Mediterranean, when part of the Brest fleet was reported at sea. Combined with news that French troops from the Army of Reserve were appearing in the Alpine passes, this suggested a grave threat to Melas's Austrians in Italy, and Pitt wavered about sending more troops to Minorca after all. Might not more be achieved by sending 8,000, 10,000 or even 12,000 additional troops to the Mediterranean than by any other operation? He was strengthened in this idea by a talk with Dundas which disclosed how very unready were the forces in the west: 'the state of our preparations . . . on this side of France is so wretchedly backward and the exertions for pushing them so languid, as to leave (in my judgment) little chance of our doing any thing in that way that can influence the fate of the campaign. We may *yet* be in time to send to Italy what may render success decisive, or retrieve disasters that might otherwise be irreparable.'[29]

The scare evaporated, for the squadron from Brest returned to port. But the threat in the Alpine passes remained. 'Reports had been received in Italy', ran the dispatch received from Vienna on 2 June, 'of the march of General Berthier towards Savoy; but the corps which he commanded was estimated at 10,000 men, and nobody carries it beyond 15,000; and if the force was not much more considerable General Melas was not apprehensive of any ill consequences from his approach.' Grenville was not deceived by this anodyne report, and from other information (perhaps from France) he was convinced that the threat was much greater than the Austrians believed. He rightly guessed that the advancing Army of Reserve would be supported by part of Moreau's army from Germany. But Pitt's interest subsided. He still wondered whether the troops waiting at home to exploit the Belle Île attack might be shipped to the Mediterranean; but with the Brest squadron back in port 'it does not now press as I supposed it would'.[30]

The next letters from Minto in Vienna were contradictory and confusing. Melas was marching back from the Riviera to the Po with reinforcements to encounter Berthier, but 'felt

[29] Dropmore, VI. 6.
[30] FO 7/58, Minto's of 20 May; Dropmore, VI. 242-3.

no sort of uneasiness'. Later he was said to be still at Nice preparing to assault the French bridge-head on the Var; yet the French force crossing the high Alps was now said to be 18,000 strong, and 'some imagined that Bonaparte accompanied this corps in person'. A small body of French had already appeared in the Val d'Aosta, but the direction of the rest of the force was still unknown — whether by the Swiss passes into Lombardy, or by the Mont Cenis to Piedmont, or to reinforce Suchet on the Var. But still Melas was said to feel 'no uneasiness'.[31]

If the Austrians were so complacent, the British ministers naturally had no conception of how time was pressing. Grenville was still talking of the assault on Belle Île as a diversion whose effect would last for several weeks in western France. To be fair to Grenville, he realized that British strategy was falling between two stools, as he had predicted when the Mediterranean expedition was emasculated in April.[32] If we had at this moment, he wrote, twelve or fifteen thousand men in the Mediterranean (as he had wished when he fought to keep the expedition intact) they would decide the campaign. To send them now was much less promising; yet even this he thought was better than keeping the home forces in England, under the pretence of a build-up in Belle Île which was not really intended or actively pursued.[33]

This was an indictment of Dundas. If he was serious about the Belle Île diversion, the preparation of the assault force should surely have been long since completed, whatever the condition of the forces which were to follow it up. Even now the old story of insufficient landing craft was being repeated, for the transports which brought the assault battalions to Quiberon Bay had no flat boats on board.[34] The troops were still arriving in bits and pieces: the Queen's and the 36th Foot from England in the first days of June, followed by the 92nd Highlanders; the three battalions from Ireland not till 13 June, and they of dubious quality. All these were encamped at Houat, where Maitland was pondering about intelligence

[31] FO 7/58, Minto's of 23 and 28 May, received 4 and 8 June.
[32] Above, p. 89.
[33] Rose, *Pitt and Napoleon*, 271-2; Dropmore, VI. 242.
[34] Spencer, III. 334.

from the Chouan Georges that the garrison of Belle Île was much stronger than had been supposed, certainly 4,000 and possibly double that number. With his force complete, however, he decided to risk the assault, and issued his orders on 15 June, actually the day after the battle of Marengo. The landing was timed for the 19th, a date which the naval commander, Sir Edward Pellew, particularly wanted since it was the double anniversary of his promotion to post-captain and his capture of the French *Cleopatra*. 'He therefore thought he must continue fortunate on that day,' a battalion commander noted, 'an instance of the superstition that prevails amongst seamen.'[35]

It was not to be. A storm blew up, and Pellew cancelled the attack. On the following day Maitland postponed the operation indefinitely, for a message from Georges informed him that the enemy garrison was 7,000 besides militia. If this was true, Maitland's 4,200 infantry of all ranks were too few to win a general action in the field even if they forced a landing, and Maitland would not risk re-embarking a defeated force under fire. He would therefore wait for the reinforcements he daily expected. He did not give much credit to Georges's report, and he was right, for the garrison of Belle Île appears to have been no more than 3,000–4,000 and in a state of destitution. But the ministers' trust in Georges was such that Maitland felt he must act on his information; 'and also', Lord Dalhousie recorded, 'in the event of his meeting with a check, it is obvious all blame would be heaped on him'. Naturally; on who else but the commander? Pellew, however, sympathized with Maitland, particularly since he was far from impressed by the quality of the troops: 'Under all the circumstances I think he is right, although I wish the messenger had been drowned.'[36]

So the assault force disembarked on Houat again after three days at sea in warships and transports. The only encouraging feature of the affair had been the good relations between the

[35] Fortescue, IV. 778-9; SRO, GD 45/4/16, Dalhousie's journal, 18 June.
[36] Hall, *Pichegru*, 284; SRO, GD 45/4/16, Dalhousie's journal, 20 June; Spencer, III. 344-5. Colonel Nightingall had a very bad opinion of the British troops, and thought Maitland had only 3,300 really effective men (Add. MSS 37924, f. 33). When the British attacked Belle Île in 1761, their first lodgement on the island's inaccessible coast had been defeated.

two services, which was not to be taken for granted. All the army officers who had been embarked in warships spoke warmly of 'the attention and civility shown them on board by the naval officers'.[37]

That seemed to be the end of the Belle Île operation; for on the following day Maitland received an order to send his entire force to the Mediterranean.

4. *The Road to Marengo*

Events had now passed out of the Cabinet's control. By 8 June reports from all quarters showed that Moreau was detaching powerful forces from Germany, and that the Italian front would bear the weight of the French offensive. Bonaparte intended to achieve superiority there 'by every effort and sacrifice', wrote Dundas. Britain had to respond, and he suddenly withdrew his opposition to reinforcing the Mediterranean. On the 10th he circulated a memorandum to the members of the Cabinet, urging that the additional force of two battalions he had agreed to send to Abercromby (but had not yet sent) should be raised to 4,000. This would give Abercromby 10,000 men to aid the Austrians.[38]

Predictably the only objector was Windham, who argued that the reinforcement could not reach Italy before the campaign was decided, while its absence would cripple the western operations. The other ministers agreed with Dundas in principle, though the question of shipping was raised. On the 15th, however, news arrived of Maitland's first postponement of the Belle Île assault. Here was an opportunity to send the Mediterranean reinforcement swiftly, without waiting to assemble shipping. Maitland's 4,000 men with transports were still uncommitted, and Dundas agreed with Pitt to send them to the Mediterranean. Without delaying to seek the King's approval, Dundas sent off the order, and with it an instruction to Abercromby to use his whole 10,000 to aid the

[37] SRO, GD 45/4/16, Dalhousie's journal, 21 June; Brodie of Brodie journal, I. 3–17.

[38] Add. MSS 57444, Herries journal, 8 June 1800; Dropmore, VI. 246; Add. MSS 40102, ff. 50-1.

Austrians; perhaps by taking over the defence of the western
Riviera to relieve Melas's left wing, and occupying the mountain passes to prevent the enemy in Provence from reinforcing
Bonaparte. Melas would then be free to mass his whole army
against Bonaparte in the Po valley.[39]

None of this was to have any bearing on the drama in
the plains of the Po: it was already weeks too late to stop
Bonaparte, and the interest of British planning now lies only
in the light it sheds on the war ministry and its mounting
problems. One of the stresses which were beginning to be
piled on the ministers was their deteriorating relations with
the King: for George III's interventions in the next three
months are a factor in the ministry's collapse in the following
winter. In the present crisis the King objected to the diversion
of Maitland's battalions to the Mediterranean. Surely, he said,
it would be wise to pause till it was clear that the dispatch of
so large a force would be useful. In a day or two the mails
would reveal whether Genoa had surrendered and bring news
of Melas's movements. When Dundas received this remonstrance, the order to send off Maitland's troops had already
gone; but the absence of a Cabinet minute gave force to the
King's objections, and made it necessary to consult the
Cabinet formally.[40]

When the news for which the King was waiting arrived, it
was bad. Though Masséna had surrendered Genoa, the Paris
papers reported extraordinary progress by Bonaparte in the
Po valley, and Moreau had detached two crack divisions from
Germany to reinforce him. Dundas was not shaken in his
wish to send the force to the Mediterranean, but when the
Cabinet reviewed the war news at midday on 19 June it
decided otherwise. Every available man must now be used to
increase the pressure in the west. Instead of reinforcing
Abercromby, the western attacks must be pressed with all
speed and energy. Maitland should be reinforced as fast as
possible with 6,000 men and a battering train so that he

---

[39] *GL* 2171; WO 6/21, pp. 21, 67; Add. MSS 37924, ff. 31, 33.

[40] Duke University Library, MS XVIII F, 17 June, King's note to Dundas, circulated to Cabinet. 'If Mr. Dundas is of this opinion', Lord Chatham replied to
Dundas's proposal. 'no further consultation can be necessary, and the order should
go instantly.' The King's objection changed the picture (Add. MSS 40102, f. 52).

could besiege the Belle Île citadel; when the island fell, nearly all the regular forces in Ireland should be sent there; and the royalists should be informed that 20,000 men would assemble in Belle Île to aid them. At home 4,000 men were to join the Dutch brigade in Kent for a diversionary attack on the coast of Holland.[41]

Dundas did not conceal his disappointment, but in face of the King's doubts and with divisions in the Cabinet he did not feel able to press his view. An order went off to Maitland immediately cancelling the dispatch of his force to the Mediterranean. It arrived too late. The first order had reached Maitland on the 22nd, the transports were ready, the troops embarked at once. Maitland gave Lord Dalhousie two dozen of claret and the command of the force; and Dalhousie pushed for Minorca with orders to lose not a moment on the voyage.[42]

Dundas cannot have been sorry that the cancelling order miscarried. In his desire to reinforce the Mediterranean he was probably looking beyond the immediate war crisis to the likelihood that England would soon have to hold the Mediterranean alone. As he observed darkly to Lord Spencer, he could imagine many circumstances in which it would be of the greatest importance to have the force in the theatre. His prediction would soon be realized.[43]

In this farcical fashion ended the British efforts to aid the Austrians. On 24 June news arrived from the Customs Collector at Dover that Melas had been defeated ten days earlier at Marengo, and had signed an armistice at Alessandria by which he withdrew a hundred miles to the Mincio and abandoned the whole of Liguria, Piedmont and Lombardy to Bonaparte.[44] All Suvorov's gains of the previous year had been lost, and the hope of a victorious invasion of France was obliterated. No longer could any reasonable person hope for

---

[41] Add. MSS 57444, f. 55, Herries of 18 June; FO 74/30, Wickham's of 28 May, received 18 June; Dropmore, VI. 249-50; Add. MSS 37879, f. 192; *GL* 2175n.
[42] *GL* 2175; Spencer, IV. 285; SRO, GD 45/4/16, Dalhousie's journal, 22-3 June.   [43] Spencer, IV. 285.
[44] Add. MSS 57444, ff. 56-8; Add. MSS 58861, 24 June, King to Grenville.

a decisive Coalition victory; and Bonaparte, who had been surrounded by plotters speculating about his successor, was now firmly established as the dictator of France. Ten days after the battle he appeared unexpectedly in Paris to reap the political harvest.

While this catastrophe was preparing, not a single British soldier had been in action in Europe. Even Belle Île had not been attacked; and in the Mediterranean, where a British force might have released enough Austrian troops to turn the scales in the close-run battle of Marengo, neither commander nor orders had arrived in time. How had this extraordinary disgrace occurred?

It is easiest to blame the ministers. Their divided views had delayed agreement on a plan; and when the plan was settled after many alterations, it was not simple and harmonious, but fragmentary, tentative, a compromise. And it was too late. To affect the Marengo campaign, the Mediterranean expedition should have sailed from England about the middle of March instead of late April, to be in action on the Riviera by the middle of May.

But there were deeper reasons for the delays than divided counsels and tardy departments. Delay was the price of the Coalition. The uncertain shape of the alliance in the autumn and winter, with Russia and Austria at loggerheads; the ice which held up the couriers in the German estuaries; Thugut's reluctance to disclose his plans or express a clear and steady view of how the British could help: these were the underlying causes of delay. Naturally Grenville was to stress this in retrospect to the Austrians. 'If', he wrote,

in the beginning of the present year, M. Thugut could have brought his mind to treat with us as allies, and to say distinctly that he might want our assistance in Italy, Sir R. Abercromby and his army — at its present amount — might have arrived before Genoa as soon as the Austrian operations began there, and would unquestionably have saved Italy.

This Thugut would not do, and the troops were consequently not sent till the period which suited our plans.[45]

This was selective but not unfair. The Austrians had expressed no interest in the British Mediterranean expedition, or in

[45] Dropmore, VI. 300.

royalist co-operation in Provence. Indeed when the royalist General Willot finally joined Melas at Turin, after a detour from Germany to Vienna at Thugut's insistence, Melas refused to co-operate with him. It became clear to Willot that the Austrians had no intention of crossing the French frontier in the south; and the doubts of Austrian co-operation in Provence which had caused Dundas to reduce the British expedition were amply justified.[46] The Austrians had no wish for a British presence on the coveted Genoese Riviera.

As for the timing of the British operations, they were designed to aid an Austrian invasion of France in due course, not to meet an early emergency. Napoleon's seizure of the initiative and his irruption from the Alps were no more foreseen by Grenville and Dundas than by Melas; and perilous amphibious landings could not be attempted till the Austrians were ready to take some of the pressure of the French. It was not to provide relief against a French offensive that the Mediterranean expedition was designed, but to crumble the French defensive positions on the Riviera from the rear. Whether, if the expedition had arrived in time, it would have caused a larger Austrian force to march to Marengo is not as certain as has sometimes been claimed.[47] Would Melas have grasped the opportunity? He had no reason to trust the quality of a British force; nor did he recognize the peril which faced him. The commander who fought Bonaparte in pitched battle without calling in his detachments and garrisons, and then so readily signed an unnecessary armistice, did not show the energy and resolution to make the most of a British force.

Even if there had been a common allied war plan, the British role could only have been a minor one. In the Mediterranean a British force of limited size could at least have contributed directly to Austrian operations. But in the west the small and poorly trained British army would have had to fight

---

[46] See Mitchell, *Underground War*, 241-2. Jackson's dispatch from Turin reporting Willot's reception was received in London on 26 May (FO 67/29, Jackson's of 30 April).

[47] The case was persuasively argued by the British staff officer Sir Henry Bunbury (*Narratives*, 39-42), in a characteristic passage in which effect flows inevitably from cause. Fortescue (IV. 775) and Rodger (*Second Coalition*, 246) follow him.

alone. And it would have been hampered by the crippling conditions of amphibious warfare, restricted by the shipping shortage and dependent on sea-borne supplies. British aid in the west could be little more than a marginal diversion.

And Bonaparte knew it. He knew that without massive insurgent aid the British could make no speedy impression on western France. And while the Coalition had been fighting its internal diplomatic battles in the winter, he had deprived Britain of insurgent aid in the *Vendée militaire*. Once that was done, he could afford to strip the western coasts while he sought his *Hauptschlacht* beyond the eastern borders. By early April, long before the British were capable of making even a demonstration, he had withdrawn from the west the core of his Army of Reserve.

And this was at the heart of the allies' problem: the initiative lay with Bonaparte. He had the interior lines, for speedy communication and for military movement: a demi-brigade could reach Dijon from Paris in fourteen days. He had almost undivided direction of the war, for this was the first Napoleonic campaign in which he was effectively head of the state. Though Moreau was still capable of obstructing his plans in Germany, Bonaparte had all the resources of the state at his command; and he had the resolution and the power to weaken western France while he achieved his concentration at the chosen point of gravity. None of the allies anticipated the swiftness of the Napoleonic offensive. Not the Austrians — Thugut, Melas or Kray. Not the British: not even the much-praised Sir Charles Stuart, who showed no sense of urgent danger as he assembled his expedition and buried his uncle and quarrelled about Malta. The British government was planning for a steady build-up of pressure on many fronts. But once the Army of Reserve was concentrated at Dijon, nothing would distract Napoleon. He was committed to an offensive which must be decisive; and a victory which would solve his problems everywhere.

PART TWO:
PEACE WITHOUT VICTORY

CHAPTER VI

Dundas Ascendant

1. *Reappraisal*

Six months had passed since the British ministers' rejection of Bonaparte's peace overture: now a few hours of precarious battle had swept away their logic. The troops Lord Grenville had described as ragamuffins had beaten the high-spirited armies of Austria, and Bonaparte was no longer a dubious adventurer but the master of France. At home he had proved his statecraft in pacifying the Vendée, and had begun to heal the wounds in French society. From Milan the victorious First Consul addressed a rhetorical letter to the Emperor, purporting to be written on the battlefield of Marengo 'surrounded by about 15,000 corpses', and offering a general armistice and peace. He denounced the selfishness of England which alone protracted the war.

The British rejection of the New Year overture had been bitterly attacked in Parliament, and the defeat at Marengo naturally revived the opposition's clamour for peace. This time their wish was echoed in government circles, where distaste had already been expressed for the language with which Grenville had repelled the Consuls' overture. 'I hope we may not repent our last message to Bonaparte', Cornwallis wrote a month before Marengo; and Lord St. Vincent felt likewise. 'Now the Union is carried', he declared at the beginning of June, 'there is no object to continue the war; and the sooner you make peace the better, for this Royalist system is pitiful, and contemptible.' Such opinions from distinguished fighting men were formidable; and their ranks were strengthened from the government benches by the news of Marengo. 'Peace we must have I am sure', said George Rose, the Secretary to the Treasury. 'Such a peace (with almost all the expense of war) as we can now obtain is formidable to look at. I do not at this moment more deeply regret the irritating expressions used to Bonaparte than I did when the answer was sent to his question.' Even the bellicose George Canning doubted the country's will to continue: 'Do you think people will agree to go on with the war for terms? Not they, I fear . . .'. The answer to his question was supplied by Edward Cooke, the Irish Under-Secretary: '. . . a peace will be demanded by the nation upon every account'.[1]

With all this Pitt and his colleagues scarcely had the heart to disagree, though they spoke up defiantly in Parliament. Pitt probably saw no better prospect ahead than to sue for peace jointly with Austria, and remembered that only a month earlier he had had to defy the Bank of England by sending specie to Germany to support the faltering bills of exchange for paying subsidies.[2] Even Lord Grenville admitted that public opinion might demand a gesture towards peace; and if the alliance was to be held together, Austria must be supported even to the point of negotiations. On a mere telegraph report of the French victory, a Cabinet meeting agreed to join in peace negotiations if asked by Austria. The ministers recognized that the terms were likely to be bad, and the settlement impermanent; but only by showing willingness to agree to a reasonable peace could they induce Parliament and the country to carry on the war.

This advice the King received with sorrow. The Austrians, he predicted, would suspend all military efforts at the prospect of negotiations; and if peace resulted, it would be more dangerous than continuing the war alone behind the moat of the Channel. 'Peace . . . can be nothing but an armed neutrality, which is a most hazardous situation. . . . While French principles are victorious no peace can be safe.' He protested that to take great political decisions on a French telegraph report without waiting to learn the extent of the disaster was at least premature. But his views were brushed aside, and a dispatch went off authorizing Minto to agree to a joint negotiation. The King did not forgive the action, and from now on he became steadily more alienated from his ministers.[3]

For the time being, then, the British government continued

[1] Cornwallis, III. 236, 270; Add. MSS 36708, f. 7, 3 June, St. Vincent to Nepean; Pretyman MSS, T 108/44, 25 June, Rose to Tomline; *Parl. Hist.* XXXV. 394-8, 401-28; Add. MSS 38833, f. 4, 26 June, Canning to Frere; Castlereagh, III. 341.   [2] Sherwig, 133-4.
[3] Keith, II. 121; *GL* 2181; Add MSS 58861, 28 June, King to Grenville; Dropmore, VI. 256; FO 7/59, 27 June, Grenville to Minto.

to conduct its affairs on the premiss that the Coalition went on. The Austrians were still fighting in Germany, though the news from the front was bad; and on 4 July a treaty of alliance arrived from Vienna after months of delay. It was ironic that it should arrive at such a moment: Thugut had signed the treaty on the day before he received the news of Marengo, and the British government found itself shackled to Austria at the very moment when Austria collapsed.[4] The Austrians were to receive £2 million as a loan over the next six months, interest-free till the war was over; and neither party was to enter into secret negotiations with the enemy or make a separate peace. The ratification went through the usual delays that Grenville had learned to expect from Vienna; and Parliament was kept sitting in the hope that the ratified treaty would arrive, though all its other business had been completed with the royal assent to the Irish Union. The angry ministers debated whether to prorogue Parliament or lay the treaty before it unratified.[5]

To Dundas all this agonizing seemed useless, for the crisis he had long foretold had come. The continental war was collapsing, he did not believe Austria would recover, and England's strategic plans were in disarray. For the moment, however, he offered no fresh appraisal, and till the middle of July British war plans were still aimed at supporting the Austrians. Lord Grenville assured Vienna that 25,000 troops would make diversions on the French coast; Sir Charles Grey was offered the command of the force; and a brigade marched from the Bagshot camp to reinforce Maitland's assault on Belle Île. Already, however, Belle Île itself was being re-examined. General Grey was consulted by the Duke of York and advised him that 20,000–25,000 troops would be needed for the assault, on the principle that an investment of the citadel would require a force three times the strength of the garrison. This alarming proposition combined ill with the news that Maitland's existing force of 4,000 had all gone to the Mediterranean. In the light of this Dundas doubted whether

---

[4] Though backdated to the 20th the treaty was signed on 23 June; the first rumours of Marengo did not reach Vienna till the 24th. See Duffy, 412n, which questions Sherwig 132.

[5] *Parl. Hist.* XXXV. 430-54; Dropmore, VI. 262.

the Belle Île operation could proceed, and he summoned Maitland home to consult him. In the meantime he announced that he was about to put forward new ideas on the conduct of the war, and began his mission to reorient British strategy.[6]

The strategy which unfolded in the next three months forms a pattern already foreshadowed when the continental western front had collapsed in 1795, and it was to be repeated in clear-cut form when the Peace of Tilsit ended the Third Coalition in 1807 and ranged the continent against England. The collapse of each successive coalition faced Britain with the prospect that France would challenge her naval supremacy, by concentrating French resources on the sea and enlisting Europe's other navies: it was the old nightmare of eighteenth-century statesmen. England faced the choice of protracted, and indecisive or perhaps disastrous maritime warfare, or an immediate peace. For war she needed to strengthen her naval power and her economy, and for peace to improve her bargaining power.

The strategy to meet these needs developed in three phases. First, emergency measures to weaken enemy naval power, by attacking enemy squadrons in harbour and removing neutral fleets from the French grasp. Next, to secure the naval bases needed for maritime command, and deny them to the enemy. And finally, colonial offensives for several purposes: to protect and expand the trade which financed the British war effort, the goal which Dundas had been promoting for many months; to make British colonies safer from attack; and to provide bargaining strength for future peace negotiations. Thus the continental collapse of 1795 had been followed by the seizure of the Cape and Ceylon, Dutch possessions commanding the ocean route to the east which must be denied to the enemy; and offensive warfare had been renewed in the Caribbean. The full pattern was to be unrolled in 1807 after the Peace of Tilsit. Neutral fleets were brought away from Copenhagen and Lisbon; the Russian Mediterranean fleet was driven into the Tagus and blockaded; and a raid was

[6] FO 7/59, 27 June, Grenville to Minto; Grey Papers, 2120a; *GL* 2184; WO 6/21, p. 24; Add. MSS 37924, ff. 37-8.

projected against the Spanish squadron in Port Mahon. Madeira was occupied to forestall the French in this Port-uguese outpost. For the phase of colonial offensives an attempt was made to concentrate a striking force at Gibraltar; and attacks were being prepared against Spanish America when the revolt of Spain against Napoleon's occupation created an opportunity for the British army in Europe.

Such was the pattern which Dundas was now preparing as the Second Coalition collapsed. Spanish fleets were to be attacked in harbour. Malta was to be secured for the British navy. The core of the design was to concentrate Britain's disposable forces from England and the Mediterranean into a single army at Gibraltar, the point from which it could be launched towards any quarter of the globe.[7]

In his concern for naval security Dundas had a natural ally in the First Lord of the Admiralty. We have seen Lord Spencer under attack from his colleagues for too readily adopting the views of the naval officers on the Board; but he had acquired a sound understanding of the navy and its needs, and writing of those naval colleagues St. Vincent commented that the First Lord 'is now a better officer than any of the three ever was'. For some time Spencer had been worried by the pro-longed commitment of warships to blockading Malta, caused by the failure to find enough troops to finish the siege of Valletta. 'I have long lost my patience on the subject', he had recently complained to Lord Keith. He was now concerned by the enemy's battle-power at sea, and wrote to St. Vincent off Brest enquiring whether the Spanish squadron in Ferrol could be attacked by a military force. St. Vincent replied that Ferrol was the least vulnerable place in Spain; but that Cadiz, Carthagena and the Canary Islands were all within the grasp of Abercromby's Mediterranean striking force.[8]

---

[7] 'It will be a fortunate circumstance if a considerable body of troops can be speedily assembled at Gibraltar', Dundas wrote to the King (*GL* 2184). He returned to the theme after the expeditions against Spanish ports were launched: 'The services at present assigned to them are probably of a very temporary nature, and . . . by the end of September at the latest . . . the two corps united will be at Gibraltar, available for any further operation to which such a body of troops may be applicable.' (SRO, GD 51/1/725/1, August memorandum by Dundas.)

[8] Spencer, III. 357-8, 361; IV. 89, 113, 115-16, 124; Add. MSS 38708, f. 9, 28 Aug. 1800, St. Vincent to Nepean. For contemporary criticism of Spencer's deference to his naval colleagues, see *Strategy of Overthrow*, 16, 122.

Spencer's enquiry was made the day after Dundas had declared his intention to put forward a new strategy, and was
probably inspired by him. Some days passed, however, without the promised initiative from Dundas, while he waited for
events to ripen. On 13 July came a warning from Vienna that
the Austrians would be forced into a general armistice leading
to peace negotiations. Britain could not object to the armistice, and in Grenville's view she must stand by her promise
to join in a negotiation; for though Britain was capable of
continuing the war indecisively on her own she could not,
without Austria, force the enemy to change their government and restore tranquillity to Europe. The Cabinet therefore agreed to acquiesce in an Austrian armistice; to join
in a peace negotiation if necessary; and to pay the first
instalment of the Austrian loan. The Austrian treaty was
now laid before Parliament though the ratification had still
not arrived.[9]

British policy was in an uncomfortable imbalance. On the
one hand the Austrian alliance was cemented; yet it was now
virtually certain that all fighting would cease on the continent
(and in fact the Italian armistice had already been extended
to Germany). This was the moment for Dundas to move into
his attack on Britain's continental strategy. Was there any
point in pursuing operations on the coast of France in support of a non-existent continental campaign? Even the Belle
Île attack could not be mounted till late in the season if
the force demanded by General Grey was really necessary.
Dundas posed the question on 20 July, the day when Maitland arrived from Quiberon Bay. On the 21st he conferred
with Maitland; and on the same day came news of the armistice in Germany, and an account from Wickham which
reversed the impression hitherto held that the Austrian
army was still in fighting spirits. He reported general dissatisfaction and despondency: Kray's army was 'absolutely
null', and in Vienna the peace party would gain strength.
This news made the British diversions on the coast of France
seem even less attractive; and on the following day Dundas
proposed a total strategic reversal. In this paper he laid down

[9] PRO 30/8/339, Minto's no. 37 of 28 June; Dropmore, VI. 257-8, 268; *GL*
2193-4.

the lines which British strategy was to pursue for the rest of the war.[10]

2. *Dundas's Strategy*

Dundas's plan was, in its essence, 'a shake at the naval strength of the enemy', the capture of Malta, and a military concentration at Gibraltar for an offensive in Spanish America: fleets, bases, and colonies, the classic pattern in times of isolation. As soon as Grenville received the paper he summoned the Cabinet, and on 24 July it accepted the first part of the plan, an attack on the naval arsenals of Spain. The fleets in Brest were invulnerable, Dundas explained; but (in spite of St. Vincent's opinion) General Pulteney believed that Ferrol could be attacked. The Cabinet agreed to try it. The force in Quiberon Bay would be reinforced to 12,000, to attack Ferrol if there were 'a reasonable prospect of success'. From there the force would proceed to Gibraltar to meet Abercromby's Mediterranean army, and the combined forces would attack Cadiz.

With this decision the Cabinet reorientated Britain's offensive forces from diversionary operations on the coast of France to attacks on enemy fleets in harbour. The Cabinet acknowledged that too little was known of the places to be attacked; nevertheless it had taken the first step towards the dissolution of Grenville's continental strategy.

'I would not however stop here', Dundas went on. Whether or not the attacks on enemy harbours succeeded, the end product of the plan was a concentration at Gibraltar of 20,000 troops, whose further operations Dundas would design to meet the new political situation. The obsession with supporting the French royalists and the Austrian army had to cease, for the political foundations of that strategy had gone. Britain faced a choice of fighting on alone, or joining Austria in making peace. Either course demanded a strategy of colonial offensives, which would 'tell effectually either with a view to peace or war'. If England fought on, she had to show

[10] Dropmore, VI. 258, 272-3; PRO 30/8/338, Minto's of 6 July, received 21 July; FO 74/30, Wickham's of 27 and 28 June, received 21 July; Weil, 333; Add. MSS 40102, memo. by Dundas of 22 July.

her enemies that they could enjoy no prosperity without conceding an acceptable peace. If she joined Austria and sued for peace immediately, she must strengthen her bargaining hand by striking a blow at once before the end of the campaigning season. The peace settlement would probably make the eastern seas safe by leaving the Cape and Ceylon in British hands; but the West Indies would become more vulnerable than even at the end of the American War, unless the British possessions there had been strengthened in the meantime. France would demand the return of all her lost possessions, and Britain's finances and public opinion would make it impossible to reject these demands and continue the war. If Martinique, St. Lucia and Guadaloupe were returned to the French, they would be able to seize the whole of the British Leeward Islands at the start of the next war; and even Jamaica would be less safe than in the past with Toussaint's black empire of Saint Domingue as a neighbour.[11] The only escape from this situation was to conquer an equivalent, some colony of wealth and strategic importance to be exchanged or retained at the peace.

Dundas had two proposals to meet this need. First, to conquer Cuba. Rich in produce, and important in war because it lay to windward of Saint Domingue and commanded the Windward Passage, it fitted Dundas's description. His second proposal was his old favourite, the trade of South America. By occupying some position such as the River Plate Britain could force open the Spanish colonial markets, or bargain for freedom of trade in South America. That would lead to a general opening of the colonial trade of the world; and for many years to come the country best placed to exploit free trade would be Britain.

Much of this paper was a repetition of what Dundas had been preaching for months; but now he could hope that his colleagues would be converted by the Austrian disaster. It was not yet to be. Many of the Cabinet still clung to the hope of an Austrian resurgence, or believed that a joint negotiation

[11] Add. MSS 40102, Dundas's memo. of 22 July 1800. An undated paper, printed as an appendix by Dunfermline and attributed to Sir Ralph Abercromby, contains some features of this plan, and significantly gives priority to the opening of South America rather than the removal of the French from Egypt.

required a continuing posture of military support for Austria. In spite of the continental armistice the first instalment of the loan was being paid so that Austria could repair her damaged armies; and paid not in bills of exchange but in scarce specie. To Grenville and others it seemed vital that the British army should remain available for European operations. Dundas could obtain no concession to his plans for overseas offensives except that part of the army about to assemble at Gibraltar should attack Tenerife. Most of the force was to remain concentrated at Gibraltar and wait for future orders.[12]

3. *The Alienation of the King*

On the day of these Cabinet decisions the King was reviewing the army in camp at Bagshot, where he supposed that it was preparing to embark for Belle Île. Great was his astonishment that evening on his return to Windsor to find a Cabinet minute from Dundas announcing that the troops were to attack Ferrol. He had had no warning and no explanation. What grounds were there to suppose that it could be done? It was only three weeks since the King had reproached Dundas for the muddle which had sent the force in Quiberon Bay to the Mediterranean. 'Orders and counter-orders are too freqently given', he had complained, 'which puzzle the services and create much confusion.'[13]

This time the King was not merely puzzled, but angry. He was already upset by the Cabinet's willingness to join in peace negotiations;[14] and it was intolerable to learn that the country's military plans were being overturned without his receiving notice or explanation. And without an explanation he would not consent. 'Not having before heard of an expedition against Ferrol and on what grounds of supposed success it is to be undertaken, nor what force will remain in this country after sending so large a force out of it, I cannot give any answer till I have received the data on which to form an opinion.'[15]

[12] *GL* 2194, 2202; Add. MSS 37879, f. 203; Duffy 419.
[13] *GL* 2184.   [14] *GL* 2193.
[15] *GL* vol. III, p. 382, n. 3; and no. 2203.

It was many years since the sovereign had rejected a Cabinet minute. But he was entitled to courtesy, and he expected notice of important measures before they went to the Cabinet. His ministers were becoming increasingly overbearing and neglectful; and as head of the army he found it particularly hurtful to receive a military decision presented without notice or explanation as a *fait accompli*. It would probably end in another slipshod muddle.

On the following morning Dundas was to visit the Duke of York at Swinley to settle the details of the Ferrol expedition, and at six o'clock he was stepping into his carriage at Wimbledon when the King's reply was handed to him. It stopped him in his tracks. Without the King's assent the operation was suspended, and precious time was being lost. There was only one thing to do; the King's letter must be referred to the Cabinet, and Dundas's horses were headed towards London. But neither Pitt nor Grenville was in town, and the Ferrol plan remained in suspense while messengers went off to Dropmore and Holwood to find them. Five or six precious days were to be lost by the dispute.

Dundas was already ruffled by the Cabinet's rejection of his plan to seize Cuba, and the King's attempt to obstruct an operation which his colleagues had actually accepted made him feel trapped. 'Most of you', he told Grenville, 'being of opinion that we ought not to send any force out of Europe (the reverse of which is my decided opinion), and the King and those in whose councils he confides being of opinion that our force is to go nowhere (which is the plain English of all this), my situation is become too ridiculous to be longer submitted to.'[16]

A reply from Pitt was soon on its way from Holwood; a letter which glowed with the Prime Minister's best qualities of moderation and good sense. Pitt excelled as a conciliator. He was astonished and hurt, he assured Dundas, by the rejection of the Cabinet's advice; but he did not believe the

---

[16] *GL* 2203; Dropmore, VI. 277-8. One of the colleagues with whom Dundas was in collision was Windham. 'Since the circumstances are such', he wrote to Minto on 8 August, 'as not to admit of anything decisive, my opinion, in the present state of things, is that we should do nothing.' (Nat. Library of Scotland, MS 11140, f. 180.)

King could persist, and instead of wasting time collecting the Cabinet Dundas should write immediately to the King, or go to Windsor in person with a temperate statement of the case. Pitt suggested the points to be made: that Belle Île would have taken just as many troops from home defence as the Ferrol expedition; some blow had to be struck quickly; and the judgement of a reputable officer that the Ferrol operation was practicable was good reason for allowing him to attempt it. 'These topics calmly stated must I trust have their effect. If not there is only one left, in which I most decidedly join, that of begging his Majesty to find servants whose judgments he can trust more than ours.'[17]

Dundas accepted his friend's advice. Back at Wimbledon in the evening, he sent off a letter at eleven o'clock at the end of a long and agitating day, defending the Ferrol expedition in the manner Pitt had advised. He revealed that his adviser was Sir James Pulteney, to whom the final decision to attack would be left; and ended with an exhortation on the lines suggested by Pitt. They felt 'that if an army collected at so much expense, and by so unusual exertions, was to remain inactive during the whole of the remainder of the season, the spirit of the country would be let down, your Majesty's government justly censured, and the impatience and clamour for peace *on any terms* increased every hour'. He appealed for the King's confidence 'at a moment when it is so essentially necessary in every particular, and in none more than the conduct of the war'.[18]

Dundas's letter travelled through the night to Windsor, and was waiting when the King rose on the morning of 26 July. His reply, meticulously dated at 7.10 a.m. was intended to be conciliatory.[19] He explained that his response to the Cabinet minute had been written in haste and was not meant to be shown to the Cabinet; and he admitted that any operation which would postpone peace with France was desirable. The rest of the letter, however, only increased Dundas's annoyance. The King said he was concerned to avoid the waste of life which had marred recent expeditions, particularly the

---

[17] *GL* 2203n.   [18] *GL* 2203.
[19] This letter is dated 28 July in *GL* 2205; but internal evidence points to the 26th, and the original in Add. MSS 40100, f. 272, appears to read 26 rather than 28: compare the handwriting in the letter of 28 July timed 7.23 a.m.

Helder expedition of the previous autumn, through lack of planning and preparation. Since Pulteney thought the Ferrol attack was feasible he should be allowed to consult Lord St. Vincent, but their advice should be considered by the Cabinet. In the meantime the troops in Quiberon Bay must be brought back to a home port and properly equipped for foreign service.

These proposed delays, and the criticism of his military administration, made Dundas frantic. 'I hope in God the wind will remain in its present quarter', he told the Duke of York; 'for if it should quickly change so as to prevent sailing from Portsmouth, the consequences may be very unpleasant at this advanced period of the season.' He drafted a reply to the King in which he threatened to resign, and Pitt had to deflect the storm by writing to the King himself. He pointed out that the approach of autumn made speed essential. The expedition had to be launched immediately, and the details left to Pulteney and St. Vincent; and for secrecy the rein-forcements must be sent out to Quiberon Bay as though for the Belle Île attack instead of the whole force assembling in England. While he waited for the effect of these arguments on the King, Pitt pleaded with Dundas to soften his tone. The King's note did not justify his resignation, and he begged him not to mix policy with personal pique. 'Tho' I admit you have reason enough to be personally displeased, I am sure you are above indulging that feeling especially at such a moment. And we must allow something more than usual for the effect in all other business of the irritation on the King's mind from our pressing upon him unwelcome tho' necessary counsels on the subject of negotiation.'[20]

Again Dundas let Pitt guide him. He scratched out eleven lines to which Pitt objected, and at 10 p.m. on 27 July he fired his final shot at Windsor Castle. He told the King that speed and secrecy forbade the delay that the King proposed. He was sorry that the King had disapproved of his procedure; but he had always allowed major measures to be matured by the Cabinet before submitting them to the King. Even with the final lines obliterated the end of his letter was a stern constitutional remonstrance. 'Having stated this much in

[20] *GL* 2203n, 2204 and n; Add. MSS 40102, f. 48.

apology for his own conduct, Mr. Dundas begs leave with the utmost humility, and the most profound respect, to state to your Majesty that in his poor judgment the appropriation of the national force must, in time of war, like every other resource of the Empire, be subject to the advice and responsibility of your Majesty's confidential servants.'[21]

This protest need not have been written, for the King had already climbed down in response to Pitt's letter, and no longer insisted on bringing home the troops in Quiberon Bay. The way ahead was clear, and on 31 July orders went out to the commanders to launch the Ferrol and Cadiz attacks. 'Our immediate exertions', ran the instruction for Abercromby, 'should be directed as much as possible to the destruction of the Enemy's Naval Forces.'[22]

The King had made it plain that by disputing the Ferrol minute he was not only asserting his constitutional rights and demanding good manners from his ministers. He was also expressing his anxiety at the recent slipshod and over-hasty way of mounting expeditions; he had already urged that the Belle Île operation should be properly assessed and prepared: 'Dear bought experience ought to teach us that if soldiers have not the conveniences that are necessary, . . . it is impossible that they can support the fatigues of service, and I cannot forget the old saying of loving more haste than good speed.' And as a parting shot when he withdrew his opposition to Ferrol: 'The success of any enterprise must in the end depend on the arrangements being duly prepared . . . After the sanguine expectations of some with regard to Belle Isle after five months its being found impracticable, gives reason for pausing on a new project till it is more fully explained.'[23]

These shots were well aimed to hurt; and Dundas has often been criticized for launching the Ferrol expedition without first collecting intelligence about the enemy's defences. Yet one must consider the circumstances. Bonaparte had not a

[21] *GL* 2205. The eleven obliterated lines, which I have not deciphered, are in the draft in Add. MSS 40100, f. 271.

[22] WO 6/21, 31 July 1800, Dundas to Pulteney; Keith, II. 133–5.

[23] Duke University Library, MS XVIII F, 17 June, King to Dundas; *GL* 2205.

single enemy in arms on the continent, and would soon be
able to challenge Britain's maritime command with a coalition
more formidable than that of 1780 in the American War. The
resources of Spain and Holland were again at France's disposal;
Portugal was threatened with invasion; and a new Armed
Neutrality was foreshadowed in the Baltic under the protection of Russia. The battle of Marengo therefore faced the
Cabinet with a great emergency, comparable with the Tilsit
crisis of 1807 which sent a fleet and army to seize the Danish
navy at Copenhagen. To this national crisis Dundas's colleagues
were slow to respond; and when he did force them to take a
limited action, it was obstructed by the King. Dundas saw
that risks must be taken and corners cut. The raids on the
Spanish ports were a crash programme, with no time to seek
intelligence before the autumn gales even if it could have
been done without impairing secrecy. The orders were therefore conditional: 'a reasonable prospect of success' was the
commanders' guideline. They were to make sure of re-
embarking in case of failure; had discretion to 'relinquish the
attempt as too hazardous'; and were not to risk the destruction of their forces.[24] If they succeeded, Britain's power to
continue the war would be strengthened; if they called off the
attacks, little would be lost except pride; and in either event
the final product of their voyages would be a striking force
in the Straits of Gibraltar, well placed to launch offensives
in the Mediterranean or the Americas during the winter. In
the great emergency which followed the battle of Marengo
Dundas had refused to stand supine. And he passionately
desired a success, to hearten the British public and impress
the watching courts of Europe. 'I fairly flattered myself', he
wrote later to Abercromby, 'that one brilliant act of British
enterprise would intervene to check and soften the uniform-
ity of calamity and defeat . . . Such an event was much
wanted.'[25]

The loss of a week in mounting these urgent operations,
and the King's criticisms of his past administration, left
Dundas in an angry mood. Pitt too was rattled, to the point
of talking of resignation, for he was feeling the strain of the

[24] *GL* 2202; WO 6/21, pp. 74-8.　　[25] SRO, GD 51/1/774/19.

crisis brought on by Marengo. 'It is really provoking', he wrote to Grenville, 'to find a disposition equally to object to all means of making peace or making war.'[26]

The King appeared to forgive the quarrel. 'The entering into a paper war is not in the least my intention', he told Dundas: 'it can answer no good purpose and [is] certainly no agreeable occupation.'[27] But he remained resentful. Twice in ten days his opinions and prejudices had been trampled on, and he was irritated by what Malmesbury called Lord Grenville's 'authoritative manners' as well as by Dundas's neglect of form. In the following month he was to make a tentative move to find alternative ministers. Windham, whom he congratulated on his absence from the Cabinet which agreed to treat jointly with Vienna, was summoned with Lord Malmesbury to join him in August on his summer holiday at Weymouth, with the idea that they might replace Pitt and Grenville as Prime Minister and Foreign Secretary.[28] The King came to no direct explanation with his visitors; but the fabric of government had been shaken, and coming events would widen the fissures.

4. 'The grand question of peace or war'

Six weeks after the battle of Marengo Dundas had swung the Cabinet to the first phase of his alternative strategy. By the end of July he had drawn the British army away from the continental war, and engaged it in operations against the enemy's navies. But as those orders went out, a new naval danger appeared in the Baltic, and force was deployed to meet it.

Back in the spring of 1800, as the rift between Britain and Russia widened, the British minister in Copenhagen had warned Lord Grenville that the Armed Neutrality of 1780 was likely to be revived: the naval powers of the Baltic would unite to challenge the British blockade. Since then the Tsar Paul's hostility had grown, and when the expelled ambassador Sir Charles Whitworth arrived from Petersburg towards the

---

[26] Dropmore, VI. 258, 279.   [27] GL 2205.
[28] Windham *Diary*, 429; Malmesbury, IV. 22-3.

end of July he was full of stories of Paul's eccentric manners and instability. Of this Paul had just given a striking demonstration when, from trivial pique, he had expelled the British *chargé d'affaires* in the wake of Whitworth. 'One should not be angry with infants', pleaded the Russian ambassador Vorontsov; but worse would surely follow, and from this time Russia was treated as a potential enemy. General Abercromby's instructions to admit the Russians to Malta were reversed and he was ordered to exclude Russian troops from the island when Valletta surrendered, for fear that they would close the port to the British fleet.[29]

That Denmark might seek Russian support against the British exercise of belligerent rights at sea had been apparent for some time, and at the end of July the crisis came. British cruisers in the mouth of the Channel attempted to search a Danish convoy bound for the Mediterranean; shots were exchanged with the escorting frigate *Freya*, which struck her colours to superior force; and the convoy was brought in to Deal. On 29 July the Danish minister in London demanded that the British captain be disavowed, the convoy released, and the *Freya* repaired at British expense.

How should the British ministry respond? To defy the Danes could bring on a Northern League and close the Baltic to British shipping. Access to European markets would be closed; and in this year of dearth 75 per cent of the country's corn imports came from Danzig. Yet the government could not give way; for it was not the first clash with a Danish convoy, and Grenville believed that for Britain the right to search convoys was 'a question of little less than its independence, affecting all its sources of greatness, and shaking the very foundations of its naval power'. Twenty years earlier in the midst of the American War Lord North's government had declared war on Holland rather than allow her to join the Armed Neutrality and supply the French navy with stores. Seven years later on the news of the Peace of Tilsit

[29] FO 7/59, 17 July 1800, Grenville to Minto; FO 65/47, f. 125; Gower, *Private Corr.*, 281; Dropmore, VI. 259, 261, 279-87; Keith, II. 135-8. Paul's foreign policy has been obscured or misrepresented by successive Russian governments. It forms no part of my subject; but Ole Feldbæk ('The Foreign Policy of Tsar Paul I . . .') has argued that it was, though grandiose, not inconsistent. Hugh Ragsdale's racy *Détente in the Napoleonic Era* is also interesting.

George Canning would send an army to seize the Danish fleet; and even in the present crisis he would have liked to divert Pulteney's Ferrol expedition to Copenhagen.[30] But Canning was not yet in the Cabinet, and Grenville was more cautious. Though the right of search could not be renounced, the use of force might bring the navies of Russia and Sweden to the aid of Denmark's twenty-five ships of the line. A more circumspect course was adopted. Sir Charles Whitworth was sent off to Copenhagen to demand an end of resistance to search at sea. He was supported by a squadron under Admiral Dickson equipped with bomb-vessels and gunboats; but the Admiral was not to use force unless his squadron was attacked or British shipping seized, and Whitworth's instructions allowed him to temporize. Nevertheless the government knew that the worst was possible, and took precautions. A cutter sailed for Elsinore to warn the British shipping to leave the roads. Consul-General Shairp cut short his leave and returned to Russia to hasten the loading of British cargoes and get them clear of the Baltic. And in extremity Admiral Dickson's orders were to destroy the ships and arsenal at Copenhagen.[31]

The danger in the Baltic played a part in frustrating Dundas's wish for a colonial offensive. The threat of a northern confederacy had helped to propel the British govenment in its drift towards a joint peace negotiation in conjunction with Austria;[32] and if the British striking force were disengaged from the continental war and sent out of Europe this would give the Austrians grounds to conclude a separate peace without regard for British interests. That the Austrians expected British military support to continue in spite of the armistice was made clear by Lord Minto, who urged diversionary attacks on the enemy coasts. He added that the Emperor had asked for Abercromby's Mediterranean army to be landed at Leghorn; a request which he had passed on to Abercromby. The British response to this pressure was a

---

[30] Canning MSS, 29 July, Canning to Pitt.
[31] *GL* 2209; Dropmore, VI. 287; FO 65/47, 9 Aug., Grenville to Shairp. The whole affair is admirably described in Ole Feldbæk, *Denmark and the Armed Neutrality 1800–1801*, 48–52.   [32] FO 7/59, 17 July, Grenville to Minto.

compromise between Dundas's eagerness to attack the enemy fleets and Grenville's anxiety to preserve the army's striking power in Europe. Dundas ordered Abercromby to ignore Minto's requisition to land at Leghorn, and any other demand which would interfere with the attack on Cadiz; but he told him that in the present crisis no instructions for further operations could be issued, and that after the Cadiz attack he was to return to Gibraltar and wait for orders. Thus Grenville was able to assure Vienna that if the Austrian army reopened hostilities, the British forces in the Mediterranean would be available to aid them. To justify the Cadiz attack he explained that the army could not be left idle during the armistice and must be used to strengthen British security; but he assured the Austrians that no decision had been taken to use them in any way that would prevent them from acting in Europe.[33]

For the time being, then, British strategy remained half-enmeshed in Coalition warfare, and the army was poised uncomfortably between continental and maritime commitments, chained to a policy which would not let go of Europe. Till the questions of peace and war were clearer, Dundas would not be allowed to complete his alternative strategy by launching a colonial offensive.

For strategy rightly remained the servant of policy, and the issue which was to split the ministry in the next six weeks was whether to negotiate for peace. At the end of August the choice was presented in an embarrassing and dangerous form, when the British ministers' offer to negotiate jointly with Vienna recoiled on them.

The offer had reached Vienna at a critical moment. After the German armistice was signed in mid-July, the Emperor had sent the Comte de Saint-Julien to Paris bearing his answer to Bonaparte's highly coloured offer of an armistice and a peace. In six days of negotiation Saint-Julien was outwitted by Talleyrand, and without authority he signed preliminaries of peace on 28 July.

How was the Austrian government to receive this doubtful blessing? The British offer to join in negotiations resolved the

[33] PRO 30/8/339, Minto's of 18 July, received 30 July; WO 6/21, p. 90; FO 7/59, 8 Aug., Grenville to Minto; Dropmore, VI. 300; Keith, II. 135.

question. Thugut opted for a joint negotiation, disowned Saint-Julien, and proposed a tripartite peace conference. Bonaparte reacted swiftly. While Lord Minto's report on these transactions travelled slowly northwards across Germany to catch the packet-boat in the Elbe, the French dispatches went directly westwards to Paris and on to the Straits of Dover. On 24 August Bonaparte's version of Austria's peace proposals arrived in London with an offer to extend the Austrian armistice to Britain. The offer was transmitted through Monsieur Otto, the French resident agent in London for the exchange of prisoners.[34]

Lord Grenville had no hesitation about accepting a peace conference, and even appointed his brother Thomas to be the British plenipotentiary if it took place.[35] But an armistice was another matter, unprecedented and dangerous. No British government in the past had agreed to suspend naval hostilities during peace negotiations; for the pressure of maritime power operated slowly over months or years and could be undone in days. An armistice would allow Bonaparte to resupply his arsenals with naval stores, and redeploy his blockaded battle squadrons; revictual Valletta to stand another two years of siege; and rearm and reinforce the Army of Egypt to secure the French occupation till peace was signed.

If maritime considerations prevailed, the answer was clearly no. But the French offer could not be isolated in this fashion, for Bonaparte had linked his proposed naval armistice to the continental armistice with Austria. If the blockaded German fortresses of Ulm, Ingolstadt and Philipsburg were to be victualled during the armistice, and the Austrian field armies were to receive reinforcements, then Bonaparte argued that he should receive equivalent concessions from the British. Otherwise he could not allow the Austrians to take advantage of an armistice during protracted peace negotiations. No armistice at sea, none on land; the French armies would resume the offensive.

Many points could be made in reply, for Bonaparte's parallel between a land and sea armistice was specious. But debating points weighed nothing against Bonaparte's threat

---

[34] Louis Guillaume Otto, 1754-1817, a native of Baden.
[35] FO 7/59, 30 Aug., Grenville to Minto.

of force. The inescapable dilemma was that France could take the offensive, and Britain could not. Otto revealed that his offer of an armistice was an ultimatum, and required an answer before 3 September. It was already 29 August, and with the King at Weymouth no answer could possibly be given within the time limit. On 4 September, however, when the offer had expired, Otto announced a respite till the 11th when, if no armistice had been agreed, Bonaparte would resume his offensive and impose a separate peace on the Austrians.

Bonaparte could certainly execute his threat, for all reports agreed that the Austrian armies were still in a deplorable state and needed more time to recover. If they were attacked now, the Emperor would be driven into a hasty separate peace as he had been three years earlier at Leoben. This prospect did not intimidate Dundas or the King; for both of them regarded Austria as a broken reed, and they did not want to buy concessions for their reluctant and slippery ally by surrendering British conquests in a joint negotiation. The Foreign Secretary, however, disagreed, still clinging to the hope of saving the Coalition; and though far from wanting peace, he was prepared to buy time for the Austrians by negotiating. Moreover it was still possible at this stage to negotiate with firmness, while experience showed that it would be much more difficult to stand firm for British interests at a later stage under duress of public opinion. Thus though it was only a fortnight since Grenville had dismissed a naval armistice as unthinkable, he was now willing to take that treacherous path for the sake of Austria.[36]

And Pitt? An enigma, as usual, sympathizing with every point of view but committing himself to none. The clues to his real opinion, however, point towards peace. 'His intentions about peace were quite satisfactory', the pacific George Rose reported after an 'unreserved' talk with him. Pitt's refractory acolyte George Canning, though far from pacific, explained to Lord Wellesley that negotiations were unavoidable and it was best to take the initiative before the government's

[36] *GL* 2193-4; PRO 30/8/339, 24 July, Minto to Grenville (received 7 Aug.); and FO 7/59, 8 Aug., Grenville to Minto; Dropmore, VI. 311; *Parl. Hist.* XXXV. 540 *et seq.*

hand was forced by public opinion.[37] Indeed public discontent was rising fast. The West Riding manufacturers were petitioning for peace, and there had been food riots in Yorkshire in the first half of the year which the volunteers had shown reluctance to put down. In August the promising harvest was drowned in torrents of rain for the second year in succession. The grain shortage would continue, and farmers and corn-factors began to hoard in the hope of still higher prices. Pitt had feared for a long time that public support for the war would fail, and his fears were confirmed when the disastrous news of Marengo caused the funds to rise in the hope of peace. Lord Malmesbury's diary later recorded his conviction that Pitt had been driven towards peace by financial fears: 'I always perceived these to supersede in Pitt's mind every other considerations, and that even when he declaimed the loudest, and with the greatest emphasis, for a continuation of *war*, his real and genuine opinion went for *peace*.'[38]

Pitt therefore desired a joint negotiation, as Grenville did; but while Grenville's concern was to keep Austria in the war, Pitt's real wish was to make peace if he could. He feared that blunt refusal of a naval armistice would cause Bonaparte to impose a separate peace on Austria, leaving England alone to negotiate her own terms from a weaker position. He was therefore inclined to take the armistice talks further with the hope of finding a compromise. From this the King strongly dissented. He regarded an armistice on any terms as out of the question, and even a peace conference as dangerous. If there had to be a negotiation, he wished the British envoys to treat it as window dressing and assume that it would fail. But he regarded any negotiation as a betrayal of the true aims of the war.[39]

The Cabinet which considered Otto's respite on 4 September met in the absence of two strong opponents of an armistice.

---

[37] Pretyman MSS, T 108/44, 20 Aug., Rose to Tomline; Canning MSS, 24 Aug., Canning to Lord Wellesley.
[38] GL 2243, 2245; Frere, I. xlviii; Malmesbury, IV. 53; Stevenson, *Popular Disturbances*, 177, 178.   [39] GL 2228, 2230, 2232.

Windham was with the court at Weymouth; and the powerful
Dundas had departed under pressure from his doctor and
family to take the waters at Cheltenham, intending to go on
later to Scotland. The ministers still in London sent the Secretary of the Admiralty to see Otto that evening. He returned
with detailed armistice proposals, and by receiving them the
Cabinet stepped on to the slippery path of negotiation. Otto's
terms were impossible; but rather than reject them outright
and abandon Austria to destruction, Pitt and Grenville guided
their colleagues into drawing up a counter-project. They
agreed to lift the blockade on French naval ports; but no
naval or military stores were to enter, nor any warships to
leave. Malta and Alexandria would be placed on the same
footing as the German fortresses, where only fourteen days'
provisions at a time were allowed to enter and all additional
means of defence were excluded.[40]

Lord Grenville's report of the counter-project was waiting
at Weymouth when the King and his companions returned
from an excursion on the evening of the 6th. The news was
'disagreeable', and though after much discussion with Windham and the Lord Chancellor Loughborough the King gave
his most unwilling assent, he required Grenville to ask the
Cabinet in his name whether the counter-project was its
ultimate offer. Loughborough assured Pitt of his support for
the armistice, in view of Austria's vulnerability and of unrest
at home; 'for I am perfectly convinced that your judgment
of the temper of the public is as just as it had proved to be
upon similar occasions'. But this was not the view of Windham,
who believed that a flat rejection of the French terms would
be popular at least with the commercial world.[41]

Windham's reaction was mild compared with Dundas's.
Though Dundas had resigned himself to an ultimate peace of
compromise, that did not mean accepting whatever terms the
enemy offered; and he believed that negotiations under the
shadow of Marengo could only lead to 'an unsafe and dishonourable peace'.[42] That was where the naval armistice was
likely to lead. The news of the Cabinet's counter-project
brought back the insomnia which he had been shaking off at

[40] *GL* 2235; Stanhope, III. 240-1; *Parl. Hist.* XXXV. 551-5.
[41] *GL* 2235 and n.   [42] Feiling, 215.

Cheltenham; and his mind churned with anxiety through two long nights before his Under-Secretary Huskisson arrived with an appeal from the Secretary of the Admiralty, Evan Nepean, to return to London. Nepean was appalled by the prospect of a naval armistice, and implored Dundas not to go to Scotland, for if ever he was needed in London it was now. Dundas resolved to return to London immediately.

This was the moment when Dundas entered the decisive battle to shape the country's policy: a battle to prevent the naval armistice and to commit Abercromby's army to colonial warfare. He rushed off a letter to Grenville to record his dissent from the counter-project. That offer, he told Nepean, 'put the conduct of both war and negotiation in the hands of the enemy. . . . I am not a fit adviser or partner in such Councils. I can neither accord with our arrogance and presumption in times of apparent prosperity, nor can I descend to pusillanimity in moments of occasional adversity.' Those bitter words were aimed at his closest colleagues.[43]

[43] SRO, GD 51/1/726/1, 7 Sept., Nepean to Dundas, *GL* 2242n; Add. MSS 40102, f. 71, 14 Sept., Dundas to Loughborough; SRO, GD 51/1/726/2, 9 Sept., Dundas to Nepean.

CHAPTER VII

The Conflict on Egypt

1. *Options for the Expeditionary Force*

Dundas's sudden return to London brought together the two strategic issues which divided the Cabinet: the armistice, and the destination of the forces which were converging on Gibraltar. For weeks the ultimate destination of the expeditionary force had hung in suspense. The government had swayed between the poles of national policy; between using the army's offensive power to support the Austrians and promote a joint negotiation, or using it to strengthen Britain's colonial and commercial interests for a solitary war or a separate peace. But did these political options relate to military realities? Could Britain afford to use the army offensively anywhere, or were Abercromby's forces to be sucked into defensive commitments and once again forgo the initiative? At home there was the abiding fear of invasion, with reports of landing craft assembling at St. Malo while from Ireland Cornwallis demanded replacements for the troops withdrawn for the Ferrol expedition. Dundas maintained that the forces at home were adequate, and anyway his plans for operations outside Europe assumed optimistically that the expeditionary force could be home by the spring.[1]

A more clamorous tocsin was sounded by England's ancient ally Portugal. Bonaparte's victory at Marengo had released the means to intimidate the Portuguese, with French troops to back the threat of a Spanish invasion. The Portuguese government was pressing the British to reinforce their small garrison at Lisbon; a demand which Dundas wanted to reject out of hand, arguing that against the Spaniards alone the existing force was enough, while against the French no reinforcement would avail. Once again he was fighting the tendency to over-insure a defensive commitment: 'we shall err egregiously if we give a single thought to

[1] *GL* 2229, 2240; Castlereagh, III. 373–6; SRO, GD 51/1/725/1; PRO 30/58/3, August 1800, draft for Abercromby.

Portugal'.[2] But this pragmatic denial of Britain's obligation revolted the high-principled Grenville, and he continued to press hard for aid to Portugal.

The graver threat in the north was dissipated, however. At the end of August Whitworth was negotiating successfully with the Danish government about neutral rights at sea. Contrary to the British assumption, the Danes had not intended the *Freya* convoy as a challenge; for though they were negotiating a renewal of their expired commercial treaty with Russia, which included the principles of the Armed Neutrality of 1780, they were not yet ready to resist the British searching of convoys. It would be some time before Russian aid could arrive, nor was the Danish fleet prepared for war. When Whitworth arrived in Copenhagen he discovered that a Danish mission was on its way to Petersburg to seek Russian help, and realized that the Danes were playing for time while they equipped their warships and waited for the Russian reply. After ten days of unsatisfactory parleying, he presented an ultimatum and withdrew to the British fleet. Admiral Dickson's bomb-vessels took station close to the city; and on 29 August, when an instruction to use force was on its way from London, the Danish government gave way and agreed to compromise. The *Freya*'s convoy was released, the question of search was deferred, and for the time being the Danes would cease to convoy their merchantmen. When the Tsar Paul learned what had happened there would be trouble; but without surrendering their belligerent rights the British had bought time in the Baltic till the spring.[3]

Thus one of the pressures to keep Britain's expeditionary force in Europe was warded off. Dundas had been determined for at least four or five months that the force should be used for colonial warfare and not in Europe. Hitherto he had been planning attacks in the western Atlantic, to make the British West Indies safe and open trade with Spanish America. Undeterred by his colleagues' coolness he had pursued his plans against Cuba and other Spanish possessions, and about 24 August had obtained at least a qualified approval from the

[2] Dropmore, VI. 309; FO 7/59, August, draft to Minto; Add. MSS 38736, f. 135, 3 Sept., Dundas to Huskisson.
[3] Felbæk, 52-66; *GL* 2228, 2230, 2234.

Cabinet. 'So; Cuba is right after all, is it?' Canning asked Pitt sharply. Dundas began his preparations, consulting the Admiralty about transports and seeking the views of Cornwallis. The Lord-Lieutenant sent a long reply from Dublin on 7 September, guardedly concluding that with a reasonable prospect of success the objects were important enough to be attempted. In the meantime orders had been drafted for Abercromby. He was to have absolute discretion to make or call off the attack on Cuba, with alternative objectives in Guadaloupe, the Canaries, Porto Rico, Caraccas and the River Plate. The operation was conditional on his being able to send home 10,000–12,000 men to Britain early in the spring; therefore 'those conquests which can be accomplished with the utmost expedition, the least bloodshed and expense are to be preferred.'[4]

These were Dundas's plans at the beginning of September, and as late as the 24th the King still believed that Abercromby was destined for the Caribbean.[5] But during his holiday at Cheltenham Dundas's concern for Egypt had begun to revive. The threat to Portugal made him ponder the security of Portugal's Indian bridge-heads at Diu and Goa, so close to two dangerous native powers, the Mahrattas and the Afghan empire of Zeman Shah. Dundas was also disturbed by signs of growing understanding between Bonaparte and the Tsar, for he had long been suspicious of Russian ambitions in Egypt and feared a partition of the Ottoman empire. On 26 August a dispatch from the minister at the Sardinian court reported Franco-Russian discussions on a joint invasion of India.[6]

It may seem curious that Egypt had found no place in Dundas's recent strategic papers, which were wholly concerned with the Americas. Perhaps he had been lulled by the hope of a voluntary French withdrawal, which had nearly

---

[4] *GL* 2223, 229; Canning MSS, 25 Aug., Canning to Pitt; Matheson, 287; Cornwallis, III. 293; PRO 30/58/3, drafts by Dundas for Abercromby.

[5] *GL* 2246.

[6] Dropmore, VI. 312–13; Matheson, 287; Spencer, IV. 187; Wellesley *Dispatches*, I. 688; J. R. Rose, *Pitt and the Great War*, 387; FO 67/29, Jackson's of 26 Aug. from Leghorn.

been achieved at the beginning of 1800 by the Convention of El Arish, of which more in a moment. Yet since his first suspicion in 1798 that Egypt was Bonaparte's destination, he had been tormented by the danger of a French occupation. In the long term he feared the commercial advantages which it would give the French. With Egypt under their control they could expand across North Africa and turn it into a virtual homeland granary, to overcome the grain shortages in the southern provinces of France. Egypt itself, Dundas was advised, could grow most of the colonial produce at present supplied by the East and West Indies, and it commanded the caravan trade of Cairo with Asia Minor. With access to the Red Sea France could restore her Indian trade and undersell the British East India Company in European markets.[7]

More immediate than the trade war was the military threat to India. It needed only a small French force to shake the balance of power in India, and naval opinion had not dismissed the danger when Bonaparte invaded Egypt in 1798. It was feared that he had arranged with Tippoo Sahib of Mysore and the Governor of Mauritius to collect shipping in the Red Sea. If there had not been time for that, Dundas imagined that the French would march from the Syrian coast to Aleppo and down the Euphrates, and so along the coast of the Persian Gulf to India: here he might have paused to consider Grenville's advice to make his strategic appreciations 'with a map in your hand, and with a calculation of distances'.[8] In the event these threats did not materialize. Bonaparte's invasion of Syria was stopped at Acre; the Red Sea was sealed by a naval force from England; and the capture of Seringapatam in May 1799 destroyed the French ally in India. But even the death of Tippoo did not allay Dundas's anxiety. Soon afterwards, referring to Grenville's reconstruction of his European offensive in the autumn of 1799, Dundas lamented 'the total forgetfulness we seem to labour under with regard to Egypt'. There were other native powers to reckon with besides

[7] SRO, GD 51/1/768 has a memo. of 20 April 1798, and many other papers on Egypt written before the French expedition was known to have left Toulon. A paper of about 1803 in the Nelson papers, Add. MSS 34932, ff. 239–48, elaborates the danger. See also Wellesley *Despatches*, I. 688, 692, and Barham, III. 12.

[8] Quoted in *Strategy of Overthrow*, 7. For a discussion of the various routes from the Mediterranean to India, see Ingram, *Commitment to Empire*, 47 *et seq.*

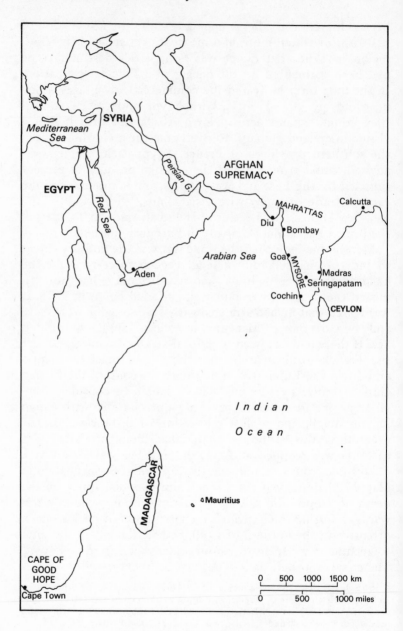

Map 5. India and its Approaches.

Mysore, and the British naval screen could not be maintained for ever. In peacetime the British defences would be rapidly dispersed and the seamen demobilized, not to be quickly reassembled; while the French in Egypt would have the means to collect the shipping they had lacked in the Red Sea. A French colony in Egypt would be a perpetual threat to British India.[9] To all this, however, Lord Grenville seemed indifferent, and he admitted his ignorance. He 'sees nothing beyond the Rhine', as Husskisson complained.[10]

The Convention of El Arish, of which news reached England in March 1800, presented the clash between Grenville and Dundas in its sharpest form. Contrary to his orders, Admiral Sir Sidney Smith had promoted an agreement between the Turks and Bonaparte's successor Kléber, by which the Army of Egypt would return to France under safe conduct with its arms and baggage. Dundas saw this as an opportunity to clear the French from Egypt and discharge the British obligation to the Turks; while for Grenville it meant unleashing the veteran French army on England's European allies. The clash was resolved by muddle and mischance. During Dundas's absence in Scotland at Christmas the government had learned that such a convention was in the wind, and had ordered the Mediterranean fleet to intercept the French transports and turn them back; and though this order was rescinded when it was realized that Sir Sidney Smith had pledged British faith, Kléber had already heard of it. Breaking the armistice, he attacked and routed the Turkish army at Heliopolis on 20 March 1800.[11] So the Convention was undone, and the French remained in Egypt; and Kléber's assassination in June 1800 left the command in the hands of General Menou, a passionate colonialist who had turned Muslim and married a local baker's daughter. No more was heard from the French of evacuation; and till the news of Marengo Grenville and the majority of the Cabinet were happy to keep the French army locked up in Egypt.[12]

    [9] Wellesley, *Despatches*, I. 689-91; Dropmore, VI. 39, 312-13; Stowe Papers, box 303, 4 Oct. 1798, Dundas to Grenville. See above, p. 37.
    [10] *Strategy of Overthrow*, 7n; Buckingham, *Courts and Cabinets*, III. 37.
    [11] Stanhope, III. 204-5; Windham *Diary*, 419; Spencer, IV. 89, 186; Dropmore, VI. 79, 32-3; *GL* 2120; above, p. 46.
    [12] Rose, *Pitt and Napoleon*, 271; *GL* 2176.

Dundas, however, lamented the lost opportunity. 'My words had almost stuck in my throat when I defended that measure in the House of Commons', he told Lord Spencer. At the beginning of September his reflections in Cheltenham on the Indian situation brought him back to the subject. 'I was in Scotland at the time', he explained to the Governor-General's brother Henry Wellesley. 'I have always doubted the wisdom of it, and if we get into negotiations the evacuation of Egypt will be a great stumbling block. If the war continues another year, I rather think it ought to be the primary object of our share in the war.'[13] That time-scale was now to be drastically shortened.

2. *Dundas to the Battle*

While Dundas was still absent at Cheltenham the ministry had continued to temporize about Abercromby's destination, able to do so because the force was still committed to the raids on Ferrol and Cadiz. But on 10 September came news which demanded a decision. The blow against Ferrol had been launched — and had failed humiliatingly. General Pulteney had landed his troops, but after reconnoitring the landward defences of the port from the crest of the coastal hills he had re-embarked. The navy were furious; but experienced soldiers supported his judgement that the fortifications were too strong to be escaladed, and he had not enough troops to cover a siege and bombardment. Though the ministers were disappointed they supported his decision, for his orders warned him not to risk his force; and the Commander-in-Chief's secretary Colonel Taylor rejoiced that whatever the next point of attack might be, and however faulty the information, Pulteney would not allow his force to be thrown away.[14] The point was cogent. If Pulteney had smashed his force against the bastions of Ferrol, or had let himself be prevented from re-embarking by a change in the weather, the major operation for which the combined expedition was ultimately destined would have been ruined.

[13] Spencer, IV. 126.   [14] WO 6/21, p. 136; Burges, 22.

Whatever the truth about Ferrol, Pulteney was now on his way south to join Abercromby, and the Cadiz attack might be launched at any moment. What then? The future of their combined forces needed an urgent decision. Winter was fast approaching, and 22,000 men could not be left floating in the Straits of Gibraltar without water or orders. When Pitt and Grenville discussed Abercromby's further operations in the light of the news from Ferrol, Grenville was still determined to help the Austrians by sending the army to Leghorn. Pitt liked the idea; but he did not expect the Austrians to stay in the war much longer, and then Britain's only striking force would be dangerously far away on the coast of Italy.[15] These leisurely speculations were interrupted by the furious arrival of Dundas from Cheltenham on 14 September. Ready for battle against the naval armistice, he was equally prepared to fight for the future of Abercromby's expedition.

Dundas arrived in London to find the armistice talks in suspense, while Otto referred the British terms to his government. But whatever instructions Otto might receive, the British counter-offer had opened new fissures in the ministry. Dundas found himself aligned with the King and Windham against the Prime Minister and the Foreign Secretary, and his confidence in Pitt had been shaken to the roots. Talking to Pitt on his return, he found him so agitated by the subject that he forbore to say all that he felt; but the fact remained that when Dundas had set out for Cheltenham Pitt had claimed to be strongly against an armistice, yet now he was seeking one. Could he ever be trusted again? If Austria were attacked and knocked out of the war, could Pitt even then be trusted to reject a naval armistice? No doubt Dundas saw Grenville's influence behind Pitt's wavering views. He even learned that Grenville believed he could remove Bonaparte from Belgium and Holland by negotiation.[16] 'I can only express my wonder that he should entertain such an idea', he exclaimed to Loughborough. He feared worse; that Grenville would cede Britain's overseas conquests to

[15] Dropmore, VI. 317.
[16] Confirmed in the instructions Grenville prepared for his brother Thomas's planned mission to negotiate with France and Austria (Add. MSS 38357, ff. 54 *et seq.*)

obtain slightly better terms for Austria. And in vain; for Thugut had indicated that if peace were made he would renew the war as soon as he could safely do so, and Britain would then have all her conquests to win again. The time had come, said Dundas, for Britain to pull out of the continental commitment, and wait to see what new alignments might emerge from the present chaos: 'We have nothing to gain and much to lose by entwining ourselves round the desperate fortunes of Austria.'[17]

Yet still Pitt and Grenville clung to the hope of keeping Austria going. When Otto's reply to the British counter-project arrived on 16 September, it contained inadmissible new proposals, yet they felt that France must have some ulterior reason for drawing out the negotiation instead of crushing the Austrians without further delay. Was Bonaparte simply trying to influence British public opinion with pacific gestures? Or was he propelled by the clamour for peace inside France? In either case time was being gained by prolonging the armistice talks, and if the Austrian army could be shielded from attack till the middle of November, major operations were supposed to cease in Germany and the Tryol and Austria would be safe till the spring. To win this respite Pitt and Grenville were willing to agree to a naval armistice of limited duration.[18]

Dundas, however, scrutinized Otto's latest offer with suspicion. A report had just come in from Madrid that, far from wishing to evacuate Egypt, Bonaparte was planning to reinforce Menou's army. Running his eye over Otto's terms, which were virtually a reiteration of his original proposals, Dundas came upon a defence of the armistice which rang upon his fears: 'and although she should make use of it to sent a few thousand men more to Egypt, do not the places belonging to the Emperor daily acquire, in like manner, fresh strength upon the continent?'[19]

Here was the answer to the riddle: it was to reinforce Egypt

[17] *GL* 2242; Add. MSS 40102, ff. 71-3, 14 September 1800, Dundas to Loughborough.
[18] *Parl. Hist.* XXXV. 556 *et seq.*; *GL* 2243; Dropmore, VI. 329, 332-3; FO 7/60, 26 Sept., Grenville to Minto.
[19] Dropmore, VI. 304; *Parl. Hist.* XXXV. 558.

that France was continuing the negotiation, and Bonaparte was determined to retain the country in the peace. His hold must be broken before the peace conference began; and Dundas embarked on a single-handed battle to sent Abercromby's expeditionary force to Egypt.

3. *Conflict and Decision*

On 18 September, two days after receiving Otto's proposals, Dundas proposed in the Cabinet to send the major part of the expeditionary forces to Egypt.

The Cabinet's reaction was procrastinating and indecisive; evidence of divided views and uncertain leadership. It was objected that Dundas was proposing to send only 15,000 men, though Sir Sidney Smith had advised that not less than 20,000 European troops would be needed to dislodge the French. The most popular alternative was to send Abercromby's army to aid the Austrians at Leghorn on the western side of Italy; but the Austrians had told Colonel Hope that to help them the force must be sent up the Adriatic to Venice. It was objected against both destinations that neither at Venice nor in Egypt could the force be summoned to the defence of Portugal. Windham as usual put forward a point of view entirely his own, that the whole force should be brought home to the British Isles to wait on events.[20]

Dundas was appalled by the discussion. With the summer already past and Abercromby's mass of transports still bobbing in the perilous mouth of the Mediterranean, too much time had already been wasted in discussing his destination; yet even now the Cabinet had dispersed without a decision. His colleagues were wavering between four distinct options; and feeling as he did that every day's delay was dangerous, he circulated another of his long papers to stress the cost of leaving the French in Egypt. If they remained in undisturbed possession, the Sultan would feel that the British were sacrificing his interests as they had already done by sabotaging the Convention of El Arish. If his resentment caused him to make a separate peace and cede Egypt to the French, their

[20] Add. MSS 37924, Windham MS diary, 17–18 Sept. 1800.

occupation would be permanent; for Otto had made it clear that they would not exchange the country to recover other possessions they had lost during the war, and the British public would certainly not fight on for Egypt. As for the European war, for the sake of which Egypt was being neglected, Dundas argued that it was time to pull out: 'Further efforts in that direction will be fruitless. We must now see to our own interests.' That meant backing the Turkish ally at the expense of the Austrian. 'Action must not be postponed on any consideration whatever.'[21]

But still the Cabinet hesitated. Confirmation had just come in from Lisbon that the Spanish invasion of Portugal was certain, with the aid of French infantry; and Grenville and Camden insisted that Portugal's need must override every other object. 'I think as matters now stand', wrote the high-minded Grenville, 'we have no choice whatever our wishes may be, yours for acting in Egypt, and mine for acting in Italy; but that we must unavoidably, not less from motives of interest than of good faith, protect the best and steadiest of our allies.' Even the normally sympathetic Lord Spencer, who was always conscious of maritime needs and shared Dundas's concern for India, turned up a new reason for delay: the winter weather on the Egyptian coast.[22]

These disheartening replies drove Dundas to desperation; for on that very day fresh proposals from Otto confirmed the French determination to keep Egypt. Otto pretended to agree that Malta and Egypt should be treated like the German fortresses; but his latest offer did no such thing. Malta was to be victualled at the rate of 10,000 rations a day, nearly three times the strength of the garrison; and six French frigates were to be allowed to run cargoes to Alexandria without inspection. It was as though the German fortresses, which it had been agreed should receive no additional means of defence, were to be allowed to admit covered waggons equivalent to the cargoes of six large ships.[23]

[21] J. H. Rose, *Pitt and the Great War*, 387; Rylands Library, Engl. 907, n. 28, 19 Sept., memo. by Dundas; Dropmore, VI. 327.
[22] Dropmore, VI. 328-9; Add. MSS 37924, ff. 57-8; SRO, GD 51/1/776/2, 21 Sept., Grenville to Dundas; Cambridge University Library, Add. 6958/14, 21 Sept., Camden to Pitt; Spencer, IV. 185-6; PRO 30/58/3, 21 Sept., Spencer to Pitt. [23] *Parl. Hist.* XXXV. 559-61.

Faced with these proofs of Bonaparte's intentions, Dundas implored Pitt to be firm. Unless the Cabinet could be forced to take a clear view of its war aims, strategic priorities would be blurred and pressing decisions put off. At present Pitt's colleagues were advocating half a dozen contradictory policies: no peace without a Bourbon restoration; no peace with an unstable French government; negotiations with the present *de facto* regime in France; negotiations only in conjunction with Austria; separate negotiations in which Britain would barter her conquests to secure her own interests. Dundas urged Pitt to force the Cabinet to decide between these options. 'It is earnestly hoped that Mr. Pitt will take these observations under his serious consideration before it is too late.'[24]

The appeal was ignored, and perhaps the questions were too divisive for Pitt to force on his colleagues. The strategic debate continued without a firm foundation of political aims, and on 23 September the Cabinet resolved to give priority to Portugal. Though it was agreed that a force should be brought to the Red Sea coast of Egypt from India, an attack from the Mediterranean was excluded by Spencer's assertion that shipping could not lie off the Egyptian coast in the winter; and Venice was also ruled out because the force would be out of reach in an emergency. Windham again took his own line, urging the recall of the army to England for his favourite strategy of supporting the French royalists. But against Windham, if on nothing else, the triumvirate were united. Pitt, Dundas and Grenville all told him that the time for the royalists had passed. It was an acrimonious meeting.[25]

The upshot was that 15,000 men of the force at Gibraltar were to go to Lisbon. To Grenville the massive aid to Portugal meant that there would be no force to help the Austrians; but honour and principle always weighed with him, and he accepted the obligation to a faithful ally. For King George the decision ruled out a Carribbean expedition, and he rejoiced:

---

[24] Versions with some differences in Stanhope, III. 242-3, and *E.H.D.*, XI. 110-11.
[25] Add. MSS 37924, f. 60; FO 7/60, 26 Sept., Grenville to Minto. For the previous history of the Red Sea expedition, see Ingram, *Commitment to Empire*, 99, 358, 379.

'the West Indies . . . has ever proved the obstruction (*sic*) of every corps sent there.' But Dundas saw that for the sake of a useless gesture to Portugal Egypt would become French.

Still, however, he persevered. Two years earlier, when he had failed to convince Grenville that Bonaparte's expedition was bound for Egypt, he had vowed never again to let his better judgement be swept aside. 'In future', he had written when he was proved right, 'if other Departments will not concur with me in such measures as I think necessary . . . I must be positive on the subject, and act by agents of my own.'[26] Now was the time to seek such agents; and while he waited for the right moment to renew the fight in the Cabinet, he pursued his researches into the problems of navigation raised by Spencer. Officers who had served east of Malta were consulted: Lord Hood, Captain George, Captain Troubridge. Advice was sought from the Levant trade. The log-books of warships which had served in the eastern Mediterranean were fetched from the archives and scanned. These sources disposed of two naval objections to the Egyptian expedition. The difficulty of an autumn passage from Gibraltar to Egypt had been exaggerated; so had the winter weather on the Egyptian coast.

But how to convince Lord Spencer? To do so Dundas had to tunnel beneath the bastions of the Admiralty, as he and Pitt had done in 1798 to obtain a fleet for the Mediterranean. The perfect agent for this was his Under-Secretary William Huskisson, who had long been a confidential friend of Evan Nepean, the Secretary of the Admiralty.[27] To Nepean Huskisson was sent, bearing Dundas's evidence, and a short conversation exposed the source of the First Lord's opinions. It was the very officer on the Board of Admiralty who had tried to block the reoccupation of the Mediterranean two and a half years earlier, Spencer's professional colleague Admiral William Young. If Young's advice had prevailed at that time Nelson would not have sailed for the Nile; if it prevailed now, the French would remain undisturbed in Egypt. Yet Young spoke from ignorance. He had never been further up the Mediterranean than Corsica and knew nothing of Egypt; and the only

[26] *GL* 2246; Add. MSS 38735, ff. 110–11, 27 Aug. 1798, Dundas to Huskisson.
[27] SRO, GD 51/1/769/1, 11 Sept. 1798, Huskisson to Dundas.

authority for his opinion seemed to be a forced construction of a single paragraph from Sir Sidney Smith.

But the civilian Spencer habitually deferred to his naval advisers: how was he to be detached from Admiral Young's advice on this occasion?[28] Nepean showed him Dundas's evidence, but it made no impression. Spencer simply replied that 'the fact did not signify, as the plan had been abandoned from other considerations'. Very well, Huskisson wrote to Dundas, so the expedition was not to take place in the healthy winter months and at a time when the enemy were believed to be weak in numbers and morale. But let the government at least be clear about its reason. 'If the expedition must be relinquished to enable Portugal to take care of itself, let it stand firmly upon that ground; but I would almost stake my life that there is no solid foundation for the objection to which you have now submitted.'[29]

Fortified by Huskisson's report, Dundas prepared for a fresh onslaught in the Cabinet. He managed to persuade Pitt that the Egyptian weather was not a problem, but was unable to move the First Lord. Though Spencer shared Dundas's concern for Egypt, he disputed the reassuring report on the Egyptian weather, and raised new objections. There were not enough troopships, he argued on 28 September; and it would be fatal to send off a weak and hastily prepared force at the wrong time of year and before the force from India could reach the Red Sea. Such an expedition 'will only expose us to disgrace and defeat', and strengthen the French claim to Egypt. He urged Dundas to await the outcome of the Portuguese crisis, and attack Egypt at a later date with maximum force.[30]

In spite of Spencer's immovable resistance, Dundas sensed that the tide was turning in the Cabinet. He had almost carried a majority with him at the last meeting, and since

[28] For Spencer and Young see *Strategy of Overthrow*, pp. 16-21.
[29] Nat. Library of Scotland, MS 3835, ff. 198-201, 26 Sept., Huskisson to Dundas; SRO, GD 51/1/774, 6 Oct. 1800, Dundas to Abercromby, and 29 Sept., Troubridge memo.; WO 6/21, p. 128; PRO 30/58/3, 19 Oct., Lord Hood to Pitt; Add. MSS 40102, f. 91.   [30] Spencer, IV. 126-31; *GL* 2252.

then Otto had made the French designs on Egypt explicit and garnished them with threats. He was prepared to compromise about Malta; but on Egypt there could be no accommodation. He read aloud part of a dispatch from Talleyrand, which emphasized the interest of France in the Army of Egypt and declared that its security was the main French reason for seeking a naval armistice. Their aim, said Otto, was to send 1,200 men and 10,000 muskets to Alexandria. If the British refused an armistice on these terms, Bonaparte would attack and crush the Austrians. Naples and Sicily would then be swiftly occupied, and from their ports France could supply Malta and Egypt freely.[31]

While Otto's threats were frightening the Cabinet into line with Dundas on Egypt, Grenville's determination to stand by Austria was shaken by an ignominious Austrian surrender. Bonaparte had again exploited the time-lag between London and Germany to play off the two allied powers, and while he was demanding maritime concessions from England as the price of prolonging the Austrian armistice, he was extorting other concessions from the Austrians for the same purpose. On 19 September General Moreau informed them that England had refused to treat for an armistice and that hostilities would therefore begin in Germany. This he said on instructions from Paris, though Grenville's counter-project had been received there nine days earlier and the talks in London were continuing. Fooled by Moreau's lie and terrified by the threat of a French attack, the Emperor bought an extension of the armistice by surrendering his three blockaded fortresses, whose revictualling Bonaparte nevertheless continued to use as a lever in the London negotiations.[32]

This convention was signed behind the back of William Wickham, the British representative with the Austrian army. In Vienna Lord Minto denounced it as disgraceful, and Thugut resigned the Foreign Ministry rather than be a party to it. In London the shock was severe, and even Grenville's loyalty to the Austrian alliance was shaken. It was Dundas's opportunity. On 30 September, the day after the news arrived in the French papers, the Cabinet met to discuss the question of the Irish

[31] *Parl. Hist.* XXXV. 567-79; *GL* 2252.
[32] FO 7/60, Minto's of 24 Sept.; Dropmore, VI. 334-5.

Catholics (a subject which was soon to drive fissures across the already divided Cabinet). Dundas seized the opportunity to reopen the subject of Egypt.[33]

Even now Dundas's battle was not over, and the discussion was acrimonious though he made some progress. It was agreed that the threat to Portugal had been exaggerated, and the reinforcement for Lisbon was pared to 10,000, leaving 12,000 with Abercromby. But still the Cabinet havered about his destination. It was agreed to send the force in the first instance to Minorca, and from there to order it eventually either to Egypt or to aid the Austrians in the Adriatic. This was indecisive enough; but a suggestion that if the Austrians made a separate peace the force should be recalled to the west was more than Dundas could swallow. He refused to be the agent to execute the plan and absented himself from the meeting on the following day, sending instead a letter to say that if the force was to be strangled by such a proviso it had better come home immediately. He asked Grenville to circulate the latest dispatches from the Levant, from which he maintained that Grenville had drawn the wrong conclusions; and he told Pitt that he would no longer bear the sole responsibility for keeping the expedition at Gibraltar, and was writing to exculpate himself with Abercromby. Never had Dundas seemed to be so alienated from his colleagues.[34]

Yet sensing as he did that the balance was tilting in his favour, Dundas's anger may have been calculated. If so, it seems to have succeeded. Two days later on 3 October, suddenly and without any explanation that has come down to us, the Cabinet changed its mind and agreed to send an army 15,000 strong to Egypt immediately. This meant paring Pulteney's force for Lisbon to 8,000 and borrowing a further 1,500 men for Abercromby from the Mediterranean

---

[33] Minto's report of the convention did not reach Grenville till 8 October; but reports in the French press of the surrender of the fortresses were copied in the English newspapers by 29 September and were unhesitatingly believed by Grenville (FO 7/60, Grenville's of 8 Oct.; Dropmore, VI. 334-5).

[34] Add. MSS 37924, ff. 64-5; *GL* 2256n; Add. MSS 40102, ff. 83-4. Dundas did indeed suffer blame for collecting the great force where it could not be supplied with water. 'But,' wrote the Duke of Richmond, 'I suppose Mr. Dundas drinks himself so little that he does not consider it as at all necessary for an army.' (Add. MSS 51802, 8 Feb. 1801, to Lord Holland.)

garrisons.[35] The decision was carried by a bare majority, with Grenville still fighting for more aid to Portugal, and Windham arguing that Abercromby's force should be brought home. It was Pitt who tilted the balance, firmly opposing Grenville's pressure to send more troops to Portugal and throwing his weight as chairman on the side of Dundas. By now he regarded the French presence in Egypt as the main obstacle to peace.[36] Lord Liverpool later regaled a friend with his version of what happened at the meeting. Pitt, he said, regarded the Egyptian expedition as a vital preliminary to the peace negotiations he desired. Seeing that there was opposition, he called out contrary to custom for the opinion of Lord Liverpool whom he knew to be in favour. The vote was nearly equal; but according to Liverpool Pitt counted in favour of the expedition three members who had not voted, and thus decided the question. Grenville and Windham angrily insisted on recording their dissent.[37]

Thus after months of hesitation and doubt the destination of Britain's striking force was settled. It was the final layer of the strategy which Dundas had been patiently constructing over the past six months, and he rejoiced a few days later when the armistice negotiations petered out in the wake of the Emperor's surrender of his fortresses. This virtually signalled the end of military aid to the Austrians and of Britain's involvement in the continental war. The King shared Dundas's relief, as he quaintly confided: 'the dear bought conquests in the East and West Indies may [be] given up for the ideal support of continental connections and, contrary to the watchword in the Seven Years War that America was conquered in Germany, that our conquests will be lost by our allies in Germany.'[38]

---

[35] It would be idle to apologize for the Cabinet's unsteady arithmetic. Part of the difficulty was perhaps the old confusion between 'effectives' and men present and fit of duty; or the separate counting of officers, sergeants and drummers; or the omission of artillery, which were administered by the Board of Ordnance.

[36] 'Peace on fit and honourable terms would not be found impracticable', he wrote to Addington on 29 September, '. . . were it not for the mention of Egypt' (quoted in Ingram, *Commitment to Empire*, 380).

[37] *GL* 2256; Add. MSS 37924, f. 66; Glenbervie, I. 159-60. The whole Cabinet except Westmorland were present. Glenbervie's record of Liverpool's story is uncorroborated; but in matters where corroboration is possible, Liverpool's reminiscences to Glenbervie are reliable.

[38] Dropmore, VI. 332; *Parl. Hist.* XXXV. 583-4; *GL* 2247; SRO, GD 51/1/774/19, Oct., Dundas to Abercromby.

Judged as policy the decision to send the expeditionary force to Egypt was correct. But as a military plan it has been bitterly criticized, for faulty intelligence and miscalculations of time and space.

4. *The Military Plan*

Liberated from the long suspense, Dundas plunged into the mass of correspondence which launched the expedition. The Red Sea plan to send a force from India, which had been in contemplation for the past two years, was at last put under way: a dispatch to Calcutta ordered Lord Wellesley to send a thousand European infantry and two thousand sepoys to Aden, to be joined there by a British battalion from the Cape. A courier set out overland to Constantinople to alert Lord Elgin and the British officers serving with the Turks. General Pulteney was ordered to take 8,000 men of the force at Gibraltar to Lisbon; but the Portuguese were warned that Britain would not be able to defend them against a strong French attack, and that the British troops were liable to be recalled if the British Isles were threatened. To his old friend and relation Abercromby, tossing on the seas in a warship somewhere in the mouth of the Mediterranean, Dundas sent his plans for the main force in an enormous bundle of dispatches and private letters which were remarkable for their candour. He explained his reasons for mounting the expedition. Though he was opposed to joining the Austrians in a general peace congress, he favoured opening separate negotiations with France as soon as possible. In such negotiations Britain's colonial gains would not compensate for the French possession of Egypt; for 'their first object is at any rate the preservation of Egypt, and they expect to find it a compensation for the loss of their colonial greatness in other quarters, and the means of creating a great revolution in the commercial and political world.'[39]

[39] WO 6/21, pp. 157-60; Add. MSS 38736, ff. 182-93; Add. MSS 37924, f. 68; Dunfermline, 245; SRO, GD 51/1/774/23. The Red Sea expedition from India had probably first been put forward by one of Dundas's Scots connections, Colonel Sir Thomas Maitland: see SRO, GD 51/1/768 and 770; Dropmore, IV. 413-14.

Dundas's plan, based on the advice of Captain Home Popham, was to assemble the expedition at some island in the eastern Mediterranean where it could collect intelligence, take on board fresh vegetables and cattle, and buy the horses which could not be shipped from England. When his force was ready, Abercromby was to sail for the coast of Egypt and seize a beach-head.[40]

There was a number of false assumptions in the planning. As so often happened with maritime expeditions, the calculations of time and space were wildly astray. Dundas hoped that Abercromby would reach the Egyptian coast in December, and the force from India in February; and that Egypt would then fall so rapidly that Abercromby could be back in Portugal by April or May.[41] These calculations ignored not only wind and weather but the state of Abercromby's transports. After months at sea, many of the ships needed repairs, and all needed water and fresh victuals before they could sail for the Levant.

More serious were the errors about the enemy. In the previous January enemy correspondence from Egypt had been intercepted which represented the French army as being reduced to 15,000 men, destitute of ammunition and military supplies, and so homesick that their commander would be unable to offer serious resistance. These papers had been thrown overboard from a polacre captured off Toulon, but had failed to sink. Their reliability was not questioned, though it should have been; for the French commander General Kléber had motives for painting the gloomiest picture of his situation. He was negotiating with the Turks to evacuate the country, and needed to justify his actions to the French government by exaggerating his troubles. Moreover Kléber's account was contradicted by a British observer. Sir Sidney Smith's secretary visited Cairo and concluded that the French army was at least 20,000 strong and in good order. Dundas, however, while accepting Kléber's dispatches at face value, threw doubt on his own witness, suggesting that he was trying to justify the Convention of El Arish by exaggerating the strength of the enemy. This was the very argument which

[40] SRO, GD 51/1/775; Dunfermline, 248; WO 6/21, p. 104 ff.
[41] Dropmore, VI. 361; WO 6/21, pp. 157-60.

should have been used to test the reliability of Kléber; but on the contrary Dundas argued that the difficulties which had induced Kléber to sign the Convention must still be operating; and all his Cabinet colleagues except Windham seemed to have agreed. The King even pushed his optimism to the point of believing that 5,000 British troops would be enough to eject 'the remains of the debilitated French army'. On such wild calculations Dundas framed his orders.[42] Abercromby's 15,000 men were to besiege and capture Alexandria, whose garrison Dundas put at only 3,000; and by now the other French troops in the country must be reduced to 10,000, which after deducting garrisons would not be enough to disrupt the siege. There was no doubt, Dundas assured Abercromby, of the enemy's 'extreme and almost unanimous wish to go home'.[43]

The error was grotesque. The French were more than twice the strength Dundas predicted, and 30,000 would eventually be repatriated. Nevertheless several favourable factors were to redress the balance. About the enemy's morale Dundas was not far wrong, and one defeat in battle would destroy their fighting spirit. Moreover the death of Kléber had given the command to an incompetent: Menou would make many mistakes and further undermine his army's unity. And the Turks, of whom Dundas advised Abercromby that 'much is not to be expected', proved to be capable of exerting considerable pressure on the enemy. Though Sir Sidney Smith described them as a 'multitude of barbarians within an inch of famine or insurrection', they were numerous and keen for plunder.[44] The French were deadly afraid of falling into Turkish hands; and when the tide of war turned against them, they preferred to treat with the British and go home rather than put themselves at the mercy of the Turks.

Thus the fortunes of war helped to redress Dundas's error. Yet a more substantial point must be made in his defence. Political aims had launched the expedition, and they governed its conduct. The British army was not being hurled against

---

[42] SRO, GD 51/1/768, 14 Jan. 1800, Huskisson to Dundas; GD 51/1/774/23; Add. MSS 37924, f. 64; *GL* 2252.   [43] WO 6/21, pp. 104 ff.

[44] SRO, GD 51/1/774/23; Spencer, IV. 93–4; Sidmouth Papers, 27 June 1800, Sir Sidney Smith to Lord Wellesley.

the enemy's centre of gravity in a decisive *Hauptschlacht*, but seeking limited advantages to improve a negotiating position. This could be done on several levels, and to strengthen the British negotiators' hand it was not essential that the French should evacuate the country. In sending Britain's only offensive force to the distant Levant, Dundas was launching what he called 'a limited plan of operations'. He advised Abercromby not to advance into the interior when he had occupied the ports. If all turned out for the best, the Alexandria garrison would surrender and be granted free passage home, and the rest of the French army might then yield to its homesickness in the Egyptian hinterland and accept repatriation. Even if this did not happen the diplomatic advantages of having a British army in the Levant would be great. Its mere presence in striking distance would enable the negotiators at a peace conference to claim that Britain was in a position to dispute the possession of Egypt. Better still, if Abercromby occupied the ports, Britain would have a clear right to consider Egypt as a divided possession, and the French would be entitled to no equivalent for evacuating the interior other than the British withdrawal from the coast. Thus 'every other advantage of the negotiation, as far as relates to sacrifices and restitutions, will be on our side.'[45]

The expedition was therefore no wild adventure, but a measured act of policy. And recognizing that conditions in the distant theatre of war could not be foreseen, he gave the commander absolute discretion to postpone the landing, and expressed complete confidence in his judgement. 'In your hands', he told his old friend, 'I feel the interests of the country safe. . . . No false point of honour or feeling will induce you to attempt what is too hazardous to be attempted.' Yet he knew that in pursuit of a great object Abercromby would 'not to be startled by those difficulties to which characters of less energy or less standing than your own may allow themselves to yield.'[46]

[45] Dumferline, 248-9.   [46] Dunfermline, 251.

CHAPTER VIII

The Undermining of Pitt

1. *Dundas's Burden*

A week had passed since the decision to invade Egypt. The expedition had been set in motion, and Dundas was free to return to Cheltenham and give the waters a longer trial, cheered on his journey by the news that Valletta had surrundered to the British reinforcements, and the long blockade was over. The Grand Harbour could be used by the Egyptian expedition, and some of the troops at Malta could be added to Abercromby's force.[1] Still better for the Egyptian operation was the news from Lisbon. The Spanish threat had receded, and the Portuguese government would be content with a smaller reinforcement. Pulteney's force was therefore cut to 5,000 men, giving Abercromby 3,000 more for Egypt. Dundas was so sanguine that he asked Abercromby not to take them to Egypt if he could do without them.[2]

Dundas needed all his optimism, for he was oppressed by the burden of pushing the Egyptian decision through the Cabinet. He had been 'uncommonly urgent in pressing these opinions'; and if the expedition failed 'the responsibility does and ought to rest upon me, as many doubts and objections have been stated against it by persons of great respectability'.[3] And what a responsibility! As Home Popham had warned him, the eyes of all Europe would be on the operations. The honour, martial reputation and feelings of the nation would be at stake. Success would give great weight to peace negotiations; 'but I dare not calculate the evil consequences of a reverse'.[4]

The history of amphibious expeditions was not reassuring; and on 22 October Dundas learned of yet another fiasco to add to the Helder, Belle Île and Ferrol. Abercromby and

---

[1] Add. MSS 37924, f. 67; Add. MSS 40101, f. 84; WO 6/21, pp. 131-4.
[2] FO 63/33, Arbuthnot's of 30 Sept. 1800; Add. MSS 40101, f. 86; WO 6/21, pp. 134-6.   [3] Dunfermline, 249-50.
[4] SRO, GD 51/1/775, 19 Sept., note by Popham.

Lord Keith had failed at Cadiz. They had formed up the fleet and transports, summoned the Governor, embarked the first wave of troops in boats — and had called off the assault and sailed away.

The commanders offered conflicting explanations: yellow fever in the city, and uncertainty about the weather. In either case consultation between the two services had evidently broken down. 'What a disgraceful and what an expensive campaign we have made,' exclaimed Lord Cornwallis. 'Twenty-two thousand men . . . floating round the greater part of Europe, the scorn and laughing-stock of friends and foes.' With peace negotiations in the air and the northern powers threatening war, the farce at Cadiz would be immensely damaging to Britain's reputation. 'How mortifying', Lord Carysfort lamented at the hostile Prussian court.[5]

Indeed as the old century expired the British army's reputation touched bottom. Its successes in the American War had been obscured by the loss of the United States; and at the beginning of the French Revolutionary Wars its half-trained battalions had been swept away in the Austrian débâcle in the Netherlands. In Holland in 1799 skeleton regiments filled at the last moment with militiamen had been measured against the well commanded and experienced French. And the present year had been sullied by a succession of flops along the coast of Europe. Was the army even fit to keep order at home? 'Our army', Lord Buckingham sneered to his brother the Foreign Secretary, 'is as little applicable to our civil, as they are to our military purposes.'[6]

The jibe needs to be qualified. The army was on an upward road, with a sound drill book and a conscientious Commander-in-Chief. It had excellent new men from the militia, and experiments with light infantry and riflemen were bearing fruit. Nevertheless it was not yet ready for war. Lord St. Vincent had judged that Maitland's troops at Belle Île were 'not up to a difficult enterprise'. 'Unfortunately', he added, 'the whole infantry of the country is in the same state and totally unfit for a service of hardy enterprise.' Senior generals agreed, but had a clearer notion of what was wrong. The

[5] Cornwallis, III. 300; Dropmore, VI. 382.   [6] Dropmore, VI. 265.

regiments had needed a settled period of summer training, but had been hustled on board crowded transports to float round the coasts of Europe. 'The troops are none of them fit for actual service at present', Cornwallis had warned in the spring, 'although in a few months with proper care and training they might become excellent.' The Duke of York said virtually the same to the Cabinet. Cornwallis continued to lament the premature use of these troops, raised by extra-ordinary efforts but 'by no means at present fit for service'. He accused the ministers of treating the reconstructed army 'as a child is to pull to pieces a new plaything'. We should not go lightly in quest of adventures, he warned Dundas in September on the eve of the Egyptian expedition, with regiments still in an unformed state and commanded by un-trained and inexperienced officers. Cornwallis was eager for peace; and he did not believe that the army in its present state was capable of improving the terms.[7]

It was in the face of these warnings that Dundas sent Abercromby's force to Egypt to meet the veterans of Bonaparte's Army of Italy. He coula. count on Abercromby to make the best of his resources, for no general in the army was more capable of collecting good brigadiers and training his troops; and he would have some seasoned regiments from the Mediterranean garrisons to leaven the troops from England. Nevertheless Dundas must have known the risk of measuring these troops against Bonaparte's, homesick though the French might be. Nor were his spirits sustained by his colleagues. Windham had told him in the heat of the Egyptian discussions that he had lost one army in a contest with yellow fever, and was now sending off another to fight the plague. Dundas's anger with his fellow-ministers rang through his letters to Abercromby. He had seen the country's military resources squandered and neutralized to support 'the tottering fortunes of Austria' and 'the desperate speculations broached by the Royalists'. He had been 'decidedly adverse to the whole principle' of a naval armistice. The Egyptian expedition had been delayed by 'differences of opinion between me and one or two members of His Majesty's Government'. On his holiday

[7] Spencer, III. 346, 361; Cornwallis, III. 218; *GL* 2112, 2113 (the Duke of York's views, for which see p. 78 above).

in Cheltenham he snarled back at Windham: 'Six weeks of
the best time of the year were lost in Cabinet deliberations,
which I submit to, as I suppose it is a necessary evil, but it
tells always heavily against the person who holds the pen on
such occasions.'[8]

Windham too was angry, and not only with Dundas. He
had protested bitterly to Pitt at being kept in ignorance about
the Belle Île plan, for in spite of his special responsibility for
the royalists he had not been informed when Georges Cadoudal
was sent out to join Maitland. This was not the only occasion
when he had been kept in the dark about military operations
of which he claimed a right to be informed. His failure to
prevent the Egyptian expedition provoked him to recite old
grievances and to thrust at Dundas and Grenville. Those who
distrusted Frenchmen and would not believe in a French
insurrection, he complained to Spencer, had nevertheless
relied totally on Dutchmen to raise an insurrection in Holland;
and now they were transporting their faith in local insurgents
to the Levant: 'We now take it for granted, that we are to
have the co-operation and friendship of all the inhabitants of
Egypt.' While Dundas grumbled about his colleagues to
General Abercromby, Windham was complaining of Dundas's
uninformed optimism to Admiral Blankett in the Red Sea.
'Those who are full of confidence . . . know very little of what
they are talking about, and calculate much more upon the
sanguineness of their own wishes than upon any knowledge
or information.'[9]

The underlying cause of Windham's anger was the rejection
of his own view of the aims and strategy of the war. This
'apostle of Burke'[10] had always been a determined opponent
of a compromise with revolutionary France, towards which
he could see that Pitt was drifting: two years earlier he had
privately damned Pitt for his 'low, mean and narrow views'
of the struggle. 'I still hold that we are never completely
ruined but by a peace', he now told Admiral Blankett; and
from this conviction stemmed his strategic views. Instead of

[8] Add. MSS 37924, f. 64; SRO, GD 51/1/774/19 and -/23; Add. MSS 37879,
29 Oct., Dundas to Windham.
[9] PRO 30/58/3, 5 June, Windham to Pitt; Spencer, IV. 131-2; Add. MSS 3
37880, f. 1.   [10] Glenbervie, I. 114, 122.

looking for colonial bargains the government should bring the army home, ready to seize a fresh opportunity to aid the royalists on the coast of France. 'If that course had been pursued, we should long since have seen the legitimate monarchy restored in a part at least of France. . . . Upon the other system . . . the utmost we have to hope is, the difference of a few possessions one way or the other, in a peace that is to leave the French masters of Europe.' It was a fair description of the future Peace of Amiens. His royalist philosophy rejected the imperial priorities which Dundas had been imposing on the Cabinet over the past six months, for even Marengo and the surrender of the German fortresses did not shake his faith in continental operations: 'All blows not aimed at the body of France are thrown away.'[11]

Dundas might shrug off the criticisms of the capricious and lightweight Windham; but the King was another matter. Dundas and George III had recently found common ground in their objections to joining the feeble Austrian government in peace negotiations; but the Egyptian decision thrust them violently apart again. The King consented to the expedition with strongly expressed reluctance; and he told Dundas that the dissent of Grenville and Windham did not surprise him, for Egypt 'would prove a burial ground to as great an extent as St. Domingo'. This was an unkind thrust at Dundas, the architect of the costly West Indian expeditions; but in Egypt the King feared famine rather than disease. He was harking back to the American War and the immense difficulty of supplying the army beyond the Atlantic. To this Dundas answered that Abercromby would be able to draw on the fertile Ottoman lands in Syria and the islands of the Levant; nevertheless he expressed his 'very severe regret' at the royal disapproval, which he concealed from his colleagues. The King never mentioned the expedition to him again till news of victory came eight months later; and long afterwards

[11] Add. MSS 37880, ff. 2-3; Nat. Library of Scotland, MS 11140, f. 178, 11 July, Windham to Minto ('how foolishly we have managed all our operations on the coast of France'). The violence of Windham's private feelings about his Prime Minister were expressed in a letter of 20 April 1798 to Lady Anne Barnard: 'No distinction of right or wrong, nor to consider anything otherwise than as it affected his own situation, confining even that to the mere possession of personal power' (Rylands Library, Mems. of Lady Anne Barnard V. 31).

Dundas told a friend that the royal letter of displeasure had weighed on his mind beyond anything he had ever experienced. In spite of support from the Duke of York, Dundas went into the winter oppressed by a load of responsibility which none of his colleagues wished to share. His firmest support in launching the expedition had come from Pitt, and Pitt was now a broken reed.[12]

2. *Pitt and the King*

If the sanguine Dundas was so dejected by the royal displeasure, it could crush the oppressed spirits of Pitt. Since the early spring his health had not been good, and the three months since the battle of Marengo had been passed in continual stress. Canning had reported the confusion which flowed from the disaster in the unpleasant jeering tone which he often used about his protector. 'What do you think of the Italian news?' he asked his idle Foreign Office friend Hookham Frere as the bad tidings accumulated. 'And what consolation does Pitt point out after looking at the map in the corner of his room by the door? Does he make out that Bonaparte is in a scrape? that old Melas has not lost his head? — or will recover it? — and that Moreau is advancing no faster than Kray chuses to let him?'[13]

The time had not yet come for Pitt to roll up the map, but kinder friends than Canning pitied his disappointment. 'Mr. Pitt bears it with fortitude', George Rose reported to the Bishop of Lincoln; 'my feelings for him personally weigh me down.' The weeks that followed saw Pitt wrestling with the disputes over peace negotiations and the King's resistance to the Ferrol expedition. Both questions brought him into collision with his sovereign, and it upset him. 'He is not well', Rose reported. 'I have had a long conversation with Sir Walter [Farquhar] about him, and he agrees with me his illness arises more from his mind than anything else.'[14]

[12] *GL* 2256, 2261; Glenbervie, I. 233; SRO, GD 51/1/779, 5 Oct., Duke of York to Dundas; Pratt MSS, [29 Oct. 1801], Dundas to Camden.

[13] Add. MSS 38833, f. 2.

[14] Wellesley *Papers*, I. 129; Pretyman MSS, 25 and 30 July 1800, Rose to Tomline.

George III had been resentful of his ministers' actions on a number of occasions since the early summer. He had criticized Dundas's military administration: the dispatch of expeditions inadequately trained and equipped, the sudden diversion of Maitland's force from the Bay of Biscay to the Mediterranean, the hasty operation against Ferrol. He had protested against the decision to negotiate jointly with Austria in July, and the vacillation over a naval armistice in September; for, in his view, both these proceedings wavered from the true purpose of the war, and reflected Grenville's determination to cleave to the 'broken reed' of Austria. And he had opposed the Egyptian expedition. After the Ferrol trouble Pitt had growled that the time might come to beg the King to 'find servants whose judgments he can trust more than ours'. And indeed the King had put out feelers for an alternative ministry.

Yet the King's impatience with his ministers was not solely due to their policies. With some of their individual views he was in sympathy. If he disliked Grenville's loyalty to Austria, they were not far apart about the purpose of the war, 'to save Europe and Society itself'.[15] Dundas's military arrangements might not be impeccable, but he was sound in his distrust of the Austrian alliance. Underlying the differences on policy, however, was the King's accumulating resentment against the manners of the ministers who had held office for so long. The military 'job' Dundas had tried to fix behind the King's back for Lord Granville Leveson still rankled;[16] so too no doubt did the attempt to spring the Ferrol expedition on him, and the constitutional rebuke Dundas had seen fit to send him on the subject. Grenville's peremptory manners had also alienated the King. As for Pitt, rumours were widespread that he had offended by his neglect of customary form. Even his colleagues were shocked by his slighting of the King and his neglect to explain business to him. Lord Camden recorded 'unwillingly' that the Prime Minister had often spent six weeks in London without coming to Court. Camden ascribed this behaviour to Pitt's poor health and exhaustion, but 'a long train of this conduct certainly in a degree estranged the King from him and induced him to think of him personally with less interest'.

[15] Taylor *Papers*, 49.   [16] Above, pp. 16–17; Glenbervie, I. 181, 202.

There had been a time when the King would have put up with Pitt's lack of respect because he was the only barrier against Charles Fox, but this was no longer so. The power of Fox had been destroyed by the Portland group's coalition with Pitt in 1794 and Fox's subsequent secession from the House of Commons. From the ministerial ranks the King could now find an alternative Prime Minister; and he would soon have cause to do so, for the Catholic question was about to explode.[17]

At the moment when Pitt was being battered by the Cabinet storms over the naval armistice and Egypt, the first gusts of a new hurricane stirred the waters. The Cabinet of 30 September, at which Dundas seized the opportunity to force an acrimonious discussion of Egypt, had been called to consider Ireland. The issue was the so-called 'emancipation' of the Catholics, their relief from the political disabilities which they and the Protestant dissenters had suffered throughout the British Isles since the seventeenth century. Pitt proposed to repeal the religious tests required of office-holders, and replace them with a civil oath of allegiance. It was the price he owed the Irish Catholics for the union with Ireland.

In the autumn of the previous year it had become apparent that Pitt's plan to achieve the union on the basis of the Protestant ascendancy was foundering, and the Irish Secretary Lord Castlereagh had come over from Dublin to communicate Cornwallis's advice as Lord-Lieutenant that the Irish Catholics must be reassured. They were not necessarily inimical to the union, believing that an imperial Parliament at Westminster might be more inclined to relieve them of their civil disabilities than the bigoted legislature in Dublin. The Cabinet discussed the question in Castlereagh's presence, and though some members were doubtful about admitting Catholics to all the higher offices, and anticipated hostility from the King and in certain Protestant quarters, no one dissented from the principle. 'As far as the Cabinet was concerned', Castlereagh was assured, 'his Excellency need not hesitate in calling forth the Catholic support.'[18]

---

[17] Glenbervie, I. 181, 415; Malmesbury, IV. 33; Willis, 255-6.

[18] Castlereagh, IV. 8-11. On the nature of the obligation to the Catholics, see

Armed with this assurance Cornwallis solicited Catholic support for the union, though he claimed that he avoided explicit promises of relief. Yet from the beginning Pitt had recognized the difficulties of honouring the pledge, and characteristically avoided facing the problem: no minute of the Cabinet meeting was taken, and the King was not informed. George III indeed would be the main obstacle. He had always held that to remove the religious tests would violate his coronation oath to preserve the Church of England, in spite of contrary advice given in 1795 by the Lord Chief Justice and the Attorney-General. He continued to assert that Catholic relief was 'beyond the decision of any Cabinet of Ministers', and when Dundas reminded him of the distinction between the Crown's executive and legislative capacities, he dismissed the argument with the retort, 'None of your Scotch metaphysics, Mr. Dundas!'

Absurd though the King's position may have been, the force of religious fears on an unstable mind was dangerous; and Pitt's determination to overcome his resistance was doubtful. Concealing the Cabinet's discussion, he felt free to assure anti-Papist peers that they could vote for the union 'with a perfectly safe conscience'. Of this Cornwallis and Castlereagh were unaware, but they observed with some bitterness that the ministers were trying to slip out of other obligations which the Lord-Lieutenant believed he had been authorized to incur. Asked by Cornwallis to approve the creation of new peerages, Pitt had resorted to his favourite evasion by leaving a vital letter unanswered, thus allowing the Lord-Lieutenant to infer assent which had not been given; and in due course the Duke of Portland followed this with a rude and open disavowal for which Lord Camden had to persuade him to apologize.[19]

Pitt's inability to be explicit was therefore much in Castlereagh's mind when he arrived in London in September to tidy up some of the consequences of the union. He firmly reminded

the letter to Castlereagh from his private secretary Alexander Knox, the theologian (ibid., 32).

[19] Holland, *Memoirs of the Whig Party*, I. 162–3; Castlereagh, III. 326–8, 330–3, 337, 343, 350. Grenville referred in a political memoir to Pitt's 'fondness in every difficulty for complicated expedients' (Ehrman, 202).

the Cabinet of the Catholic question, and explained Cornwallis's anxiety that the measure should be proposed by government and not by the opposition. But with the union safely achieved the Cabinet changed its tune. At the meeting on 30 September there was still general sympathy for tithe relief and a state salary for the Irish clergy (an arrangement which had worked well in Canada for the past twenty-five years). But Lord Chancellor Loughborough now declared himself the adamant opponent of political relief, though he had voiced no dissent in the previous autumn. Westmorland, a former Lord-Lieutenant of Ireland, was an old opponent of concession; Lord Liverpool supported him; and Portland and Camden were wavering. Pitt, presiding over what was now revealed as a divided Cabinet, was favourable in principle but pessimistic about the difficulties ahead. Everyone saw that there would be trouble from the Church and probably the Law; the King was absent at Weymouth; other interests ought to be sounded before a final decision was taken. . . . The meeting trailed off without a decision.[20]

There was still time in hand, however, before the first meeting of the Union Parliament in January 1801; and Castlereagh returned to Dublin supposing that the next four months would be used to prepare the gound for a Catholic Relief Bill. The matter was too delicate to be broached to the King for the first time in a letter, and Pitt undertook to speak to him as soon as he returned from Weymouth. He also promised to sound important people who might be difficult.[21] That the King would be awkward there was no doubt, and if he knew that the Cabinet was divided he would be immovable. He had to be approached quickly, and his mind prepared before the Lord Chancellor and his allies could foment his prejudices. But Pitt was in a quandary. There were other matters to clear up; and in particular he had to explore the question further in the Cabinet to see whether its members could be sufficiently united to overcome the King by firmness. If they were not, he must determine whether to press ahead, or stop short of political emancipation and tackle the less contentious questions of tithes and clerical stipends. He

---

[20] Add. MSS 37924, f. 65; Ashbourne, 304; Castlereagh, IV. 11; Glenbervie, I. 257-8; Willis, 248-50.   [21] Willis, 250.

also had to decide what constitutional safeguards to incorporate in a bill; and consider whether the measure could pass the House of Lords, where the Protestant vote would be reinforced by four Irish bishops and twenty-eight Irish representative peers.

Faced with this programme of action, Pitt did nothing. He neither took the matter further in the Cabinet, nor spoke to the King. Lord Camden attributed his 'culpable neglect' to inform the King to his knowledge that the Cabinet was not united.[22] No doubt this and other difficulties were discouraging; but his procrastination was storing up more trouble. His delay has been attributed to his pragmatic temper, or his balanced sense of priorities, or his political tact. But the abrupt manner in which he was eventually to attack the question suggests a different explanation. His dilatoriness reflected a state of mind which could not cope with further stress: a paralysis of the will.

3. *The Isolation of Pitt*

The end of September 1800 was Pitt's crossroads, the intersection of all the pressures which were bearing down on him. He was at odds with Dundas and Grenville over the naval armistice; with Grenville, Windham and Spencer over the Egyptian expedition; and with the King over both, while a more furious collision was approaching over the Catholic question. There had never, the Speaker Addington was to declare, been a more divided ministry. And the irritation of Pitt's mind under all these stresses was beginning to show. When Lord Liverpool, on the collapse of the armistice negotiation, declared that he had always been against it, Pitt snapped angrily, 'And I was decidedly for it.'[23]

And now a different crisis was bubbling which Pitt told Addington he regarded as more formidable even than the question of peace or war. By the middle of September there had been widespread riots in the midland towns and Bristol against the high price of bread; and while cavalry moved

<hr />

[22] Willis, 251.   [23] Glenbervie, I. 160, 277-9.

towards the provincial trouble centres, the capital itself was seething. Placards called out crowds to demonstrate against a rise in the regulated price of the loaf, and an appeal from the Lord Mayor brought the Home Secretary hastily back from the court at Weymouth. Fortunately the Volunteers were capable of standing up to the mob if not to the French, and the crowds in Soho and Westminster were contained; but a petition from the Corporation of London for the early recall of Parliament blighted Pitt's hopes for a restful autumn. George Rose persuaded him to agree, for even if no significant measures resulted, a parliamentary discussion of the corn crisis might reassure the public. 'These are uncomfortable speculations', Pitt lamented, 'and I am not the better for brooding over them during the confinement and anxiety of some weeks past.'[24]

Pitt was now a constant anxiety to his friends. Dundas warned the King that the Prime Minister was not fit to carry on through the winter with any energy unless his health improved; and he told Grenville that he was returning to Cheltenham only to lure Pitt there in collusion with their physician Sir Walter Farquhar, in the hope of enticing him to travel the further forty miles to the best of all health resorts at Bath.[25]

Farquhar was now constantly in and out of Pitt's house, wondering how to make his patient fit for the early session of Parliament. He and Rose continued to insist that Pitt's illness was caused by the state of his mind; and this belief was strengthened by Rose's discovery that Pitt was in deep financial trouble. On 18 October he was shown a list of debts and distresses which 'actually sickened me'. Pitt was threatened with the bailiffs for a debt of £60, and unpleasant publicity was likely for a further £400. The country house at Holwood must go, said Rose. 'Palliatives will not do . . . Mr. Pitt must go to the root of the evil.'[26]

There were reasons enough for an anxious mind; but could

[24] Stevenson, *Popular Disturbances*, 177-8; *GL* 2243, 2245, 2254; Rose *Diaries*, I. 281-2; Stanhope, III. 244-6. For the government's response to radicalism in London, see also J. A. Hone, *For the Cause of Truth*, 92-9, 116-17.
[25] *GL* 2264; Dropmore, VI. 34.
[26] Pretyman MSS, 30 July and 18 Oct. 1800, Rose to Tomline.

anxiety alone account for Pitt's illness? He was suffering from loss of appetite and vomiting, 'and is a good deal shook; he cannot carry a glass of beer to his mouth without the aid of his second hand'.[27] Nerves, perhaps? But Pitt had a long history of medical disorders, ever since a severe illness at the age of fourteen had interrupted his Cambridge studies for a year. Throughout his life he suffered from attacks of upper abdominal vomiting; and loss of weight and emaciation attacked him in the mid-twenties when he was Prime Minister. These symptoms, it has been suggested, indicated a recurring upper gastro-intestinal lesion, and he was also afflicted with episodes of painful arthritis and gout.[28] His was not a physique to support prolonged stress.

What treatment could he be persuaded to follow in the short interval before the recall of Parliament? He refused to go to Bath or Cheltenham, with the unanswerable objection that wherever he might go he could not leave his anxiety behind him. Eventually he was persuaded to spend a fortnight with the Addingtons at Woodley, their country house near Reading, where Farquhar visited him, rationed his drink, and decided he should remain there rather than go to Cheltenham. 'He wants rest and consolation', said Addington, 'and I trust he will find both here.' With fresh air, regular exercise and less wine Pitt soon felt better, no doubt helped by Rose's arrangements to avert immediate financial disaster. He left Woodley on 5 November to meet the House of Commons, feeling much the better for his holidays; 'but I doubt whether they have been sufficient to enable me to face the session, and I am not comfortable at its approaching so near.'[29]

Dundas returned from Cheltenham and was not reassured by the Prime Minister's condition. He told Lord Glenbervie that Pitt's mind had matured too early and was wearing out, and the conversation left Glenbervie with the impression that Pitt had suffered a breakdown or was on the verge of one. Stories were in the air that he was actually mad, whatever that might mean, though Rose denied the rumours,

[27] Ibid., 10 Oct., Rose to Thomline.
[28] R. Guest Gornall in *The Practitioner*, 179 (1957), 607–12.
[29] Stanhope, III. 246; Pretyman MSS, 20 Oct., Rose to Tomline, and 2 Nov., Pitt to Tomline; Dropmore, VI. 358; Farington *Diary*, I. 293.

maintaining that there was nothing wrong with Pitt but depression of spirits, the effect of overwork on a frail physique. Glenbervie, however, was later told by Farquhar that Pitt would not go to read the King's Speech to the Cabinet at Lord Grenville's before the opening of Parliament, and had said he thought he could not bring himself to face the House of Commons.[30]

Pitt's condition recalls the later years of Lord North's ministry. Towards the end of the American War North had shown increasing symptoms of a breakdown of will and nerve, a growing reluctance to grasp nettles and take decisions. Pitt had this in common with North, that each had taken office in peacetime, when low-key qualities were required: a capacity for compromise, the art of dropping a timely word here and there, a grasp of financial detail. Each had to hold together a conglomerate ministry which was not united by legislative goals or party discipline. Their role did not call for the kind of leadership required in war, nor test them under great stresses. Pitt was indeed a man of some courage and moral stature, with a considerable list of legislative and administrative achievements to his credit; yet like the political managers who had preceded him — like North and Newcastle — he was no war leader. As he confessed himself, 'I distrust extremely any ideas of my own on military subjects';[31] a disclaimer warmly endorsed by some well placed observers. Like his predecessors, he relied on his Secretaries of State to give positive direction to the war. But unlike Newcastle and North he chose, not one powerful colleague to direct the war, but two.

And Dundas and Grenville could scarcely have been a more disparate team. In temperament as in policy they were poles apart. I have speculated above[32] about whether Pitt had created this dichotomy deliberately to give himself the casting vote and the final power of decision, or whether it reflected his bent for expediency, compromise and drift: an inability

[30] Glenbervie, I. 167, 174-5, 180; Rose *Diaries*, I. 212-14 (the extract from his daughter's diary is evidently misdated 1800 for 1801). The perspicacious Keith Feiling (221) regarded Pitt as being 'on the verge of a bad nervous breakdown'.   [31] See *Strategy of Overthrow*, 5.

[32] Above, p. 39.

to make up his mind who to back, an incapacity to impose decisive leadership in matters of war and national policy. However this may be (and I incline to the second explanation), the past year had seen the differences between Dundas and Grenville polarized into two radically different views of the nation's ends and means. And paradoxically, Pitt could now rely on neither of them for the support he desperately needed.

For if Pitt felt unable to face the House of Commons, he was certainly in no condition to carry his disunited Cabinet into peace negotiations. How soon negotiations would begin depended on Austria. If she fell out of the war and a joint negotiation ceased to be feasible, separate British negotiations would have to wait till the Egyptian campaign and the northern crisis were settled. Nevertheless peace could not be postponed for long; and when the time came Pitt would not be fit to contend with the bellicose convictions of his Foreign Secretary. If Lord Grenville had promised the Austrians a joint negotiation, he had done so only to preserve the war-alliance and reassure British opinion, and not because he believed peace to be necessary. As late as 2 December, in a darkening situation, he still saw no reason to seek peace or even to conciliate the menacing Prussians. 'Our means are ample', he assured his brother-in-law Lord Carysfort; 'the country is in good heart; the distress for provisions is the only real difficulty with which we have to contend.'[33]

How was Pitt to convert this dedicated seeker of victory to his own belief that peace without victory would soon be forced on them? Grenville's temperament made it improbable that Pitt would succeed. Like many self-contained men Grenville lavished on animals the warmth he withheld from humans. He would go out of his way to speak to an old cart-horse at Dropmore, but he could not handle people. Subordinates disliked him, complaining of his jealousy, arrogance, and what Canning called his 'disagreeableness'. A Cabinet colleague described him as not ill-tempered, but 'in his outward manner offensive to the last degree'; and a distinguished diplomat called him 'the most close character possible — never relieved his mind by trusting *any one*'. His lack of human

[33] Dropmore, VI. 400.

warmth was reflected in the rigid principles which guided his diplomacy, unsoftened by sympathy for the private feelings of foreign sovereigns and statesmen. 'Lord Grenville', wrote Huskisson, 'is the last man in the world to allow them a due weight.' As Grenville himself confessed, 'I am not competent to the management of men.'[34]

Argument could not shift this unapproachable man from his convictions; and knowing his inflexibility, Addington a year later refused him an interview to discuss the peace terms. 'He is very honest in morals', he said, 'but in argument the most unfair that can be imagined, and never to be shaken.' This unbending obstinacy must be what Cornwallis meant when he described him, from observation in the Cabinet, as 'a most dangerous minister'. The King regarded his obstinacy as a family trait. Grenville, he said, took up his opinions entirely from himself, and would listen to no argument against them; yet some months later he might, after reflection, change his views, and would then be angry with those he had forced into his opinion if they would not change back with him.[35]

This deafness to argument undermined, the usefulness of his clever mind. With all his industry, said old Lord Liverpool, he could never see a question in all its bearings; 'and consequently his judgment can never be right'. Lurking among the Chiltern beechwoods at Dropmore, this blinkered mind was steered by the tramlines of principle. 'He acts always on what is right in the abstract', said Lord Malmesbury.[36]

Pitt was singularly ill-fitted to cope with this rigid opponent of compromise and pragmatism. He was a master of conciliation and persuasion; but his relations with his cousin were peculiar. 'Pitt gives way to him in a manner very extraordinary', a Foreign Office subordinate had remarked some years earlier; and Lord Malmesbury had complained during the peace negotiations of 1797 of Pitt's 'weakness in regard to Lord Grenville'. These observations were echoed in Dundas's

[34] Burges, 172, 319-20; Gower, I. 257; Auckland, IV. 308; Malmesbury, IV. 44-5; Stanhope, I. 415; *Strategy of Overthrow*, 6-7.

[35] Glenbervie, I. 149-50, 269; Cornwallis, III. 270 (Cornwallis was writing after the news of Marengo, which in his view made peace a necessity).

[36] Auckland, IV. 308; Glenbervie, I. 176.

lament after the fall of the ministry at Pitt's 'facility of disposition' in the face of Grenville's importunity.[37]

The cousins were diverging now on many things. Pitt had to restrain Grenville's desire to push the Danish crisis to the point of war; and even about the grain shortage their views were dividing. They had been reared together in the free trade principles of Adam Smith; but while the pragmatic Pitt was prepared to meet the grain crisis with interventionist legislation, his cousin adhered to the most rigid principles of *laissez-faire*.[38]

It was one thing to differ, however; but to break with a lifetime's influence was another matter, and Pitt's temperament was not fitted to cope with such a collision. A shy man, he took refuge from difficult decisions and personal clashes in paper work, committees and political talk. At home his desks and tables were cluttered with neglected papers; and by immersing himself in details which he ought to have devolved on subordinates, he kept disagreeable problems at arm's length.[39] To restore harmony after a dispute was agony to him, and he therefore shrank from confrontations. The Duke of Richmond once lamented 'the shyness of your disposition, which when there has been any little rub knows not how to bring matters to rights again'.[40]

Grenville's rigidity and Pitt's shyness could be a disastrous combination. Pitt would not be able to talk Grenville into proposing peace terms which there was any hope of the French accepting; yet it was psychologically hard for him to break with his cousin and friend. He should have found a crutch in Dundas, that 'strong-minded, warm-hearted, friendly man' and 'unshaking undaunted rock of support'. Dundas had been the well of firmness and decision on which the flexible Pitt had drawn; the older man to whom he had even

[37] Burges, 172; Adams, *Influence of Grenville*, 65; Ehrman, 132-3; above, p. 39.

[38] Windham *Diary*, 430; Dropmore, VI. 288; Stanhope, III. 247-9.

[39] Dropmore, VI. 259; Glenbervie, I. 128, 149; Lovat-Fraser, 26-7; Harlow, II. 247-51.

[40] *GL* 1764n. I have lost the source of Richmond's remark; but see also Ehrman, 109-10, 584-7, the latter passage a strikingly perceptive analysis of Pitt's relationships.

perhaps looked for a father-figure.[41] But Dundas had lost confidence in Pitt over the armistice negotiations. Nor was he the rock of strength he had once been. This courageous man felt old, tired and unwell. Three times in the past year his attempts to shed the Secretaryship of State had been blocked by Pitt and the King, and he had struggled on in spite of his wife's tears and his physician's warnings. He bore blame which he thought was undeserved for the failures of the Second Coalition: the Helder campaign, the Belle Île farce, the fiascos at Ferrol and Cadiz. His Cabinet battles over the naval armistice and the Egyptian expedition had drained his energy and disrupted his sleep. Ahead he faced an endless 'choice of difficulties'; parliamentary inquiries into the military failures; and the perils of Abercromby's expedition. He was a man for whom resignation might come as a relief. Even if their views had been in complete accord, he was no longer capable of propping the faltering Pitt.

4. *The Stress Accumulates*

If peace negotiations became inevitable — and Pitt saw them now as a matter of timing rather than principle — he would be encumbered with two colleagues, his closest and most influential political friends, who for different reasons would want to continue the war: Grenville for outright victory, and Dundas probably to retain colonial conquests which Pitt was willing to barter. Pitt's predicament in face of the King would then be not unlike Lord North's nineteen years earlier when the capitulation of Yorktown convinced him that he must make peace. North's closest colleagues had wanted to fight on, and to make peace he would have to drop them and reconstruct his ministry. But this the King had blocked. He would not hear of peace, and therefore would not accept a team of appeasers. Trapped by the King and deprived of all room for manœuvre, Lord North had seen only one escape from the predicament which was dragging him towards defeat in Parliament: his sudden resignation.

[41] Rylands Library, Memoirs of Lady Anne Barnard, IV. 161 ('a young man who looked up to him, for whom he had all the fondness of a father'), and VI. 5-6.

So it would be with Pitt when the moment for peace arrived. Without the King's support he could not break with his closest colleagues; and after seventeen years as Prime Minister he could not count on the support of the throne. Moreover to trample on the will of the aged and fragile head of the nation and 'common father of his people'[42] by imposing a peace on him would seem like a dereliction of duty.

As the meeting of Parliament approached, the famine grew sharper. In the poorer London parishes people were starving to death in October, while aristocratic households made small attempts to ration flour at their tables. At Oxford the undergraduates of Christ Church were reduced to tuppence-worth of bread for breakfast ('I could eat at least eight of these pieces', young Lord Ebrington lamented). Serious public men were corresponding about mixing barley with wheat in the flour, or using whole wheat as in Westphalia (too 'opening' for sedentary people, was the verdict). Lord Grenville exchanged solemn letters with the King about how to cook rice for the poor (Lady Grenville thought it better to put it in cold water rather than hot).[43]

But behind this well-meaning concern was the grim fact that wheat, which had averaged 50 shillings a quarter in 1798, was now 106 shillings; by the following April it would be over 150 shillings. Gold was flowing out of the country, for foreign corn as well as subsidies. The puzzle was to find the real cause of the dearth. Was it a genuine famine due to two poor harvests, or an artificial inflation caused by hoarding and illegal combinations? Though Arthur Young's correspondents reported an enormous shortfall, some accounts of the harvest were rather favourable. In north Oxfordshire Warren Hastings reported it to have been the most 'exuberant' for many years; another gentleman did not see one bad crop on a journey between Banbury and Chester; in Cornwall the wheat yield was four times what it had been in the previous year. If these reflected the general picture, only one conclusion could be drawn: the shortage was artificial. When the rains came in August the old corn had suddenly vanished. Farmers were refusing to thresh till the spring; dealers were assuring the

---

[42] Pitt's phrase in his speech of 5 May 1800 (*Parl. Hist.* XXXV. 151).
[43] *E.H.D.*, XI. 420-2; *Corr. of Charlotte Grenville*, 62; *GL* 2278.

millers and bakers that there was no wheat to be had. The word went round that the country was 'literally starving in the midst of plenty', while farmers and dealers wallowed in affluence; a wicked and dangerous proposition, thought Dundas.[44]

Indeed the idea of an artificial famine could be more damaging than a real dearth. The poor might bear a failed crop with becoming submission to Providence, but they would not starve quietly with the death-rate up by 11 per cent to enrich speculators. 'There is a great spirit of discontent among the poorer manufacturers', a friend in the midlands reported to Canning; 'the rich are armed and trained to exercise, and upon that alone it seems to me depends our security.' In the middle of November Windham complained that half the army was engaged in suppressing tumults; 5,000 men of the garrison in Portugal were summoned home to keep order; and Dundas could not see how to spare the cavalry reinforcements which Abercromby wanted for Egypt. A cry could be heard that the war was to blame for the corn shortage: 'the waste from fleets and armies, and expeditions which float about and do nothing', Lady Malmesbury accused. Lord Grenville's brothers were warning him that public opinion would force the government to make 'a very bad and dangerous peace; for John Bull tells you very loudly that *tel est notre bon plaisir.*'[45]

The last session of the last Parliament of the Kingdom of Great Britain opened on 11 November with a lengthy debate on the price of bread, and motions for peace and the dismissal of the ministry. Pitt made a very long speech in reply to Tierney on 27 November, and Dundas a short but very telling one which delighted Pitt and Canning in reply to Sheridan's motion for peace on 1 December.[46] Even as Dundas was speaking, the Archduke John's Austrian army in Bavaria fell on Grenier's French corps and drove it back towards Hohenlinden.

[44] Ragsdale 86; Sidmouth Papers. Nov. 1800, Warren Hastings, 18 Oct., Sir William Elford, Nov., Mr. Beake, 29 Oct., Ralph Churton, all to Addington; Matheson, 292.
[45] Canning MSS, 14 Sept., Leveson-Gower to Canning; Windham *Papers*, II. 161; Dropmore, VI. 320, 344, 380–1; *Parl. Hist.* XXXV. 610–11; Minto, III. 198n; Ragsdale 88.   [46] GL 2288.

Throughout November the game of watching the Austrians had been as tiresome as ever for the Foreign Office. The new Austrian Foreign Minister Count Louis Cobenzl was lured from Lunéville to Paris by Bonaparte, where every effort was made to seduce or intimidate him into opening a separate peace negotiation. The Cabinet suspended the next instalment of the Austrian loan while it waited for the outcome. Cobenzl returned from Paris unseduced; the armistice expired; and the eighteen-year-old Archduke John, now in command of Kray's army and convinced that Austria's earlier defeats had been due to excessive caution, advanced boldly against Moreau's superior forces with inept staff-work and a full complement of raw recruits. His initial success against Grenier drew him on through the first snows of winter into the defile of the Ebersberg forest, with his columns disconnected and unguarded by patrols. On 3 December Moreau routed him with the loss of 17,000 men. The French newspapers reporting the battle of Hohenlinden reached London on 12 December. As more information arrived about the effects of the defeat, it became certain that Austria would be forced into a separate peace. With low national morale, and with Paul moving two Russian armies menacingly towards the Austrian border, the Vienna government could not continue the struggle.

In the meantime new storms had been gathering abroad. By 28 November it was known that the Tsar had responded to the British capture of Malta by laying an embargo on British shipping in his ports, having delayed only long enough to confirm that the British had excluded Russian troops from the island. He was already negotiating for a French alliance; and now he offered the Scandinavian powers a league of Armed Neutrality, with a covert threat against the Danes if they did not hold the mouth of the Baltic for the Russians in the spring. The unfortunate Danes, who had no interest in the Malta question, saw no choice but to fall in with the Tsar's policy.

In contrast with the supple diplomacy of Bonaparte, the British had adopted a rigid attitude to the Tsar since the expulsion of Whitworth in the spring. They reasoned that conciliation had not worked with the unstable Paul, and that firmness might succeed. 'With such a *strange* character as that of the Russian Emperor', said King George, 'nothing can be gained but by shewing him he is not feared.' There was an underlying expectation that Paul's conduct would lead to his overthrow, as had happened to his father. 'His fatal distemper', the King had predicted, '. . . may occasion some horrid explosion.' That hope had not diminished. 'I should think the thing must be drawing to its crisis', Grenville predicted in December; 'I cannot conceive how so manifest a madman can be permitted to go on even so long as he has.' The Russian embargo was met with firmness. Merchants trading with Russia were forbidden to answer bills of exchange; and Abercromby was warned to be ready for war, and ordered to attack Russian ships and troops in the Mediterranean if they committed hostile acts against his own force or the Turks. The Scandinavian powers were notified that Britain would resist an Armed Neutrality with force. And preparations were begun to send a fleet to the Baltic at the end of the winter.[47]

This strong line was to be vindicated in the spring. But at the turn of the year the picture was alarming. For some time the government had been receiving warnings from its envoys that opinion on the continent was swinging against Britain; and Prussian troops had occupied Cuxhaven in retaliation for the seizure of a Prussian merchant ship. 'So we are at the point of being at war with the whole world', wrote Lord Carysfort from Berlin, 'and excluded from every port upon the continent of Europe!'[48]

[47] *GL* 2142, 2287, 2297; Dropmore, VI. 409; WO 6/21 pp. 151 ff; FO 7/61, Grenville's of 16 Dec.; Spencer, IV. 274-5. Ragsdale (pp. 114-20) argues that this tough British handling of Paul reflected a misunderstanding of his aims, which were in reality stable and conservative, and an erroneous assumption that he was pursuing the expansionist policy of his predecessors.

[48] Dropmore, VI. 334; Stowe Papers, 11 Nov., Garlike to Thomas Grenville, and 21 Jan. 1801, Carysfort to same.

CHAPTER IX

The Fall of the Ministry

1. *The Pilot Bales Out*

On New Year's Day 1801 the nineteenth century dawned in gloom. In Germany Schiller greeted it with strident verses denouncing the French imperium on land and the British tyranny of the seas, while in London the Tower guns boomed a subdued welcome as the new Union flag was hoisted for the first time, and people doubtfully wished each other a 'happy new century'. The hope seemed unlikely to be realized. 'The century is not I think ushered in by any very extraordinary prospects of prosperity', wrote Colonel Calvert from his office at the Horse Guards.[1]

Indeed it was not. Within a week there was news of an armistice in Germany on such terms that a separate Austrian peace was certain, and the peace treaty was signed at Lunéville in February. Austria's frontier in Italy was pushed back inside Venetian territory to the Adige. The Emperor recognized the four French puppet republics in Lombardy, Liguria, Switzerland and Holland; the French possession of the left bank of the Rhine; and the right of France to interfere in the reorganization of the Holy Roman Empire. In March negotiations with Naples were to bring the whole of peninsular Italy under the control of the French army, with easy access to Egypt from the ports of Apulia. From the Baltic came news on 13 January that the expected Northern Convention had been signed by Russia, Sweden, Denmark and Prussia to form an Armed Neutrality. Sir Hyde Parker had already been ordered to take a fleet to the Sound in the spring to coerce the Danes; and on 14 January an Order in Council laid an embargo on ships of the Baltic powers in British ports. The Danish islands in the West Indies were ordered to be seized; and an additional squadron was sent to the Mediterranean, lest the enemy exploit the northern crisis to seize control of the Straits and

---

[1] Verney MSS, 1 Jan. 1801, Colonel Calvert to his sister.

sever the communications of Abercromby's expedition in Egypt. Peace seemed ever more desirable, with even Canning pretending that he had deplored the repulse of Bonaparte's overture a year earlier. As for Pitt, he was only waiting for success in Egypt and the Baltic before opening negotiations.[2]

And now, with the Union Parliament about to assemble, Pitt's equivocation over the Catholic question came home to roost. On 29 December Lord Castlereagh had arrived from Ireland to prepare for the meeting of Parliament. He and Cornwallis had borne the heat and burden of carrying the Union in Ireland, and were suspicious of the ministers' sincerity about honouring their obligations. On New Year's Day, while the new flags fluttered and the guns reverberated, Castlereagh wrote to remind Pitt of the history of his pledge on the Catholic question. He was speaking for the Lord-Lieutenant Cornwallis, whose distrust of the ministers' honour probably equalled his contempt for their military judgement. Cornwallis was anxious for the calm which had greeted the Union in Dublin to continue; but it could not last 'if the evil genius of Britain should induce the Cabinet to continue the proscription of the Catholics'.[3]

Cornwallis underestimated the difficulties ahead. Charles Fox, for one, was convinced that if the King and part of the Cabinet were against emancipation, the bill would be thrown out in the House of Lords by an immense majority. But though Cornwallis knew that Lord Loughborough had written a paper against Catholic relief, he believed that Loughborough would soon find it impracticable to oppose it. Pitt's reply to Castlereagh confirmed this optimism. Cornwallis thought that the general crisis which beset the government at home and abroad would favour Catholic relief, in the same way that the Irish rebellion had led to the Union. 'Timid men will not venture on any change of system, however wise and just, unless their fears are alarmed by pressing dangers . . . If Mr. Pitt is firm, he will meet with no difficulty.'[4]

What Cornwallis did not know was the state of the Prime Minister's mind, and how grotesquely he was mishandling the

[2] Add. MSS 38833, f. 10, 2 Dec. 1801, Canning to Frere; Canning MSS, 6 Jan. 1801, Pitt to Canning.   [3] Castlereagh, III. 327; IV. 8-13.
[4] Castlereagh, III. 418; IV. 20-1; Fox *Memorials*, III. 309.

question. He had feared that Pitt would suffer a convenient forgetfulness about the Cabinet's undertaking to relieve the Catholics, but he could not know that Pitt had done nothing since September to prepare the ground for the measure. Above all Pitt had not approached the King, and had left the field open to Lord Loughborough's machinations. Having warned the King that the Catholic question was under discussion, Loughborough gave him on 13 December a copy of his long paper opposing emancipation.[5] Loughborough's paper concentrated on the political and constitutional dangers of admitting Irish Catholics to Parliament. These dangers were not negligible, and Pitt's vague talk of safeguards did not dispose of them. But there was another argument which would weigh more heavily with the King, his coronation oath; and to alarm the royal conscience Loughborough enlisted allies. More than twenty years earlier he had combined with his cousin Lord Auckland to further their ambitions by harrying Lord North during the war crisis of 1779.[6] Now he called Auckland into action again. Their purpose in unsettling the ministry is uncertain; it had more to do with frustrated ambition that with principle.[7] It may have been Auckland who enlisted his brother-in-law the Archbishop of Canterbury; certainly the Cabinet's discussions were leaked to the Primate, who began to work on the royal conscience. Thus the King knew from September onwards that behind his back a measure was being prepared to which he had made it clear that he had religious objections. It is no wonder that George III's tormented mind would soon boil over.

Yet even when Pitt agreed with Castlereagh in the New Year that the measure must now be brought forward, he still made no approach to the King, who would soon have to deliver his speech from the throne to the new Imperial Parliament. On 10 January Pitt had a long discussion about the Irish Catholics with Grenville and Dundas, with whom he was united in a plan to replace the sacramental test with a political declaration against subversive principles. Castlereagh's progress reports continued to reassure the Lord-Lieutenant, while

[5] Pellew, *Sidmouth*, I. 500-12; Stanhope, III. 269.
[6] Mackesy, *The War for America*, 247. They were at that time Wedderburn and Eden.   [7] Stanhope, III. 267.

Lord Spencer let him know that he expected the King to give way. 'We now shall turn that great measure of the Union to real profit', Cornwallis replied happily on 22 January.[8] Three days later, on Sunday 25 January, the Cabinet met for its first formal attempt to reach a decision on Catholic relief. Three opponents of the measure were absent, the Lord Chancellor, Liverpool and Chatham; and Camden and Spencer, both of them very cautious supporters of emancipation, insisted that there should be a further meeting with the Lord Chancellor present. Pitt agreed to meet again on the following day; but he proceeded, improperly in Camden's opinion, to collect the views of those who were present after an inadequate discussion and naturally had a majority. It turned out that Loughborough did not want a further meeting, and none was held; and in spite of the numerous absentees Pitt treated the meeting on the Sunday as having taken the decision. 'It was a great neglect', wrote Camden later, 'not to summon another meeting after the loose manner in which opinions were collected at the last.' It was indeed, with most of the opponents absent; and Dundas apparently told the King that he had not regarded the 'conversation' as a final decision. Had the whole Cabinet been present it would probably have emerged that the controversial measure had a majority of only one in its favour, like the Egyptian expedition; far too shaky to force the hand of the King in a matter of conscience.[9]

And still Pitt did not speak to George III. Yet someone was keeping the King informed, and in his eyes the constitutional character of the measure must have been changed fundamentally by the Cabinet decision. It was no longer an open question like the slave trade, a matter for individual consciences, but a government measure brought forward by the collective action of the Cabinet.[10] Three days passed; and on the Wednesday the bottled-up feelings of the King burst

[8] Canning MSS, 10 Jan., Pitt to Canning; Castlereagh, III. 333; IV. 21; Buckingham, *Courts and Cabinets*, III. 128–9; Campbell, *Chancellors*, VI. 356–6.
[9] Willis, 251–2; Add. MSS 37924, f. 86; Rose *Diaries*, I. 302. All six of the probable supporters of the measure were present (Pitt, Grenville, Dundas, Spencer, Windham, Camden); of the five probable opponents, only Portland and Westmorland. Loughborough, Liverpool and Chatham were all absent.
[10] Willis, 244, 253.

forth. Walking up to Dundas and Windham at the levee, he berated them about the Catholic measure. 'I heard', he said in a loud voice to Dundas, 'Lord Castlereagh is to bring forward a motion in the House of Commons respecting the Catholics, and I must say that I shall consider every man who supports that measure as my personal enemy.' It was the tactics and indeed the phrase he had used in 1783 to defeat Fox's India Bill and bring Pitt to power. 'I am sorry your Majesty should see the matter in that light', Dundas replied. The King: 'You know I have always done so.' Dundas: 'Yes, I am sorry to recollect that some measures I thought it my duty to propose in 1793 did not accord entirely with your Majesty's sentiments.'[11]

The game was up, and Dundas went straight to Downing Street to report the conversation to the Prime Minister. Pitt probably decided now that he would have to resign, for he would not be able to carry the bill with a divided Cabinet in the teeth of the King, and could not remain at the head of the ministry after giving way to the King and the intriguers who had manipulated his prejudices. Pitt had foreseen the dilemma but had not faced it. For a day or two he continued to procrastinate. There was a Cabinet discussion which tried to find a compromise in the form of 'a sort of moderate test', but the attempt was soon abandoned and Pitt told his colleagues that he must go out of office unless the bill was carried.[12] A message to the King asked for the postponement of the royal speech at the opening of Parliament, and at this stage the Speaker Addington was brought on to the scene. It measures the secretiveness with which Pitt had handled the Catholic question that, though he had stayed for weeks with Addington in the autumn, his old friend arrived in London on 22 January for the meeting of Parliament with apparently no suspicion that the Catholic question was to be brought forward. On 29 January the King wrote to ask him to open

[11] This version of the conversation was recorded by Glenbervie as having been repeated to him by Dundas five minutes after it took place (Glenbervie, I. 147). According to another version Dundas replied, 'Your Majesty will find many among those who are friendly to that measure some whom you never supposed to be your enemies.'

[12] Matheson, 299; *GL* vol. III, p. 475 n. 1. Bishop Tomline was later told by Pitt that he already knew at this time that he would have to resign. (J. H. Rose, *Pitt and the Great War*, 444.)

Pitt's eyes to the danger of emancipation. For a couple of days messages went to and fro, and Addington saw Pitt and thought he had made his point. But he was mistaken, for on 31 January Pitt at last opened the question directly with the King, in a long written exposition which made it clear that Catholic relief would be proposed by the government.[13]

Lord Camden described Pitt's paper as masterly; but if Pitt seriously hoped to relieve the Catholics, it was a strange tactical blunder to lay the whole argument before the King for the first time at the last moment and in the form of a written ultimatum, instead of trying to prepare his mind over a period of four months. Pitt bluntly told the King that the majority of the Cabinet favoured the admission of Catholics to Parliament, with certain safeguards which he outlined. On this point his own mind was unalterable, and he insisted on bringing the bill forward with the King's full concurrence and the whole weight of government. If the King objected, he must resign. If pressed, he would consent to remain in office till the immediate war crisis was overcome, without raising the Catholic question in Parliament; but on one condition. The King should not allow his name to be used by the opponents of emancipation.

This peremptory letter, broaching the Catholic question for the first time and presenting the King with an ultimatum, was apparently written without the knowledge of most of the Cabinet. Pitt consulted Lord Grenville about the drafting; but Dundas denied that he had seen the letter, and Pitt's brother Chatham had heard nothing from him on the subject whatever. Lord Loughborough claimed that none of the ministers who opposed Catholic relief had seen the letter, and was thunderstruck by its consequences.[14]

That evening, 31 January, Addington arrived at the Queen's House (the present Buckingham Palace) in response to a royal summons. The King knew of Pitt's determination though he may not yet have received his letter; and he begged Addington to rescue him by forming a new administration. Addington

---

[13] Pellew, I. 278, 285–6; *GL* 2331; the text of Pitt's letter is in *E.H.D.*, XI. 159–62.

[14] Pellew, I. 305; J. H. Rose, *Pitt and Napoleon*, 272; Rose *Diaries*, I. 303–5; *GL* 2349n; Matheson, 300–1; Pratt MSS, 4 Feb., Chatham to Camden.

went straight to see Pitt, who urged him to accept, with the words 'I see nothing but ruin, Addington, if you hesitate.'[15] It is not surprising that Pitt looked to Addington to succeed him. Four years earlier when peace had been in the air, Pitt had thought of resigning to make the negotiations easier, and had settled with the King that Addington should head the government.[16] The Speaker's visit cleared Pitt's conscience of the reproach that his resignation would leave the King to the mercy of the Foxite opposition, as North's resignation had done in 1782. Addington would be acceptable to the King, and Pitt hoped that his own colleagues would continue to serve.

As Pitt must have expected, the King's reply was a flat refusal to relieve the Catholics or undermine the Church and constitution. He expressed his 'cordial affection' for Pitt who, he hoped, would remain in office during his lifetime. 'If Pitt would stave off the Catholic question and his friends would abstain from agitating it, he too would be silent; but he neither could nor would silence others, to whom his opinion was already well known.[17]

By now Pitt was in no doubt that the King was immovable and prepared to fight; and for his part he would not drop the Catholic question to remain in office. On 3 February, peremptorily and without attempting to prolong the negotiation, he asked to be relieved of his office as soon as possible; for since the King would not effectively discountenance the use of his name, the ministry's difficulties would quickly become insuperable. On receiving this letter the King consulted Addington; and on 5 February he replied rather disingenuously expressing surprise, since he had assured Pitt of his own silence on the Catholic question. But since Pitt did not find that they understood each other, he would take steps with all speed to form a new administration.[18]

On the same day Addington began to form his government.

---

[15] Pellew, I. 287; Ashbourne, 309-11.

[16] Ziegler, 81-2; Pellew, I. 332n; Glenbervie, I. 277.

[17] J. H. Rose, *Pitt and Napoleon*, 272; *E.H.D.*, XI. 162. Bonamy Dobrée's interpretation of this letter seems to me to be simplisitic, and his comment unfair to the King: see Dobrée, *Letters of George III*, 242-3.

[18] Dropmore, VI. 434; *E.H.D.*, XI, 163; Stanhope, III. App. xxxii; *GL* 2341; Buckingham, *Courts and Cabinets*, III. 131.

He had hoped that most of Pitt's colleagues would join him, but Grenville, Dundas, Windham and Camden all resigned, professing that they were too far committed to the Catholics to remain in office. It would take time to replace Pitt's leading ministers, and the business was prolonged when the King fell ill ten days later. For five weeks Pitt and his friends continued to hold the seals of office, while a parallel administration held separate Cabinet meetings. On three occasions members of both Cabinets attended meetings on foreign policy, and one afternoon there were present two Prime Ministers, two Lord Chancellors and two Secretaries of State for War.[19] No wonder Pitt's resignation was widely regarded as a 'juggle'. When the new Cabinet emerged only four of Pitt's old Cabinet remained, none of them first rate.[20] Lord Loughborough, the evil genius of the emancipation crisis, was astonished to find that his intrigue had sawn off the branch which supported him. He was not asked to join the new government, and retired with an earldom to contemplate the end of his long and unscrupulous career.

2. *The Reason Why*

The tidings that a new administration was being formed astonished and then appalled Pitt's friends. The Irish government, which had been in the secret of the impending emancipation bill, was as surprised as any. After the Cabinet meeting of 25 January which precipitated the crisis, Castlereagh had sent such strong assurances that all was well that Cornwallis had marvelled at the prosperous turn of fortune: 'Nobody would have believed, three years ago, that Union, Catholic Emancipation, and the restoration of perfect transquillity, could have taken place in so short a time.' This hubris

[19] Aspinall, *Cabinet Council*, 149.
[20] Portland was still at the Home Office, though soon to be shunted to the Lord Presidency of the Council; Chatham remained as Lord President till transferred to the Ordnance; Westmorland retained the Privy Seal; Liverpool remained at the Board of Trade. The new Cabinet members were Henry Addington (First Lord of the Treasury and Chancellor of the Exchequer), Lord Hawkesbury (Foreign Secretary), Lord Hobart (Secretary of State for War), Earl of St. Vincent (First Lord of the Admiralty) and Lord Eldon (Lord Chancellor).

prevailed in Dublin even after the news of the King's outburst at the levee. They knew that George III could not turn to the Foxite opposition, who were deeply committed to emancipation, and they did not imagine a shadow adminstration being formed by Addington. 'Everything depends on the firmness of the Cabinet', wrote the Irish Under-Secretary Edward Cooke. Yet at that moment Addington was rallying to the King.[21]

When Cornwallis learned the composition of the new ministry, he could not believe that it would survive; for to obtain recruits it had reduced its standard as low as the new military levies. Grenville's assurance in the House of Lords that the retiring ministers would support their successors did nothing to allay his friends' contempt for Addington and his colleagues. 'It is impossible they should, even with your tuition, conduct the state', Lord Carysfort wrote to him from Berlin: 'you must resume your place. . . . Such a ministry cannot stand long, and cannot do good.' In Vienna Minto lamented that in Pitt the country was losing 'the Atlas of our reeling globe'. Dundas, pledged to support the new men, told Pitt that the elevation of a professional man to the Premiership was an affront to all the aristrocracy who supported the government, and wished that the Duke of Portland could form the ministry. There was loud laughter in the House when Sheridan described Addington as a piece of Pitt's posterior which had stuck to the Treasury bench.[22]

Responding to this outcry, Grenville thought it necessary to assure the ambassadors abroad that the sole reason for the resignation was the clash with the King over the Catholics. Dundas too asserted that there was no ulterior motives. They protested too much, and were not believed. Those of Pitt's associates who had not known that emancipation was to be forced on were stunned; others like Loughborough and Auckland who had been intriguing against the measure were equally shocked to find that they had destroyed the ministry. On all sides there was indignation that Pitt had pulled out on such slender grounds in the midst of the country's troubles;

[21] Castlereagh, IV. 17, 24-7; Cornwallis, III. 337.
[22] *Parl. Hist.* XXXV. 946, XXXVI. 824; Dropmore, VI. 458, 460; Windham *Papers*, II. 171; PRO 30/8/157, 7 Feb. 1801, Dundas to Pitt.

'withdrawing in a crisis of accumulated difficulties'. The future Speaker Charles Abbot thought it 'absolutely unjustifiable' to resign on such a point and desert the country when it was 'surrounded by domestic difficulties, and a new accumulation of foreign wars'. Malmesbury cast equal blame on the intriguers who had worked up the King's conscience and on the ministers who, after neglecting to prepare the King's mind, considered themselves ill-treated and resigned. Auckland publicly called Pitt a deserter, marvelling in the House of Lords 'that generals . . . can without motives of good and superior import, get in their post-chaise and quit their army in time of action'.[23]

But if the Catholic question was not the real reason for resigning, why had the ministers done so? In the hunt for an underlying conspiracy the field was led by Lady Malmesbury. 'The whole is a *farce*', she assured the Mintos, 'for it is impossible that Pitt's friend and creature should be his real successor, or more than a *stop-gap* till matters are settled and he may come in again.' Hers was a popular explanation — that Pitt had not sincerely intended to relieve the Catholics and was sliding out of his obligation to them by a spurious resignation. 'A juggle', said Fox; and falling back on the imagery of his favourite pastime, 'some *dessous des cartes*'. The more paranoid Protestants suspected that he had gone out of office to push the Papist claims in temporary alliance with the Foxites.

Some informed people stressed dissensions within the Cabinet: the resignation was a manœuvre by Pitt and Dundas to be rid of Lord Grenville, perhaps even with the connivance of the King who was known to be irritated by the Foreign Secretary. Or, Dundas had contrived the fall of the government, to escape the responsibilities from which he had been vainly seeking relief. Even Lord Liverpool, a Cabinet minister, thought this might be the explanation, for he could not accept the Catholic question as the whole cause of the resignation; so, too, at a later date, did Pitt's young friend Canning. Others asked whether the King had engineered the crisis to rid himself

[23] Dropmore, VI. 435; Minto, III. 190; Matheson, 301; Lovat-Fraser, 75; Pretyman MSS, 6 Feb., Rose to Tomline; Auckland, IV. 127-9, 131; Stanhope, III. 291n; Colchester, I. 232; Malmesbury, IV. 15; Glenbervie, I. 277-9; Mackintosh *Memoirs*, I. 170-1.

of the bullying triumvirs. Loughborough, in the first shock of realizing that the ministry had collapsed, suggested that Pitt had been got at after the Cabinet meeting by Dundas and Grenville. The speculations continued unresolved. 'After all', wrote Lady Williams Wynn six weeks later, 'the key to this extraordinary political enigma is still unfound.' Two years later the King himself declared that he did not believe the Catholic question to have been the real reason for Pitt's resignation.[24]

Part of the mystery can be dispelled. Contemporaries who doubted whether the Cabinet was pledged to relieve the Catholics did not know of its assurances to Cornwallis; and when Dundas declared that he could not walk the streets as a gentleman if he abandoned his pledge to repeal the Test Act, he was not simply posturing.[25] For him, as for Grenville, Windham and Spencer, the Catholic question was not an implausible sticking point when their leader Pitt took his stand on it. But the enigma is Pitt himself. It was apparently his personal decision to present the King with an ultimatum which would almost certainly lead to his resignation. There is no evidence to support Loughborough's wild guess that he had been put up to it by Dundas and Grenville: on the contrary, Dundas denied that he had seen Pitt's crucial letter, and Grenville seemed to follow Pitt rather than lead him.[26]

That Pitt was acting on a predetermined and logical policy is made less probable by his conduct after the event. 'I did not foresee the extent of the consequences to which within the week this question has led', he wrote to his brother Lord Chatham a few days later.[27] When he formally signified his resignation to the King after the levee on 11 February he is said to have cried profusely, and was much agitated when he emerged from the closet. His motive would be judged by his subsequent handling of the Catholic question. To prove his

[24] Minto, III. 199-200; Fox *Memorials*, III. 320-1, 325; Wilberforce *Private Papers*, 116; Glenbervie, I. 156-9, 181, 201-2, 277-9, 262-3, 375, 389, 415; Ziegler, 107; *Corr. of Charlotte Grenville*, 64.

[25] Glenbervie, I. 201, 279; Colchester, I. 256; Matheson, 300.

[26] Above, p. 192; J. H. Rose, *Pitt and Napoleon*, 272.

[27] Willis, 246. Lord Buckingham afterwards maintained (as Spencer had also predicted) that the King would have given way, and blamed Pitt and his own brother Grenville for resigning. (Wellesley *Papers*, I. 135.)

sincerity it was not necessary to force the issue of emancipation, but he must not desert the principle; 'otherwise', wrote Edward Cooke from Dublin Castle, 'he will subject himself to the imputation of a double game'.[28]

To stand by the principle was Pitt's first intention. He would discourage his friends from pushing it, but would give the Catholics the strongest pledge for the future.[29] Yet his purpose soon began to waver. On 18 February the King fell ill with his old malady from which he had been free for twelve years. Whatever its underlying cause, its symptom was madness. Some of the retiring ministers felt guilty about the part their resignation might have played in unhingeing the King's mind, and Pitt was 'very unwell — much shaken — gouty and nervous'.[30] To George Rose he confessed that he had intended to pledge himself never to come into office unless he had freedom to propose Catholic emancipation, but that he was 'shook' in his resolution by the royal illness. Seeing his agitation and the tears in his eyes, Rose set to work on his pliable temperament, arguing that the time might come when his pledge to the Catholics must give way to the 'higher duty' of taking office to keep out a 'Jacobin' ministry.[31] Within a fortnight Pitt was to move even further away from his principle than Rose had urged. While the King was recovering in early March Pitt sent him a promise through his doctors that he would never bring forward the Catholic question, in or out of office, during George III's reign.

The recantation, said the Irish historian Lecky, perfectly coincided with Pitt's interest and involved him in a gross breach of faith with the Catholics.[32] Pitt could defend his retraction on the grounds that the King's health required it and that his death or permanent insanity would open the way for the Prince of Wales and the Foxite opposition. His self-denial was somewhat tarnished, however, because he soon allowed himself to play with the idea of returning to office. Dundas tried to persuade him that the King's illness created a new situation which would justify his carrying on.

[28] Glenbervie, I. 169; Castlereagh, IV. 50-1.
[29] *E.H.D.*, XI. 164; Castlereagh, IV. 164; Cornwallis, III. 346, 348-50.
[30] Malmesbury, IV. 17, 20.   [31] *E.H.D.*, XI. 164; Stanhope, III. 287.
[32] Quoted in Ziegler 105.

Technically it would not have been difficult to withdraw the resignation, for Pitt and his friends still held the seals of office; and he was tempted. A message was sent through the Duke of Portland, a former colleague who had joined Addington, that if it was the wish of the King and Addington to restore the old ministry Pitt was prepared to discuss it. Addington refused to pass the proposal to the King, and added that if Pitt's friends intended to propose it to the King themselves, he hoped they would consult the royal physicians first. Pitt thereupon withdrew from the scheme; according to his biographers from a sense of propriety and of what was owed to Addington for giving up the secure and lucrative Speakership; and according to Dundas because Pitt felt the arrangement could not be accomplished without goodwill from Addington much greater than a bare acquiescence. But Malmesbury's conversations with Pitt's go-betweens Dundas, Pelham and Canning suggested a different motive. Pitt was determined that the King should make the first move and entreat him to return.[33]

Pitt's pride, as Malmesbury called it, may reveal some of the roots of the emancipation crisis. For many months past the King had been drifting away from his ministers, alienated by their policies and their manners. He had certainly had dealings behind Pitt's back over emancipation. At the end of January he used his influence to tamper with an Irish election against the interests of emancipation; and rumours abounded that he had been listening to 'underhand courtiers' and using improper channels of communication to oppose and weaken the Cabinet. 'It appeared to me when I was in England', Edward Cooke wrote to Castlereagh at the end of February, 'that there was an unfair game playing against the Cabinet. There seems to be a little Court Windsor party that were always irritating the King, always endeavouring to make him form opinions of his own, to make arrangements and appointments without the advice of his Cabinet, and who use every sinister artifice and low flattery for the purpose.'[34]

[33] Pellew, I. 235-6; Add. MSS 33107, 11 March, Dundas to Pelham; Malmesbury IV. 34-9, 43-4; J. H. Rose, *Pitt and the Great War*, 450.

[34] Bolton, 210; *GL* vol. III, p. 488n; Castlereagh, IV. 64. 'Those who stay in

This caballing formed an ominous background to the King's use of the word 'enemy' in his outburst against the emancipationists at his levee. Echoing the royal threat which had brought down the Fox–North Coalition, the King's words were the reason why Pitt's letter of resignation had to stress the King's refusal to discountenance the use of his name against emancipation. On the day when Pitt had sent his ultimatum to the King, he wrote a letter full of leashed anger to the leading caballer Lord Auckland, reproaching him with a betrayal of friendship and confidence. Within a few days Canning told Lord Malmesbury that the undermining of Pitt's influence with the Crown was the reason for his resignation. He had made so many concessions to the King in the past three years, said Canning, that his government was seriously weakened; and had he not made a stand he would have been left with only nominal power, and the real power would have passed to those who influenced the King 'out of sight'. Canning was to give several different reasons for the resignation during the next couple of years, each of them containing part of the truth; this was one of the earliest, and he repeated it eight months later. Dundas said something similar to Lady Anne Barnard: that though Catholic Emancipation was the ostensible cause of Pitt's resignation, 'the aversion the King has conceived for him is a still stronger inducement to retire'. In the following November George Rose noticed that Pitt was 'much more sore about the King's interference with the Lords of the Bedchamber, etc. . . . on the Catholic question than he was in the summer'.[35]

Earlier precedents suggested that though a measure might be forced on the sovereign against his will, the position of the ministers who had done so could soon be made untenable. Pitt was in a dilemma, torn between giving way to the King at the cost of his honour and knowing that his standing with the Crown was undermined, or making a constitutional stand for his principles at the risk of his political position. He would have been justified in making a calculated stand if he had

are dupes to the King or rather the King's secret advisers', the Duchess of Devonshire wrote (Add. MSS 33107, 9 Feb., to Pelham).

[35] *E.H.D.*, XI. 63; Willis, 256–7; Malmesbury, IV. 4, 75; *GL* vol. III, p. 475 n. 1; Rylands Library, Memoirs of Lady Anne Barnard, V. 4.

prepared for the collision in a prudent and calculating manner. But he did not; and his reckless treatment of the King and his indifference to Cabinet divisions and opposition in Parliament almost suggest that he had deliberately manufactured the collision so that he could resign. Yet this too is improbable, for indecision rather than calculation marked his conduct of the crisis, from his evasive handling of his colleagues beforehand to his surprise and inconsistency after he had resigned. In preparing for the collision he did not act like a consummate and experienced politician in full control of his actions.

If he had not planned to resign, why did he not attempt to persuade the King when the issue was forced into the open? He never spoke to the King in person, but having presented a written ultimatum resigned without further discussion as soon as the King prevaricated. 'It is indeed, doubtful', wrote Lord Holland, 'whether the King, without some morbid impression on his mind, would have resisted the representations of Mr. Pitt, Lord Cornwallis, Mr. Dundas and Lord Grenville, in favour of the Irish Catholics.' It had never been Pitt's habit to sacrifice power to principle, once it was clear that the principle could not prevail. In earlier days he had given way over parliamentary reform and Irish trade. Yet when the King obstructed emancipation Pitt neither tried to overcome the obstruction nor yielded to it, but surrendered his power forthwith though he was prepared within the month to give up the principle for which he had resigned. Lord Holland offered an explanation. Pitt would have sacrificed his principle rather than his power, 'if he had not foreseen the necessity of making a peace humiliating to his pride.' He therefore made way for a ministry of his own 'creatures and dependents' to resist emancipation and make the peace.[36]

The view that Pitt resigned to avoid making the peace is a familiar one which appears frequently in Lord Malmesbury's diary of the day, gleaned from hints dropped by Dundas and Canning. 'He was always too pacific', Canning complained to Malmesbury in March, 'but he is now quite *enfeebled* and won over, and this is the *real* reason of his declining resuming power and business.' Soon Malmesbury learned that Pitt was

---

[36] Holland, *Whig Party*, I. 120-1.

telling Addington that the country's finances required peace, and urging him to open negotiations with the enemy. 'Really', Malmesbury commented, 'what appears in the French papers and in ours, has some degree of truth, viz. that Pitt went out because he felt himself incapable either of carrying on the war, or of making peace'.[37]

'*Some degree of truth*': the experienced man of affairs did not seek for a single cause. Yet perhaps Pitt had had in the back of his mind the fate of an earlier peacemaker: the fall of his old political leader Shelburne after making the peace with France and America in 1783. The King must certainly have remembered Shelburne's fate when he wrote during the negotiations of 1797 that 'though an Englishman is soon tired of war, he is not easily satisfied with peace'.[38]

No single explanation, however, will suffice. No explanation of Pitt's resignation is complete which ignores his state of mind and health, and the many pressures which had assailed him since the battle of Marengo: disputes over diplomacy, grand strategy, and military operations; backbiting in the Cabinet; a tired and failing ministry, so divided that it could scarcely make war and could not make peace; conflicts with the King. Of these troubles the Catholic question has been rightly called a catalyst.[39] The underlying cause of the ministry's collapse was the intolerable pressure of the war on Pitt. At the time of his resignation he was said to be gouty and depressed. As his physician Sir Walter Farquhar told Lord Glenbervie, there were circumstances about Pitt's health known only to himself and Addington; and it was Addington who summed up the resignation to Glenbervie in these terms: 'the intrigues of others, and the state of health of body and mind had a great share'.[40] Pitt could see that he

---

[37] Malmesbury, IV. 39, 43, 47, 50, 53. Willis (p. 240) calls Malmesbury's suggestion 'an erroneous speculation', but Pitt's letter of 10 January to Canning, which he quotes to prove his point, does not seem to bear the emphasis he places on it.   [38] *GL* 1528.   [39] Willis, 243.

[40] J. H. Rose, *Pitt and the Great War*, 439; Glenbervie, I. 174, 320. Feiling (228) suggests that Addington's hints of Pitt's mental collapse are interested whispers later on. It may have suited Addington later on to publicize this aspect of the resignation; nevertheless Glenbervie records both Addington and Farquhar making similar observations immediately after the resignation, and even before it. Feiling himself recognizes that Pitt's mental health had been precarious in the autumn (see p. 176 above).

would soon be cornered as North had been in 1782 when peace became a necessity, by the determination of the King and a minority of his colleagues to fight on. Before this happened to Pitt, he allowed himself to become trapped in a matter of principle, between the Irish administration and a large Cabinet minority who opposed emancipation. With these stresses he no longer had the resilience to cope.

CHAPTER X

Peace without Victory

1. *The Darkness Clears*

On 14 March the King was well enough to receive the seals from Pitt and hand them to Addington, and the old ministry was out. Already, however, their successors had taken some important decisions. The first was to abandon Portugal. A Spanish army had crossed the frontier, and the new Foreign Secretary Lord Hawkesbury advised the Regent to make the best terms he could obtain. If he fought, Britain would provide a subsidy and back a loan; but having in the autumn withdrawn the force which might have defended Portugal to keep public order at home, the British were no longer capable of defending their old ally.[1]

This decision was taken at a meeting of the new Cabinet at which Pitt and Dundas were present. They also attended a meeting about 10 March on the Danish question, and approved the immediate dispatch of Sir Hyde Parker's fleet with an ultimatum before the Swedish and Russian navies could intervene. This accorded with Grenville's view that 'our fleet will be our best negotiator', and his advice to Hawkesbury when he welcomed him as his successor 'that firmness alone can extricate the country'. Hawkesbury had shown him the draft of the ultimatum, and begged him to criticize and alter it without mercy. Parker's fleet sailed from Yarmouth on 12 March, and three days later further order followed him to proceed against the war ports of Sweden and Russia.[2]

With his surrender of the seals Pitt laid down the last of his burdens, and began to recover his health. His massive debts were being dealt with. A secret subscription loan of £11,700 was raised among his friends to avert immediate trouble, and after some demur on his part Holwood, his happy home for

---

[1] Sherwig, 140; above p. 182.

[2] *GL* 2371n; Dropmore, VI. 443-4, 450, 455; Feldbæk, 139-40. The King saw and cordially approved the minute of his still unofficial Cabinet (Sidmouth Papers, 10 March 1801, King to Addington).

the past seventeen years, was sold.[3] On leaving Downing
Street he moved to a rented house in Park Place, and as
spring moved into summer people were surprised to see him
lounging through the streets of a morning, generally by himself and apparently with nothing to do. Dundas had been led
to believe that he planned to spend the summer in the country,
and was less than pleased to see him loitering about London
in daily contact with the ministers, for he knew that peace
was in the wind and feared no good would come of Pitt's
involvement.[4]

Dundas's suspicions were well grounded, for within days of
the new ministry taking office they were making a bid for
peace, and Malmesbury was assured that they had Pitt's
backing; indeed that he was positively pushing Addington
toward peace as a financial necessity. The new ministers were
hastened by news that a Russian envoy was in Paris to negotiate with Bonaparte, and on 19 March, five days after receiving
the seals, they resolved to open their own negotiations immediately. Hawkesbury notified the convenient Otto that
Britain was ready to talk peace on the basis that France
should evacuate Egypt, while Britain should retain Malta,
Ceylon, Trinidad and Martinique, relinquishing all her other
conquests.[5]

It was no time to be making such demands, for although
Bonaparte also had reasons for wanting peace he held all the
cards. He was still in unchallenged possession of Egypt, and
was making determined efforts to send relief before Abercromby's force was ready to make a landing. Much of Europe
was already closed to British exports, the Baltic was about to
be shut by the Northern League, and Portugal was being overrun. Naples was on the point of accepting an army of occupation, and from her ports at Brindisi and Taranto Bonaparte
believed he could easily supply Egypt. 'At any price we must
become masters of the Mediterranean,' he declared.[6] Above
all he counted on his understanding with Russia. He was
hoping to lure Paul with a scheme for a Russian army to march

---

[3] Rose *Diaries*, I. 404, 428-9, 474; Pretyman MSS, T 108/45.
[4] Wellesley *Papers*, I. 141; Matheson, 319.
[5] Malmesbury, IV. 50, 53; *GL* 2373; Hardman, 401-1.
[6] Sorel, VI. 79.

on India from the Caspian while the French Army of the Orient pressed on the Red Sea route. It was a preview of the schemes which were to spring from the Peace of Tilsit five years later, with the Iberian peninsula and the Spanish navy coming under French control and a great partition of the east dangling before the Russians. 'We are called to change the face of the world', Bonaparte had told a Russian envoy in December; and during the Lunéville negotiations he declared that peace with Austria weighed nothing compared with a Russian alliance to 'master England'.[7]

The tentacles of Bonaparte's ambition were spreading everywhere. On 21 March Spain agreed in the Treaty of Aranjuez not only to occupy Portugal as a lever in negotiations with England, but to cede to France Louisiana, the vast basin of the Mississippi. By arrangement with Spain France also extended her Italian boundaries south of the Po into Parma, and acquired the island of Elba which was still held by a British garrison. Napoleon had plans to incorporate the fleets of Spain for expeditions against Ireland, India, Brazil, Surinam and Trinidad, and points in the Mediterranean including Minorca.[8] In the north the Prussians occupied Hanover on 30 March and closed the last of the rivers by which British trade could enter Europe. The British government, faced with these far-flung threats, was still beset by problems at home. The gold reserves were sinking, bread prices at their peak; and the army was scattered to hold back the tide of lawlessness. From the west of England General Simcoe reported in March that 'the law of the country was totally overthrown'.[9] Bonaparte had no need to make concessions to England.

Then in the course of a fortnight his edifice was overthrown. On 2 April it was learned in London that Abercromby had forced a landing on the Egyptian coast. On the 13th came news of the death of Tsar Paul, the victim as Grenville and George III had foretold of the hereditary disease of

---

[7] Sorel, VI. 65; *Napoleon Corr.* 5315. Bonaparte's efforts to relieve Egypt have not, perhaps, been sufficiently noticed. They were wide ranging, and embraced Toulon, Corsica, and the ports of Spain and Naples. See his *Correspondence* 5299, 5304; Lecestre, 17, 19. Two fleets were dispatched during the year to attempt the relief.

[8] *Napoleon Corr.* 5327.   [9] Ziegler, 117; *GL* 2390, 2413.

assassination. Two days later an officer arrived from Copenhagen to report Nelson's victory and the capitulation of the
Danish government. The hopes of the Pitt ministry were
being fulfilled. Bonaparte's hopes of saving Egypt were un-
hinged, though he continued his efforts to send aid. The
Northern League was in ruins. Most important of all, the
death of Paul had removed France's understanding with
Russia.

In Britain the man with most cause for personal rejoicing
was Dundas. The Egyptian expedition had caused him many
a sleepless night, yet the good news of Abercromby's landing
kept him more wakeful than all his previous anxiety.[10] Abercromby had not failed him, and the British army had won the
foothold in Egypt which would allow the British negotiators
to dispute its possession. The old general had moved deliberately, first establishing a base at Marmorice on the coast of
Asia Minor to collect provisions, local craft and horses. He
sent Moore on a mission to the Turks at Jaffa, to establish
that no plan of operations could be based on the plague-
infested and disorganized levies of the Porte. He therefore
resolved to land independently to the west of the Nile in
Aboukir Bay and attack Alexandria; and while resources
were being collected, he drilled and inspected his regiments
and rehearsed an assault landing. On 8 March his infantry
brought off a brilliant opposed landing and advanced on
Alexandria.

This was the news which kept Dundas awake, but his
anxiety would have grown if he had known what followed.
By 20 March the army had fought two general actions and
was close to Alexandria. There the French were entrenched
on a line of heights with a reserve position behind them, and
the success of an assault was doubtful. Abercromby knew by
now that the enemy force was much larger than he had been
told. He had long experience of ill-found operations with inadequate resources, and viewed the difficulties ahead without
optimism. But he knew the importance of his task; his troops
had proved themselves in action; and he was determined to
make one attempt to vindicate the reputation of the British

[10] Sidmouth MSS, 2 April, Dundas to Addington.

army and achieve the political task Dundas had set him.
Reserve ammunition and equipment were brought up from
the beach-head, and the army was ready for the assault. But
Abercromby's problem was solved by the French commander.
In the early hours of 21 March Menou attacked the British
position with equal numbers, and in hand-to-hand fighting
was beaten off in what proved later to have been a decisive
British victory.

The rejoicings for the victory at Alexandria were tempered
in the middle of May when it was learned that Abercromby
had died of wounds received in close combat. Dundas's family
found the Secretary of State at his house in Clarges Street 'in
very deep affliction'. He had lost 'one of the dearest friends
I ever had and one of the best men I ever knew', he told
Addington. 'Our friendship was early, and has been unremit-
ted. Our domestic interests and feeling are twined together. . . .
When I persevered in this expedition, under many discouraging
circumstances, my chief confidence rested on the thorough
knowledge I had of the union of enterprise and judgment
which marked the military character of the General from his
first onset as a soldier.'[11]

The Grenvilles disparaged the British success, persisting in
the belief that the French force in the battle was smaller than
the British, and that Menou's force in the whole of Egypt was
even smaller than had been expected.[12] But even Grenville
could see that the battle was a turning-point for the British
army. Abercromby had at last commanded a force of the
quality he had always sought, and had had time to impose
his own professional standards on the regiments. 'Our troops
in Egypt', wrote Cornwallis when he heard the news, 'have
shown that British soldiers, when properly led, are not
inferior to our seamen.' His pleasure was widely shared. 'The
discipline of our troops has surprised everyone,' Lady Malmesbury confessed, 'for their bravery was never doubted.' 'We
appear', wrote Lord Buckingham, the head of the Grenvilles,
'to have broken that magical incincibility *sur terre* of the great

[11] Matheson, 307; Sidmouth MSS, 10 May, Dundas to Addington; Pellew,
I. 392.
[12] Grenville MSS, Buckinghamshire R.O., 7 May, Lord Grenville to Thomas
Grenville; Dropmore, VII. 17, 181.

nation; and not by one accidental advantage, but by a systematic operation, and in three distinct and heavy actions.' After the disappointments of many years past, the last British operations of the war gave proof of the 'skill and valour of the British army', and a promise of future victories.[13]

Dundas must have felt deep satisfaction in the following autumn, when the final capitulation of the French army in Egypt brought the congratulations of his friends. It was he, wrote Glenbervie, who 'under such difficulties and discouragements, had the wisdom to plan, and the firmness to carry into effect, this great enterprise'. Two former Cabinet colleagues acknowledged his courage in persisting, 'with an unwilling Cabinet at your back and the King directly adverse', as Lord Camden described it. Lord Spencer praised 'the inimitable manner in which you adhered (as I thought with so much good policy and wisdom) to the system of carrying on the war against France through her colonies'.[14]

The news of Abercromby's victory had already brought comfort to the ageing statesman: a generous retraction by George III. One hot day in June the King rode out to call on Dundas and Lady Jane at Wimbledon, and after tea he was persuaded by one of his sons to drink a glass of Madeira. 'You know', the King replied, 'I do not like wine so well as some of my family, but I will drink a glass of Madeira before I leave this house.' A quarter of an hour later he said, 'Now give me my glass of Madeira'; and raising the glass he drank 'to the health, the happiness and the prosperity of the inhabitants of this house, and particularly to the man who proposed and carried into execution the expedition to Egypt, for in my opinion when a person has been perfectly in the wrong, the most just and honourable thing for him to do is to acknowledge it publicly.'[15]

[13] Grenville MSS, Buckinghamshire R.O., 2 May, Lord Grenville to Thomas Grenville; Cornwallis, III. 362; Minto, III. 219; Dropmore, VII. 19; SRO, GD 51/1/802, 20 Oct., Glenbervie to Dundas.
[14] SRO, GD 51/1/802, 20 Oct., Glenbervie to Dundas, and /803, Camden to Dundas; Matheson, 318.
[15] The story was often told by Dundas: the version quoted is Glenbervie's, recorded a fortnight after the royal visit (Glenbervie, I. 232-3).

2. *The Preliminary Articles and their Critics*

The death of Paul and the victories at Alexandria and Copen-
hagen cleared the way for the negotiated peace which Pitt
had long regarded as inevitable, and after hard bargaining the
Preliminary Articles were signed in London on 1 October 1801.
The terms were a compromise, but not an attractive one for
Britain. Of her two dozen conquests she retained only
Trinidad and Ceylon, which had belonged to Spain and
Holland, and she withdrew her garrison from Elba. France
recovered all her colonies, while Spain regained Minorca, and
Holland the Spice Islands, her Caribbean possessions and
Cochin. The Cape was to be a free port under Dutch rule.
The Addington government had struggled to retain Malta,
but gave way to conciliate the new Tsar Alexander, and
agreed to restore the island to the Knights of St. John under
the guarantee of a third power. In return for these concessions
Bonaparte agreed to evacuate Egypt, which he no longer
possessed, and Naples and the Papal States. The integrity of
Britain's allies Portugal and Turkey was secured.[16]

Too much was left to be settled later in the definitive treaty,
or depended on the good faith of the parties, and it was with
diffidence that Hawkesbury informed his predecessor Grenville
of the terms. 'I feel as strongly as any man that new difficulties may open upon us in consequence of this event', he confessed.[17] There is little doubt that Pitt had been constantly
consulted and had urged the negotiation on, advising Addington that the state of the finances made it impossible to continue the war.[18] On the day when the Preliminaries were
signed he wrote to numbers of his friends and old colleagues
to announce the 'happy event', assuring them that he regarded
the term as honourable and on the whole very advantageous.
He saw nothing material to regret except the loss of the Cape,
and even on the importance of that he claimed that experts
differed.[19]

[16] The Preliminaries are printed in *Parl. Hist.* XXXVI. 25.

[17] Dropmore, VII. 45.

[18] Holland, *Whig Party*, I. 154; Dropmore, VII. 47; Glenbervie, I. 251, 262,
295; Stanhope, III. 351; Malmesbury, IV. 60; Pratt MSS, 29 Oct., Dundas to
Camden.

[19] Wilberforce *Private Papers*, 30; Canning MSS, 1 Oct., Pitt to Canning;

The roar of disapproval which rose from Pitt's oldest and closest colleagues was almost unanimous. Grenville led it, but Windham was the most extravagant. 'The country has received its deathblow', he told Addington; and lamented to a naval friend that 'we are going fast down the gulf-stream, and shall never stop, I fear, till, with the rest of Europe, we fall under the universal empire of the great Republic'. By the time the discussions reached the House of Commons he had grown wilder. The terms were 'the death-warrant of my country . . . We are a conquered people. . . .' The French had turned their land 'into one universal brothel', and England's intercourse with Paris would besmirch her 'with all the filth and blood of that polluted city'.[20]

In Grenville's eyes the terms were 'a desperate act' which laid the British empire open to French attack. 'This disgraceful and ruinous treaty' earned his 'entire disapprobation', leaving the country in a state of 'extreme insecurity'. It was 'the most disgraceful and ruinous measure that could have been adopted . . . marked throughout by a tone of unnecessary and degrading concession'. Camden thought his language and behaviour intemperate, but agreed with his views, like many of the former colleagues to whom Grenville sent his diatribes. The problem for most of them was how to act. Windham and Grenville told Pitt immediately that they could never agree with him about the terms, and Windham plunged without hesitation into uncompromising opposition. Most however were reluctant to discredit Pitt and make future co-operation with him difficult, though Grenville eventually followed Windham into opposing the terms. Dundas, though shocked by the surrender of Malta and the Cape, was too loyal to Pitt to enter the controversy.[21] He had long since given up any

Spencer, IV. 304-5; Stanhope, III. 351-2; Bathurst, 25; Pretyman MSS, 1 Oct., Pitt to Tomline.

[20] Windham *Papers*, II. 173; Windham *Diary*, 436; *Parl. Hist.* XXXVI. 99, 126.
[21] Add. MSS 37844, f. 253; Dropmore, VII. 50, 53, 56-9; Pratt MSS, 6 and 13 Oct., Grenville to Camden, 9 Oct., Camden to Spencer, and 29 Oct., Dundas to Camden; Bathurst, 25, 29; *GL* 2541; Canning MSS, Canning's diary for 2 Oct.; Add. MSS 58960, f. 21. In private one of Pitt's most bitter critics was Lord Spencer: '. . . to see Mr. Pitt determined to disgrace himself . . . in fact though not in name still the Minister . . . I really do not know how any Man with the least idea of the real nature of our Constitution can possibly submit to be so governed' (Pratt MSS, 14 Oct. 1801, Spencer to Camden).

hope he may have had of 'saving Europe', and the terms which left France dominant in Europe were no worse than he expected. He only cared about the maritime settlement, whose terms were a bitter blow to his dream of securing world-wide compensations for the loss of security and trade in Europe.

The opponents of the peace rested their case in part on its details: the abandonment of the Mediterranean and the routes to India; the surrender of captured colonies in return for a worthless guarantee to the Porte and a promise to evacuate Egypt which Menou had already surrendered. The Preliminary Articles were sketchy, leaving too much open to reinterpretation in the definitive treaty or to French goodwill, and the silence on commerce was particularly disturbing. The business world looked forward to the reopening of the French market and the renewal of the free trade treaty of 1786; but Bonaparte had to conciliate a powerful protectionist lobby in France. Would the vast coastline he controlled be reopened to British exports? With no mention of earlier political treaties, the way was also left open for France to refurbish the old Family Compact with Spain, and for Spain to hand over her colonies to France. And in spite of so much being left unsettled, the Preliminaries included the dreaded naval armistice, lifting the blockades so that the enemy could resupply their dockyards, redistribute their fleets and send out colonial expeditions.

Most of these criticism could be subsumed in the word *security*. It was 'a peace which gives us no security for the future'.[22] It was for security that the Pitt ministry claimed to have entered and fought the war; and if it was now necessary to abandon the Bourbon monarchy and seek a settlement with the new ruler of France, the terms Britain obtained left her security in ruins both in Europe and overseas. The government was gambling on Bonaparte renouncing aggression to consolidate internal peace and prosperity. But there was no evidence that he would do so. Half a dozen revolutions since 1789 had not brought peaceful government to the French.

[22] Auckland, IV. 144.

'They have turned over in the air, as in sport, like tumbler pigeons', Windham told the House of Commons; 'but have they ever in consequence ceased their flight?' The gamble depended on Bonaparte, whose character was 'marked by frauds of the most disgraceful kind'. The notion that his ambition was circumscribed was criminal nonsense, Malmesbury confided to his diary: his government 'knows no bounds, either moral or civil'. Lord Spencer summed up this view of the terms: 'If ever peace was precarious, this was that peace.'[23]

If the peace was impermanent it exposed Britain to extreme hazard. She would disband her forces and release her seamen, not to be easily collected again, while 30,000 French sailors would return to France from British prisons. England was buying a short interval of repose by sacrificing her security in the next conflict. Nor was there any clear point on which to make a stand if the French eroded the settlement. Would we fight if they re-entered Egypt, asked Windham. Or if they retook Malta; or overthrew Turkey?[24] Strangely, at this stage little was said about the balance of power in Europe. It was accepted that France dominated the continent and Britain was powerless to redress the balance; but the danger of France tilting the European balance further by fresh encroachments was almost ignored. The Peace of Lunéville with Austria was assumed to be a sufficient guarantee.

The fears of those who opposed the peace were largely shared by its makers. Hawkesbury's confession that 'new difficulties may open upon us' set the tone of apology in which they defended the Preliminaries. Pitt told the House that he had had no reason to change his opinion of Bonaparte; 'he was inclined to hope everything was good, but he was bound to act as if he feared otherwise'. He confessed to Grenville that the peace was 'very precarious', and that the armed forces should be kept constantly ready to renew the war. He then fell into Gladstonian circumlocutions: 'if once the question of peace or war is looked at only as a question of terms, I am far from thinking that those now agreed can, upon the whole, be denied to be honourable and reasonably

[23] Minto, III. 226; *Parl. Hist.* XXXVI. 110, 161; Malmesbury, IV. 61.
[24] Dropmore, VII. 59; Add. MSS 58918, f. 188; Canning MSS, 2 Oct., Windham to Canning.

advantageous'. His qualifications were echoed by Addington, whose private conversation was defensive and apologetic, leaning heavily on the fact of Pitt's approval and Pitt's part in shaping the negotiations. The King was resigned and scep-tical. 'Do you know what I call the peace?' he asked a visitor to Windsor. 'An *experimental peace*, for it is nothing else . . . but it was unavoidable.'[25]

Why then was a peace accepted when it was so widely regarded as dangerous? The underlying reason was domestic pressure. In July and August there had been an alarming invasion scare, which would certainly be renewed in the following summer.[26] The exchequer was shaky. And though the harvest of 1801 was good, prices took time to respond. The average price of wheat in the twelve maritime counties had peaked in March at 152 shillings a bushel (the previous wartime peak in 1796 had been 105 shillings); after falling back sharply it rose again to 136 shillings in July before falling back to a normal level of 69 shillings in October. The famine was over and rioting subsided, but the hatred of the war was not abated, and the coincidence of the fall in wheat prices with the peace was popularly taken as proof that the war had been the cause of the dearth.[27] When General Lauriston arrived in London on 10 October with the French ratification, a mob called out by a radical saddler unhitched the horses from his carriage and drew him through the streets; to the terror, it was said, of the passenger, who had learned too much about mobs in the Revolution. Members of the upper classes who accepted the necessity of peace were still disgusted by the 'senseless levity' of the public celebrations, but recognized them as 'a proof of how completely the nation is tired of the war, and for peace on any terms'. Canning's friend Leveson-Gower thought it would be amusing to oppose the peace, but bowed before 'the real enthusiasm and frantic joy which appeared in the faces of every person I met, whether farmer, labourer or

[25] *Parl. Hist.* XXXVI. 68, 72; Dropmore, VII. 49; Glenbervie, I. 267–70; Malmesbury IV. 62.

[26] The army at home was very weak: 'in our wooden walls alone must we place our trust', wrote Cornwallis, who was now commanding the eastern district. See Cornwallis, III. 379–81.   [27] Dropmore, VII. 66.

manufacturer'.[28] In the House of Lords only nine peers voted with Grenville against the Preliminaries, and Windham dared not divide the House of Commons. The distinguished officers whose opinion had encouraged Pitt's drift towards peace, Cornwallis and Moira, St. Vincent and Nelson, all supported the terms. Nelson said they were 'the almost unanimous wishes of the country' and told the House of Lords they were 'honourable and advantageous', while St. Vincent, a member of the Cabinet, called them 'a fit subject for exultation'.[29] The First Lord may have feared for the discipline of the fleet if the war continued: a month later a squadron looking foward to demobilization mutinied in Bantry Bay on a report that a force was to follow a French expedition to the West Indies.[30]

It was against this background of threatened invasion and discontent with the war that the government weighed the arguments for peace. There was nothing to be gained in Europe by fighting on. The Peace of Lunéville appeared to have stabilized the situation on the continent; and though it established 'the inordinate and frightfully overgrown power of France', Britain alone could not redress the balance. Admiral Young had summed up the blunt truth during the summer: 'With France as strong as she is now, Europe can never be secure; perhaps the great continental powers will be at length convinced of this and heartily join their forces to reduce her within reasonable bounds.'[31]

The restoration of Europe had to wait for the recovery of the great powers, and the ministry saw no other objects to justify continuing the war. The internal threat from revolutionary ideology was dead: 'we have seen Jacobinism deprived of its fascination', declared Pitt. To fight on for colonies could make little material impression on the enemy and might risk the fragile new friendship with Russia; it would further

[28] Malmesbury, IV. 61; Auckland, IV. 138, 144; Canning MSS, 17 Oct., Leveson Gower to Canning.
[29] *Parl. Hist.* XXXVI. 184-6; St. Vincent, I. 284-5.
[30] *GL* 2579n; Glenbervie, I. 307. A midshipman in the Tagus warned that there would be dismay among the seamen if the repose in their native country to which they were 'anxiously looking forward' was deferred. (Sibthorpe MSS, 23 Dec., Henry Sibthrope to his father.)
[31] Auckland, IV. 144; Canning MSS, 26 Oct., Pitt to Canning; Glenbervie, I. 268; Keith, II. 376.

strain the finances; it would collide with popular opinion. Better surely to make peace and recuperate, hoping for an epoch of prosperity, or at worst to prepare for a fresh struggle with the country united. The alternative was to fight on in the teeth of public opinion and without success, till the finances were too exhausted to maintain the military forces required for security.[32]

If these assumptions were granted, peace was right in principle, and the making of the treaty was reduced to what Pitt came to call 'a question of terms only'.[33] It is possible that the government could have improved the conditions, and it may have been precipitate in allowing itself to be hurried into signing the Preliminaries. It has often been alleged, for instance, that Hawkesbury threw away the fruits of the Egyptian campaign by being tricked into signing on the day before the news of Menou's capitulation reached London.

Too much has been made of this argument. It is true that Bonaparte had ordered Otto to complete the negotiations by 2 October or break them off, mentioning as a reason from Alexandria might not be able to hold out beyond 23 September. If this was the main reason for Bonaparte's ultimatum, he miscalculated; for Menou had offered to capitulate a full month earlier on 27 August, and if the Preliminaries had not been signed a day earlier than Bonaparte required, the news would have arrived before the signing. In any case the fact would not have been very material to the negotiation. On the one hand the surrender was not regarded as confirmed till three weeks later; on the other, it had long been inevitable. Ever since the report on 12 August of the surrender of Cairo the eventual capitulation of Menou's army had been expected; and well before that date the British ministers had been confidently planning the redeployment of the British force.[34] The Preliminary Articles did not stipulate merely the French evacu-

---

[32] *Parl. Hist.* XXXVI. 69; Dropmore, VII. 45, 49-50; Canning MSS, 26 Oct., Pitt to Canning; Glenbervie, I. 267-8.

[33] *Parl. Hist.* XXXVI. 57; Canning MSS, 26 Oct., Pitt to Canning.

[34] Cornwallis, III. 386n; Dropmore, VII. 61; Glenbervie, I. 263; WO 6/21, 10 and 22 July, Hobart to Hutchinson; Hope of Luffness MSS, 1 Aug., Dundas to Alexander Hope, and 11 Sept., Chatham to same; *GL* 2502, 2508.

ation of Egypt, which being inevitable was no concession on the part of the French, but the restoration of the country to the Turks, involving also a British evacuation which was a debt of honour to the Porte and a necessary concession to the Tsar. The British expeditionary force had not fought in vain. Its purpose had been to influence the peace negotiation; and Bonaparte would have negotiated differently if he had not known that the loss of Egypt was certain.

The belief that the Addington government threw away the victory in Egypt rests on a superficial reading of Bonaparte's correspondence. He never confided his full calculations to his correspondents; and the letter which ordered the ultimatum offers a second explanation on which greater emphasis should be placed. Bonaparte was planning to recover San Domingo from Toussaint. Expeditions were being prepared in Brest, Cadiz and Toulon, and would soon be waiting for the ratification of the Preliminaries and the raising of the British blockade. If they were held up beyond October they would lose most of the campaigning season in the Caribbean, and to postpone the expedition till the following year might force Bonaparte to recognize Toussaint and renounce the reconquest. The moment the Preliminaries were signed, he ordered the expeditions to sail. Not a single day could he afford to lose, for after April the San Domingo climate would not be fit for European troops. In that consideration, perhaps more than in Egypt, lies the reason for Napoleon's impatience.[35]

It was on the evening of 29 September that Otto delivered his ultimatum, and before the night was out the Cabinet agreed to the final terms.[36] This committee of honourable and not very experienced men had undoubtedly been out-classed by the First Consul and his well-honed instrument Talleyrand. As Metternich was to learn in a few years time, Bonaparte had a marvellous instinct for identifying and exploiting other mens' weaknesses. Metternich analysed his technique of rushing his opponents' diplomatic positions with sudden

[35] *Napoleon Corr.* 5749, 5784-7, 5863. No. 5785, an order for the formation of the San Domingo forces with the presumed date 7 Oct., may be of earlier date.
[36] *GL* 2534.

démarches, disrupting their calculations with a smoke-screen of contradictory arrangements.[37] The technique which over-whelmed Addington's Cabinet was a diplomatic version of the military tactics of the Revolution. Could the Cabinet afford to prevaricate in face of Bonaparte's time limit? The Ministers must have guessed that he had his own reasons for wanting peace; but would he rupture the negotiation if they demurred, and were any of the points at issue worth the risk of war? The Mediterranean position was past saving; for Malta had been given up to conciliate the Tsar Alexander, while Minorca had been reported by Abercromby to be in-defensible at the outbreak of a war and its fortifications to require total reconstruction at ruinous cost;[38] Egypt had to be returned to the Turks as a matter of honour and to avoid trouble with Russia. On the ocean route to the east the loss of the Cape was regrettable, but Indian authorities no longer attached as much importance to it as they had in the days before copper-bottomed ships; and the infinitely more im-portant base at Ceylon was retained to command the Malabar and Carnatic coasts, while Wellesley's defeat of Mysore had greatly increased the internal security of British India. In the West Indies it would have been desirable to hold on to the French base at Martinique; but Trinidad was an even better position for protecting the Leeward Islands, its economic value was greater, and it could become a convenient platform for operations against Dundas's favourite goals in Spanish America. None of the other captured islands that Britain was giving up would affect the security of the country or the sources of her wealth. Their retention 'would only give us a little more wealth; but a little more wealth would be badly purchased by a little more war'.

Thus Pitt defended the terms; terms which he said 'it would have been the greatest imprudence to reject . . . I can-not but think the conclusion of the treaty fortunate for the country'. The ministers in office could only echo him. 'Noth-ing', Hawkesbury told Grenville, 'could have been reasonably expected from a continuance of the war which would have justified us, under present circumstances, in rejecting these

---

[37] Grunwald, *Revue des deux mondes*, 1937, p. 369, and *Revue de Paris*, 1937, p. 834.   [38] Dunfermline, Appendix B; Glenbervie, I. 268.

terms.' Addington argued that if the terms had been refused in the teeth of public opinion, it would have become impossible to fight on. Britain's negotiating position would then be worsened by public pressure. Would the critics of the peace have chosen the alternative of war, asked Dundas's successor Lord Hobart.[39]

If the government was cowardly and defeatist in accepting this settlement, as is sometimes alleged, then it seems that Pitt must bear a heavy share of the responsibility. Whether the national finances were really in a state of collapse, as he maintained, was a question which puzzled contemporaries. A different argument for the peace was to be justified by future events. The key to the future balance of power was Britain's reconciliation with Russia. On his alliance with Paul, Bonaparte had built his plans for the defeat of England: on their understanding with Alexander the British would found their hopes of reversing the new order in Europe. The notification of Alexander's accession had been followed by an immediate truce, and peace with Russia was signed by Lord St. Helens in Petersburg on 17 June. There were concessions on neutral rights which made Lord Grenville uneasy, just as he was to become uneasy about the yielding of Malta. On the Malta question the government certainly drew back wisely in order to leap the better: they were wiser than Windham, who would characteristically have forfeited good relations with Russia sooner than lose the island.[40] By conciliating Alexander they left the way open for his later consent to the British retention of the island, and were able to renew the war in 1803 relying on Russia's friendship. A better peace, won at the price of alienating Alexander, would have been a Pyrrhic victory.

3. *The Dubious Peace*

In this manner there came about the compromise peace which Dundas had seen to be inevitable; the limited end for which

---

[39] *Parl. Hist.* XXXVI. 59–76; Dropmore, VII. 45, 49–50; Canning MSS, 22 and 26 Oct., Pitt to Canning; Glenbervie, I. 267; Auckland, IV. 140.

[40] Add. MSS 37846, f. 186.

he had geared down British strategy into limited warfare. So clear a connection between war and policy should gladden the student of Clausewitz. Yet war and policy do not slot with satisfactory precision into the categories of the theorist; and the outcome of the peace was not quite what reasoning men had expected, resembling more closely the nightmare world of William Windham's imagination than Pitt's hopes of a stable prosperity.

Not quite so. England was not destroyed or turned into a universal brothel as Windham predicted. But the hope of a stable peace had rested on an assumption which was to be falsified: that the French Revolution was over. The magic spell of Jacobinism may have been spent, but the French government had not been pacified. During the interval between the Preliminaries of London in October and the signing of the definitive Peace of Amiens in March 1802, all the unwritten expectations which had induced the Addington government to sign the Preliminaries would wither. Nothing had been said in the articles about commerce; nothing about the French boundaries recognized by the Peace of Lunéville; nothing about Piedmont, nor the independence of the satellite republics of Holland, Switzerland and Lombardy; nor about the reorganization of Germany, nor about Elba and Parma. There was nothing in the articles to restrain French colonial ambitions. In all these areas the British government found that it had been duped.

Bonaparte had hurried on the Preliminaries for reasons of which the impending surrender of Alexandria was not the overriding one. He needed an immediate truce to provide a prestigious success and give him time for the next stage in his designs: time to promulgate the contentious Concordat with the Papacy which had been signed in July; to reorganize the French Republic and affirm his personal rule; to reconstruct Germany and Italy; to reconquer San Domingo. He knew that the Preliminaries had side-stepped issues on which England and the Consulate would never agree. He did not intend to grant a commercial treaty; and he had long since determined to incorporate Piedmont with France. As soon as the Preliminaries were signed he hurried on with his plans. The coasts of France and her satellites were closed to British exports by high tariffs. With his fleets freed from the naval blockade he dispatched a great expedition to recover San Domingo from the black hero Toussaint, obtaining British acquiescence by deceiving them about the scale of the armament. He took possession of Parma and Elba under the secret clauses of his treaty with Spain which had not been revealed to the British. The Swiss and Dutch Republics were remodelled contrary to the Peace of Lunéville; and he assumed the presidency of the Cisalpine, which he renamed the Italian Republic. If the British protested that the independence of the satellite republics had been guaranteed at Lunéville, he would reply that Britain had not been a party to Lunéville, and those continental questions formed no part of the Anglo-French negotiations.

The British plenipotentiary appointed to negotiate the definitive treaty was Lord Cornwallis. A military hero, an Indian Governor-General, and a wise and temperate Viceroy of rebellious Ireland, he had qualities which it was supposed would appeal to the military ruler of France. But Cornwallis was an imperfect choice to deal with Bonaparte. In his middle sixties he was past his peak; he felt an excessive dread of prolonging the war; and he was a gentleman. He left his home in Suffolk in October 1801 expecting a short, smooth negotiation; but this guileless, honourable man of limited diplomatic experience was no match for the Bonaparte gang at Amiens, 'people with the dress of mountebanks and the manners of assassins'.[41] The French front-man was Bonaparte's amiable brother Joseph; but behind him was Talleyrand, whom Cornwallis soon summed up as 'devoid of honour and principle'. After each day's negotiations the British delegation would reduce to writing the verbal agreements they thought they had reached with Joseph, only to have their note repudiated by the French on the following morning. No powers . . . would have to seek further instructions . . . The negotiations dragged on for four tedious months while Napoleon was reorganizing Europe. The anxious Cornwallis doubted whether the French

---

[41] His son's description (Cornwallis, III. 410).

intended peace; but he was haunted by fear of war. The thought that an unguarded word or an error of judgement could cause the renewal of a 'bloody and hopeless war' preyed on his mind. All he dared hope for was a peace that was not dishonourable and would not further undermine British safety. Francis Jackson, the British minister in Paris, blamed the unsatisfactory outcome of the negotiations largely on Cornwallis's 'drowsiness' and inexperience, his incapacity to sense when the French were bluffing, and his underrating of Bonaparte's own need for peace.[42]

But Cornwallis was not backed by a resolute ministry. The Addington government, it is true, was well aware of Bonaparte's encroachments, which it watched with anxiety and some show of firmness. His duplicity towards Toussaint indicated that he was no reformed character. His expedition to San Domingo was supposed to include ships of the line equipped as transports, but it was discovered that many of them were fully armed, and a British squadron had to be sent to the West Indies to watch them with great expense and disturbance of the seamen's morale. Hawkesbury denounced Bonaparte's take-over of the Cisalpine Republic as a gross breach of faith and proof of his inordinate ambition. Bonaparte however partially distracted attention from his cisalpine coup by contriving a confrontation at Amiens over Malta, withdrawing his earlier proposal that a Neapolitan garrison should guard the fortress till the Knights of St. John were reorganized. This almost caused a rupture of the negotiations, and British commanders in the Mediterranean were warned to be ready for war. A strong letter from Hawkesbury caused the French to back off; but Bonaparte's try-on withdrew attention from his successful aggression in Italy.[43]

The government's apparent resolution was not to last. From the middle of February 1802 Addington and his daughter were seriously ill; and on 2 March, while still unfit and anxious about his daughter, he wrote a confusing letter to Cornwallis urging a speedy settlement for the sake of 'public feeling and public convenience'. On 14 March the Cabinet approved a draft treaty and authorized Cornwallis to

[42] Cornwallis, III. 420, 437, 460; Glenbervie, I. 310-11; Malmesbury, IV. 71-2.
[43] Cornwallis, III. 452, 457; WO 6/21, p. 202; WO 6/55, p. 92.

sign it, giving the French an eight-day ultimatum to sign without alteration. The real weight of this ultimatum was obscure. Hawkesbury wrote to Cornwallis after the Cabinet meeting that it was of the utmost importance 'that no further delay whatever should arise in bringing this business to its end'. If the eager Cornwallis needed any further urging to settle, he received it in Hawkesbury's explanation on 22 March: 'The Treasury is almost exhausted, and Mr. Addington cannot well make his loan in the present state of uncertainty.' By then the British government knew that the continental powers had acquiesced in Bonaparte's presidency of the Italian Republic. On the morning of 29 March messengers from Amiens brought the news that the treaty was signed.[44]

One member of the Cabinet had dissented from the instruction to Cornwallis, the Home Secretary Thomas Pelham. He felt that before the treaty was signed British security required a satisfactory explanation of the successive French reinforcements of the West Indies, and of the general intentions of the French government. He cited the many encroachments in Europe, the West Indian threat, the signs that the French planned to return to Egypt. None of these points taken alone might justify 'the dreadful alternative of war'. Yet some satisfaction should be required, before giving France all the benefits of a definitive treaty which would still require England to keep up a war establishment in the Caribbean.[45]

Pelham wondered whether to resign, but drew back from the confusion he would cause since he agreed on all other points of the treaty. His doubts were shared elsewhere, however. There was dismay in the City when the blocking of British imports to France and Holland was followed by prohibitive duties in Spain; and the feeling was widespread that the treaty should not be signed without some guarantee against further subversion of the European balance of power. 'Peace in a week, war in a month', was Malmesbury's prediction; and the King expected 'a temporary peace, for no one could expect one of any duration'. Pitt was in two minds. He admitted that he had been wrong to hope that Bonaparte's ambition was sated, for the Consul remained an insatiable

---

[44] GL 2599n; Cornwallis, III. 462, 472-7, 482; *Napoleon Corr.* 5990-1.
[45] GL 2600.

and faithless plunderer. At any other time his Italian encroachment and the West Indian expedition would have caused
Britain to go to war, and even now Pitt said it was a difficult
question whether Britain or France would gain the more by
an interval of peace. On balance, however, he favoured peace.
For England 'rest, however short, was desirable'. War would
wear out the patience of the country — his fear since at least
the beginning of 1800 — and would whittle its resources away
without making any impression on the enemy, whereas a
few years of peace would enable it to sustain a prolonged war
again. The heart of his case against war was that no help could
be expected from any of the great powers. Until they recovered, Britain would be isolated and powerless to check
Bonaparte's encroachments on the continent. Time, which
would restore Britain's finances, might bring Russia and the
German powers to her aid.[46]

Pitt's old colleagues and present critics admitted that the
country was with him. Grenville softened his attack on the
peace in the House of Lords to avoid running too much against
the feelings of his audience, and Camden declared that 'the
country anxiously panted for peace'. Parliament confirmed
his opinion: 276 votes in the Commons for the peace and only
70 against; 122 in the Lords against 16. The ministers echoed
Pitt's defence of the peace, with the same reservations.
Addington claimed that he had never regarded the treaty
with 'any sentiment of exaltation', but had satisfied himself
that it was 'upon the whole, the best measure that could be
taken'. The Foreign Secretary Hawkesbury viewed the French
encroachments since the signing of the Preliminaries with
'anxiety and alarm. . . . He did not pretend to say that the
security of the peace was no consideration; all he could ask
was, could a better peace have been secured, had the contest
been protracted longer?' Both ministers emphasized the need
to be ready to resist any further encroachment. They took
their stand against continuing the war on the absence of continental allies. When Bonaparte had assumed the presidency
of the Cisalpine Republic Prussia congratulated him, Vienna
acquiesced and Russia showed no dissatisfaction.[47] At home

---

[46] Dropmore, VII. 78, 80-2, 92; *GL* 2597; Malmesbury, IV. 64-9; Glenbervie,
I. 318.   [47] The phrases echoed Bonaparte (*Napoleon Corr.* 5990).

the British people, unable to see any progress, were weary after nine years of war and 'reluctant to continue without any definite object'. Only by husbanding her resources could Britain hope eventually to encourage the German powers to resist. In the meantime she had secured her empire by acquiring Trinidad and Ceylon, and defeating Mysore. Windham had argued that the conquest of islands did not constitute the security for which Britain had fought the war; but that fundamental security which Windham sought could not be achieved in the present situation by any peace of compromise. 'I doubt', said Hawkesbury, 'whether in this view anything short of the total subversion of the French government would satisfy; but . . . that hope can scarcely exist in rational minds.'[48]

[48] Add. MSS 37846, f. 188; *Parl. Hist.* XXXVI. 730, 758-9, 767-9, 812, 814.

Conclusion

'. . . that hope can scarcely exist in rational minds'. With those words Lord Hawkesbury confessed that the goal of security for which Britain had waged the nine years' war had not been achieved. No one dared claim that the general peace settlement of Europe promised security. The whole of the Low Countries was in the power of France, giving her deep-water bases north of the Straits of Dover with access to naval supplies by the river systems of the Rhine, Maas and Scheldt. In Spain and Portugal a dominant French influence secured not only bases but fleets, athwart the British routes to the Mediterranean, the Far East and the Americas. The outlook for British exports in European markets was bleak. Thus Britain was threatened in her trade and her maritime power. Nor was there reason to hope that the outward thrust of France would be contained by the continental powers. To the east France had extended along the natural frontier of the Rhine, had won control of the Swiss passes, and had advanced her power across the Apennines as far east as the Adige and south of the Po into Parma. These changes and the acquiescence of the major powers shook to its foundations the balance between France and the German states on which British policy had been built for two centuries.

Britain could have lived with this dismal settlement if it had been secured by a stable government in Paris, that neces-sary condition of peace which Pitt and Grenville had often proclaimed. Certainly Bonaparte had stabilized his rule and was renovating the internal life of France; but massive evi-dence had accumulated that he would not rest content with the new international order. In every direction threats could be seen; on the high seas, in the Levant and in Europe itself. Time would prove these dangers to be real, and Napoleon's ambitions would force the British government to return to Lord Grenville's uncompromising stand for a war of overthrow and a decisive victory. Grenville himself, except for a year as Prime Minister after the death of Pitt, watched from the sidelines through the long years of adversity. Ironically it was Castlereagh, a parliamentary defender of the Peace of Amiens and of the thesis that the Jacobin danger was past,[1] who a dozen years later cemented the final coalition to overthrow Napoleon. For as Grenville had foreseen, only the collective strength of Europe, united by a common goal, could contain the dynamism of the new France. Without the support of the continental powers Britain could not follow her traditional policy of preventing the hegemony of a single power or great-power domination of the Low Countries.

But besides her negative European policy of preventing hegemony, Britain had forward aims outside Europe: her drive for expanding markets linked by naval bases. Here she might have sought compensation for her failure in Europe; but here too she was thwarted at Amiens. Six months before the Preliminary Articles were signed, Dundas had been able to claim that overseas markets had been won which replaced the markets lost in the continental war.[2] But the twenty-five conquests he listed were thrown away at Amiens without recovering the markets of Europe. Dundas's desire to open world-wide sources of new wealth had been checked. The approaches to India had been weakened by the restoration of Malta to the Knights of St. John, the recovery of French influence at Constantinople, and the return of the Cape to Holland. In the Caribbean the Lesser Antilles were again overhung by the French base at Martinique, and new threats to Jamaica were likely to arise in San Domingo and Louisiana. The future of Spain's restless American colonies was un-resolved.

Nine years of war had gained nothing, illustrating again the ancient truth that the consequences of using force are unpredictable. Wars usually last longer and cost more than governments expect; and they rarely achieve the political goals that might justify the risks, the cost and the pain. This was certainly true of Britain in the Wars of the French Revolution. Perhaps her statesmen had been deluded by past successes and underrated the strategic task, because in the Seven Years War Britain had achieved both her forward aim of imperial

---

[1] *Parl. Hist.* XXXVI. 784.   [2] *Parl. Hist.* XXXV. 1072-4, 1087-8.

expansion and her negative aim of containing France. It had been done by orchestrating two concepts of strategy, the continental and the maritime; for the notion of a dichotomy between maritime and continental strategy, long entrenched in political debate, had been more polemical than real. The two strategies had not in practice been alternatives, but parallel and reciprocating efforts; and the question had not been which to choose, but how to balance them. The continental commitment in Hanover had not only defended the European balance of power, but contained French resources in Europe which might otherwise have been diverted into the naval war. Colonial offensives won territory and markets for Britain, but were also believed to undermine the French war economy to the benefit of Britain's European allies. The positive rewards of war lay in the maritime sphere, as the Elder Pitt had preached; but greater disasters were possible on the continent, as he recognized when he allowed a British army to be committed to Germany.

The success of the Seven Years War may have created an illusion about the place of warfare in British policy and about the pattern of British strategy: the illusion that Britain could always pursue her twin goals of European stability and overseas expansion by a balanced strategy combining military aid to continental allies with colonial offensives of her own. Within two decades a warning was given by the American War that the pattern of strategy would not necessarily always be so straightforward; for when Britain found herself without allies and a bridgehead in Europe, it was hard to contain a French challenge at sea. When Britain entered the Wars of the French Revolution in 1793, however, she had escaped from the diplomatic isolation which had contributed to her failure in America, and was once more a member of a powerful European alliance. In the First Coalition she attempted to repeat the balanced strategy of the Seven Years War, subsidizing her allies, buying German auxiliaries, and dividing her own army between the defence of the Low Countries and colonial offensives, with a similar debate about the right balance of effort. The argument that colonial offensives were part of the general allied strategy was maintained even by Grenville. He has been portrayed in this book as a blinkered advocate of continental warfare; yet in the debate on the Preliminaries in 1801 even he expounded the concept of a war of maritime pressure: 'whenever we were at war with France, one of our first objects must always be to cripple her marine, which could never be better done than by contracting her commerce — by depriving her of her colonial possessions'.[3]

This policy was not received with enthusiasm by allies who could not grasp that Britain's command of the sea was the necessary condition of her fighting the war at all. The policy could be defended to them; nevertheless it was true that in Britain's colonial strategy there had always been an ambivalence. Was she undermining the French economy and thereby contributing to the general interests of the alliance? Or was she pursuing her own interest in imperial expansion? In the mind of Dundas there were other reasons for the colonial strategy than to undermine the French war economy, and more important ones. Colonial warfare sustained the British economy, and furthered the pursuit of imperial and commercial expansion. Its purposes were 'to increase those resources on which depend our naval superiority . . . and provide new beneficial markets'.[4] In public discussion Dundas presented both these aims as contributions to the general welfare of the alliance; but his secret memoranda make it plain that for him commercial expansion was an aim distinct from the common purposes of the coalition. It called for a strategy which diverged from the common general war plan of the allies, much as the particular ambitions of the German powers in Poland or Bavaria or Italy caused their efforts to diverge. In the British divergence even Lord Grenville was implicated. Though he had learned from the wrecking of the First Coalition that divergent political aims could destroy a common strategy, and attempted in the Second Coalition to apply the lesson by reconciling the war aims of the continental allies, it was nevertheless he, in the Russian negotiations of 1798, who refused to allow the future 'maritime peace' to form part of the general discussion of allied war aims.

[3] *Parl. Hist.* XXXVI. 165. Even Windham recognized that continental and maritime efforts were not mutually exclusive (ibid. 748).

[4] *Parl. Hist.* XXXV. 1073-3.

By that time, in the Second Coalition, the harmony of Britain's dual strategy had broken down; and she had ceased to be able to maintain a balance between continental and colonial operations. For she had lost her continental bridge-heads and her allies in the west. In 1795 the withdrawal of the Austrians from the Netherlands and Prussia's neutraliz-ation of Hanover excluded Britain from her former bridge-heads and removed from western Europe the allies' armies to which her own small expeditionary force had been attached. This meant that on the western coastline of Europe, from the Danish Sound to Gibraltar, Britain could only intervene in Europe by amphibious assaults with her own little army and such auxiliaries as she could find and ship across the sea. A western front was not thereby precluded; but it has been shown in this and the preceding volume that to seize a per-manent military lodgment from the sea depended on two conditions: insurgent support in the invasion area, and an active eastern front to contain the main French armies.

Invasion from the sea had a further consequence, however, which disrupted the harmony of British strategy. A major assault on Europe called for such vast resources, in ships and British troops, as to preclude simultaneous operations overseas. Strategy was no longer a question of finding the right balance between continental and colonial operations, but a choice of one or the other. The strain on resources ruled out undertaking both. In this lies part of Grenville's conflict with Dundas over the deployment of British troops. Colonial warfare would cripple Britain's contribution to a coalition war in Europe; and Grenville, who saw that a coalition was the only way to the sort of victory he wanted, regarded a major British landing as an absolute duty that Britain owed to her allies. This argument Dundas rejected on both political and operational grounds. From the end of 1799 he questioned the need for total victory, and the hope of achieving it; nor did he believe that a major British front could be maintained in Europe. The demonstra-tions and island landings which were all he wished to attempt would leave resources available for overseas attacks; operations no longer designed to undermine the French economy as part of a general allied assault, but to further Britain's alternative political and commercial goals in the new markets of the world.

Such minor diversions in Europe as Dundas would allow in 1800 were quite inadequate to sustain a coalition war, or to give Britain any military standing among her allies; and later British ministries did not accept Dundas's solution, for the political perspective changed. It became apparent that no compromise with Napoleon was possible; that no end to the war short of victory would leave Britain secure. The truth was clear that in the last resort Europe must have absolute priority in British strategy; a truth to be spelt out again a century later on the Somme. The British ministries of the Napoleonic Wars did not follow Dundas's logic, but Grenville's. Whenever continental warfare blazed up, they mounted major continental expeditions: to Hanover in 1805, to Pomerania in 1807, to Walcheren in the Austrian War of 1809. All these expeditions failed, as the Helder expedition of 1799 had failed, and for the same reasons. The British force was limited in size, its mobility constricted, local aid hard to organize; and thus the British front depended on the success of the main allied armies. Napoleon could afford to screen the British invasion area with forces inferior in numbers and quality while he sought decisive victory against his major enemy, at Ulm and Austerlitz, at Friedland, at Wagram, following the pattern set in the Second Coalition at Zurich and Marengo.

Thus for Britain maritime and continental strategy became polarized after 1795, as they had never been in the past in spite of much polemical debate. A cyclical pattern emerged. A resurgence of continental warfare would lead to a British invasion of Europe, followed soon by the military collapse of the alliance and a British withdrawal into maritime warfare, while the government 'rested on its oars' and waited for the diplomatic scene to improve. The ministers were not choosing limited warfare because it was especially suited to Britain, but resigning themselves to a second best because the best option was closed.[5]

[5] The contention of Sir Julian Corbett, and later of Sir Basil Liddell Hart, that the natural British mode of conducting warfare is in a framework of 'limited' war and maritime 'mobility' was demolished by Michael Howard in his Neale Lecture, 'The British Way in Warfare: a Reappraisal'. I have examined the claims made for amphibious warfare in 'Problems of an Amphibious Power: Britain against France, 1793-1815' (*Naval War College Review*, 1978).

After the collapse of the First Coalition in 1795 there was no consistent 'right' strategy for a British government to pursue. Strategy depended as always on policy; but policy depended more than ever on the shifting strength and will of the continental powers. Only coalition warfare in Europe could lead to a decisive victory and the checking of France's overweening power; and only during a coalition war could Britain hope to maintain a military front in western Europe. Without major allies she could pursue no independent strategy of her own in the European heartland, and instead responded with opportunism to the shifting continental situation. The long defensive in the Mediterranean theatre, with great military and naval forces committed to containing France, was a symbol of Britain's imprisonment in her strategic dilemma. In retrospect the outbreak of the Peninsular War in 1809 may appear to have solved her problem. At the periphery of Europe in Portugal the British government found the conditions it had been unable to find in the heart of western Europe, and created a permanent front which was independent of major allies. Britain acquired the aid of an insurgent country in Spain, and an auxiliary army of high potential quality in Portugal; superior lines of communication and sources of supply; and a defensible bridgehead which could be sustained in adversity.

Yet the picture of the Peninsular theatre as a decisive European front is delusive. It was not to seek decisive victory that Britain flew to the defence of Portugal and the aid of the Spaniards in 1808. The Spanish navy and its bases were at stake; and honour and self-interest demanded the protection of the ancient ally Portugal, with its vital ports and rich colonies. These were maritime considerations, and war in the Peninsula alone could not decide the fate of Europe. For victory, it needed Napoleon's ambition to weld the reluctant powers of Europe into a final coalition. That coalition it was Castlereagh's achievement to hold together till the war was won: the task Grenville had identified, but had found impossible to achieve in the political circumstances of his day.

Guide to Citations

Abbreviations used in footnotes

Add. MSS	Additional Manuscripts, British Library
E.H.D.	*English Historical Documents*
FO	Foreign Office papers, Public Record Office
GL	George III: *The Later Correspondence of George III*, ed. A. Aspinall, 1962-70 (usually cited with item-numbers).
Parl. Hist.	*Parliamentary History of England*, ed. William Cobbett, 1806 ff.
PRO	Public Record Office, Kew
SRO	Scottish Record Office, Edinburgh
WO	War Office papers, Public Record Office

Manuscript Materials

Public Record Office

FO 7/57-61	Austria
FO 63/33-4	Portugal
FO 65/43-7	Russia
FO 67/29	Sardinia
FO 74/29-30	Switzerland
WO 1/298	Minorca
WO 1/411	Popham
WO 6/21	Expeditions 1800 (Secretary of State, out-letters)
WO 6/55	Minorca (Secretary of State, out-letters)
PRO 30/8/101, 104, 140, 157, 181, 197, 243, 339	Chatham Papers
PRO 30/58/2-3	Dacres Adams Papers

Scottish Record Office

GD 45/4/16-17	Dalhousie Papers
GD 51/1/529, 703, 718, 725-6, 768-70, 772, 774-6, 778-9, 802-3	Melville Papers

British Library

Add. MSS 31163, 31167	St. Vincent
Add. MSS 31171-2	Nepean
Add. MSS 33107	Thomas Pelham
Add. MSS 34932	Nelson
Add. MSS 36708	St. Vincent
Add. MSS 37844, 37846, 37872, 37876-80, 37904, 37924	Windham
Add. MSS 38237, 38311, 38355, 38357	Liverpool
Add. MSS 38735-6, 38759	Huskisson
Add. MSS 38833	Canning/Frere
Add. MSS 40100-102	Dundas
Add. MSS 41855	Thomas Grenville
Add. MSS 42772	George Rose
Add. MSS 57444	J. C. Herries
Add. MSS 58861-2, 58883, 58908, 58916-18, 58929, 58935	Grenville (Dropmore)

National Library of Scotland

Melville Papers
Minto Papers
George Rose Papers

John Rylands University Library, Manchester

Crawford and Balcarres Papers (letters of Henry and Lady Jane Dundas; and Memoirs of Lady Anne Barnard, of which the typescript copy is cited).
Pitt Papers

Various Collections

Barnard, Lady Anne: see John Rylands Library, above.
Bland Burges: Bodleian Library, Oxford.
Brodie of Brodie: care of National Register of Archives (Scotland), Edinburgh.
Canning, George: Sheepscar Library, Leeds.
Dundas of Beechwood: care of National Register of Archives (Scotland), Edinburgh.
Dundas, Henry: Duke University Library, North Carolina.
Grenville: Buckinghamshire Record Office, Aylesbury (see also British Library, above).
Grey: University of Durham.

Hope of Luffness: care of National Register of Archives (Scotland), Edinburgh
Hogendorp, G.K. van: Algemeen Rijksarchief, The Hague.
Pitt: Cambridge University Library, Add. 6958.
Pitt: William L. Clements Library, Ann Arbor, Michigan.
Pratt (Camden): Kent Record Office, Maidstone.
Pretyman: Suffolk Record Office, Ipswich.
Sibthorpe: Lincolnshire Archives Office, Lincoln.
Sidmouth: Devon Record Office, Exeter.
Simcoe: Devon Record Office, Exeter.
Stowe Papers: Huntington Library, San Marino, California.
Verney: Claydon House, Buckinghamshire

Printed Sources

Annual Register for 1798.
Auckland, Lord. *Journal and Correspondence of William Eden, 1st Baron Auckland*, 1861-2, vol. IV.
Barham. *Letters and Papers of Charles Middleton, Lord Barham*, ed. J. K. Laughton, 1907-11, vol. III.
Bathurst. *Report on the Manuscripts of Earl Bathurst*, Hist. MSS. Comm., 1923.
Buckingham and Chandos, Duke of. *Memoirs of the Courts and Cabinets of George III*, 1853-5, vol. III.
Bunbury, Sir Henry. *Narratives of Some Passages in the Great War with France (1799-1810)*, 1927.
Bunbury, Sir Henry. *Memoir and Literary Remains of Lieutenant-General Sir Henry Edward Bunbury*, 1868.
Burges, James Bland. *Selection from the Letters and Correspondence of Sir James Bland Burges, Bart.*, ed. James Hutton, 1885.
Castlereagh. *Memoirs and Correspondence of Viscount Castlereagh, Second Marquess of Londonderry*, ed. Charles Vane, Marquess of Londonderry, vols. III-IV, 1849.
Colchester. *Charles, Lord Colchester: His diary and correspondence*, ed. Charles Lord Colchester, vol. I, 1861.
Cornwallis, Marquis. *Correspondence of Charles, 1st Marquis Cornwallis*, ed. Charles Ross, 1859, vol. III.
Dobrée: see George III.
Dropmore: see Fortescue
English Historical Documents, 1783-1832, vol. XI, ed. A. Aspinall and E. Anthony Smith, 1959.
Farington, Joseph. *The Farington Diary*, ed. James Greig, 1922-7, vol. I.
Fortescue, J.B. *Report on the Manuscripts of J. B. Fortescue, Esq., preserved at Dropmore*, 1905-8, Hist. MSS. Comm., vols. V-VII.
Fox, C.J. *Memorials and Correspondence of Charles James Fox*, ed. Lord John Russell, vol. III, 1854.
Frere, J.H. *The Works of John Hookham Frere, with a memoir*, ed. W. E. and Sir B. F. Frere, 1872.

Gentleman's Magazine 1801.

George III. *Letters*, ed. B. Dobrée, 1935.

George III. *The Later Correspondence of George III*, ed. A. Aspinall, 1962-70, vols. III–IV.

Glenbervie, Douglas Sylvester, Lord. *The Diaries of Sylvester Douglas (Lord Glenbervie)*, ed. F. Bickley, 1928, vol. I.

Granville, Granville Leveson-Gower, 1st Earl. *Private Correspondence of Granville Leveson-Gower, 1781-1821*, ed. Castalia, Countess of Granville, 1916, vol. I.

Grenville, Charlotte. *Correspondence of Charlotte Grenville, Lady Williams Wynn*, ed. Rachel Leighton, 1920.

Hastings. *MSS of the Late R. Hastings*, Hist. MSS Comm., 1934, vol. III.

Holland, Henry Richard, Lord. *Memoirs of the Whig Party during my Time*, ed. Henry Edward, Lord Holland, 1852, vol. I.

Holland, Elizabeth Lady. *Journal of Elizabeth, Lady Holland (1791-1811)*, ed. Earl of Ilchester, 1908, vol. II.

Keith, Admiral Viscount. *The Keith Papers*, ed. Christopher Lloyd, vol. II, 1950.

Lecestre, *see* Napoleon I.

Mackintosh, Sir James. *Memoirs of the Life of Sir James Mackintosh*, ed. R. J. Mackintosh, 1835.

Malmesbury, 1st Earl of. *Diaries and Correspondence of James Harris, 1st Earl of Malmesbury*, ed. 3rd Earl of Malmesbury, 1844, Vol. IV.

Minto, 1st Earl of. *Life and Letters of Gilbert Elliot, 1st Earl of Minto*, ed. Countess of Minto, 1874, vol. III.

Moore, Sir John. *The Diary of Sir John Moore*, ed. J. F. Maurice, 1904, vol. I.

Napoleon I. *Correspondance de Napoléon Ier, publiée par ordre de l'Empereur Napoléon III*, vols. VI–VII, Paris, 1861.

Napoleon I. *Lettres inédites de Napoléon I (an VIII–1815)*, ed. Leon Lecestre, 1897.

Paget, Arthur, *The Paget Papers*, ed. A. B. Paget, 2 vols. 1896.

Parliamentary History of England, ed. William Cobbett, 1806 ff., vols. XXXIV–XXXVI.

Rose, George. *Diaries and Correspondence of George Rose*, ed. Revd. L. V. Harcourt, 1860, vol. I.

Spencer, Earl. *The Private Papers of George, 2nd Earl Spencer, 1794-1801*, ed. J. S. Corbett and H. W. Richmond, 1913-24, vols. II–IV.

St. Vincent, Earl of. *Letters of Admiral of the Fleet the Earl of St. Vincent . . . 1801-1804*, ed. D. B. Smith, 1922-7.

Taylor, Sir Herbert. *The Taylor Papers*, ed. E. Taylor, 1913.

Vorontsov, Count Semen de. *Arkhiv Knyazya Vorontsova*, ed. P. I. Bartenev, 1870-95, vol. VIII.

Wellesley, Marquess. *Despatches, Minutes and Correspondence of the Marquess Wellesley, K.G.*, ed. R. B. Martin, 5 vols., 1836.

Wellesley, Marquess. *The Wellesley Papers*, by the editor of the Windham Papers, 1914, vol. I.

Wickham, William. *Correspondence of the Rt. Hon. William Wickham*, ed. W. Wickham, 1870, vol. II.

Wilberforce, William. *The Private Papers of William Wilberforce*, ed. A. M. Wilberforce, 1897.

Windham, William. *Diary of the Rt. Hon. William Windham*, ed. Mrs. H. Baring, 1866.

Windham, William. *The Windham Papers*, ed. L. S. Benjamin, 2 vols. 1913.

Wraxall, Sir Nathaniel. *Historical Memoirs of his own Time*, 1836, vol. I.

Secondary Works Cited

Adams, E.D., *The Influence of Grenville on Pitt's Foreign Policy, 1787-1798*, 1904.

Asbourne, E.G., 1st Baron, *Pitt, some Chapters of his Life*, 1898.

Aspinall, A., *The Cabinet Council, 1783-1835*, 1952.

Bolton, G.C., *The Passing of the Irish Act of Union: A Study in Parliamentary Politics*, 1966.

Bowman, H.M., *Preliminary Stages of the Peace of Amiens . . . November 1799 – March 1801*, Toronto, 1901.

Campbell, John, Lord, *Lives of the Lord Chancellors and Keepers of the Great Seal of England . . .*, vol. VI, 1847.

Cugnac, G. de, *Campagne de l'armée de réserve en 1800*, 1900-1.

Duffy, C., *Russia's Military Way to the West: Origins and Nature of Russian Military Power, 1700-1800*, 1981.

Duffy, M., 'British War Policy: the Austrian Alliance, 1793-1801', unpubl. thesis, Oxford, 1971.

Dunfermline, J.A. Abercromby, Lord, *Lietenant-General Sir Ralph Abercromby, K.B., 1793-1801: a memoir by his son*, 1861.

Ehrman, John, *The Younger Pitt: the Years of Acclaim*, 1969.

Feiling, K.G., *The Second Tory Party, 1714-1832*, 1951.

Feldbæk, Ole, *Denmark and the Armed Neutrality, 1800-1801*, Copenhagen, 1980.

Feldbæk, Ole, 'The Foreign Policy of Tsar Paul I, 1800-1801: An Interpretation', *Jahrbücher für Geschichte Osteuropas*, 30 (1982).

Fortescue, J.W., *History of the British Army*, vol. IV, pt. 2, 1915.

Fortescue, J.W., *The British Army, 1783-1802*, 1905.

Furber, Holden, *Henry Dundas, 1st Viscount Melville*, 1931.

Glover, Richard, *Peninsular Preparation: the reform of the British Army, 1795-1809*, 1963.

Grunwald, C. de, 'Metternich et Napoléon', *Revue des deux mondes*, vol. 41, 1937.

Grunwald, C. de, 'Metternich à Paris en 1808-9: Mémoires inédits', *Revue de Paris*, vol. 44, 1937.

Guest Gornall, R., 'The Prime Minister's Health: William Pitt the Younger', *The Practitioner* vol. 179, 1957.

Hone, J. Ann, *For the Cause of Truth: Radicalism in London, 1796-1821*, 1983.

Hall, John R., *General Pichegru's Treason*, 1915.

Hardman, William, *A History of Malta . . . 1789-1815*, ed. J. Holland Rose, 1909.

Harlow, V.T., *Founding of the Second British Empire, 1763-1793*, vol. II, 1964.

Harvey, A.D., *English Literature and the Great War with France*, 1981.

Helleiner, Karl F., *The Imperial Loans*, 1965.

Howard, Michael, 'The British Way in Warfare: A Reappraisal' (Neale Lecture, 1974).

Ingram, Edward, *Commitment to Empire: Prophecies of the Great Game in Asia, 1797-1800*, 1981.

Lewis, Gwynne, *The Second Vendée*, 1978.

Lovat-Fraser, J.A., *Henry Dundas, Viscount Melville*, 1916.

Mackesy, Piers, *The War in the Mediterranean, 1803-1810*, 1957.

Mackesy, Piers, *The War for America, 1775-1783*, 1964.

Mackesy, Piers, *Statesmen at War: the Strategy of Overthrow, 1798-1799*, 1974 (cited as *Strategy of Overthrow*).

Mackesy, Piers, 'Problems of an Amphibious Power: Britain against France, 1793-1815', *Naval War College Review*, 1978.

Matheson, C., *Life of Henry Dundas, 1st Viscount Melville, 1742-1811*, 1933.

Mitchell, Harvey, *The Underground War with Revolutionary France, 1794-1800*, 1965.

Pares, Richard, 'A quarter of a Millenium of Anglo-Scottish Union', *History*, New Ser. XXXIX, 1954.

Parkinson, C.N., *Edward Pellew, Viscount Exmouth, Admiral of the Red*, 1934.

Pellew, George, *Life and Correspondence of Henry Addington, 1st Viscount Sidmouth*, vol. I, 1847.

Ragsdale, Hugh, *Detente in the Napoleonic Era: Bonaparte and the Russians*, Lawrence, Kansas, 1980.

Rodger, A.B., *The War of the Second Coalition: a Strategic Commentary*, 1964.

Rose, J. Holland, *William Pitt and the Great War*, 1911.

Rose, J. Holland, *Pitt and Napoleon*, 1912.

Saul, Norman E., *Russia and the Mediterranean, 1797-1807*, 1970.

Sherwig, John M., *Guineas and Gunpowder: British Foreign Aid in the Wars with France, 1793-1815*, 1969.

Stanhope, P.H., 5th Earl, *Life of William Pitt*, 1862 edn., 4 vols.

Stevenson, John, *Popular Disturbances in England, 1700-1870*, 1979.

Sutherland, L.S., *The East India Company in Eighteenth-Century Politics*, 1952.

Sorel, Albert, *L'Europe et la Révolution francaise*, vol. VI, Paris 1949.

Watkins, J., *A Biographical Memoir of Frederick, Duke of York*, 1827.

Weil, M.H., *Le Général de Stamford*, 1923.

Western, J.R., *The English Militia in the Eighteenth Century*, 1965.

Willis, Richard, 'William Pitt's Resignation in 1801: Re-examination and Document', *Bulletin of the Institute of Historical Research*, vol. 44, 1971.

Wortley, E. Stuart, *A Prime Minister and his Son*, 1925.

Yonge, C.D., *Life and Administration of Robert Banks, 2nd Earl of Liverpool*, vol. I, 1868.

Ziegler, P.S., *Addington, a Life of H. Addington, first Viscount Sidmouth*, 1965.

Index